SECRETS FROM THE TOWER

Bob Richards

An O'Hare air traffic controller's personal stories of life and aviation

NEW YORK

Ithaca Press
3 Kimberly Drive, Suite B
Dryden, New York 13053 USA
www.IthacaPress.com

Cover Design   Gary Hoffman
Book Design   Gary Hoffman
Cover photography   Jonathan Mayor

Manufactured in the United States of America

9 8 7 6 5 4 3 2

Library of Congress Cataloging-in-Data Available
Richards/ Bob
Secrets from the Tower
l, Aviation, Air Traffic Control, Autobiography

First Edition Printed in the United States of America

ISBN 0-9787113-9-4
ISBN 978-0-9787113-9-9

www.BobRichardsBooks.com

Cover: O'Hare Air Traffic Control Tower

Table of Contents

DEDICATION

To my two boys, Adam and Andy, who are the main reasons for writing this book. A father's love is oftentimes not well understood. Please know for sure that no dad loves his boys as much as I love you two.

To my wife, Kim, who has been most patient and loving with me throughout the incredible ups and downs of both our lives. She is a lifeline I've come to count on.

To my uncle, Bishop Raymond Goedert, also known as "Uncle Father Ray," who along with his brother, Uncle Father Bob, have influenced as many people as planes I've directed.

To Jim "Jimmy" Mugavero, Dave "T-Bone" Dobrinich, and John "Duke" Gregerson, three men who epitomize the meaning of the words "best friend."

To the rest of my family, who have been supportive throughout my whole life, I will *never* be able to thank you enough.

To Greg "Shadow" Taylor, advisor, fighter pilot and friend.

To *all* my brothers and sisters in the O'Hare Tower, I love you like family.

To *all* my fellow sisters and brothers in Air Traffic Control (ATC) everywhere, you are all inspirations to those around you.

Stay Positive.

Prologue

GO AROUND: *a term used when an aircraft aborts its approach for landing to then return for another approach.*

O n the morning of August 31st, 2005, while lying in my hospital bed with family members at my side, I could not have predicted or even imagined what was to happen next. My heart monitor which, until a few seconds ago, had shown a normal heart in subtle distress, was now creating wavy lines that made both the monitoring resident and ward nurses look at each other in deep concern. As I looked over at the young doctor, I could feel a weird dizziness creep into my head in a sudden rush of confusion.

I asked, "Hey, Doc, what's going on?" And then darkness.

But then I was suddenly awake again—or was I? I popped up from the first jolt of the defibrillator and could still see my wife, brother, and sister-in-law, followed by the darkness.

On the second jolt, I popped up again, only to see the doctor with paddles in hand, and many other strangers in attendance. My brain was in a state of total bewilderment. *"What in God's name is happening?"*

Again, the darkness.

And then, without warning, I could feel two hands gently holding me from behind, carrying me away. I remember not being the slightest bit afraid, and in fact, I felt very peaceful, to the point that I succumbed to whomever or whatever was floating me aimlessly around. I sensed a purpose as I drifted in total quiet and peace. Not a sound—but a feeling unlike *any* I had ever experienced. I somehow felt that the place I was being taken to would be a place I wanted to be. I knew many were touching and guiding me. I could think or feel nothing but calm.

On the third jolt, my eyes opened to see a doctor crouched over my chest with a 12-inch hypodermic. Apparently, someone in the "crash" team thought the sac around my heart might be swollen and in need of drainage. I flashbacked to that bizarre scene in *Pulp Fiction*, where an adrenaline hypo was injected directly into the heart of Uma Thurman to restart her heart. Hey, this was me! *Stop, please!* And back into the darkness I went.

By this time my wife, waiting outside the room, feared the worst. My brother and his wife were shaking as if their own lives were leaving them. It seems when death comes knocking at your door, anyone nearby can feel the vibrations. But yet again I was floating, floating, floating. This time, however, I sensed something very unnerving going on just below my feet. It *was* the room I was in, but I couldn't see what was going on—just a crowd of medically clad people working frantically, for no apparent reason. I could feel the hands that held me gripping tighter than they had ever done before.

I was communicating to that someone who held me, but not vocally or even with gestures. We were connecting by feelings. I made it clear that I wanted to go to that peaceful place I was floating to, and not anywhere near the area below my feet. All I could understand from those around me was that I *would* go back, and everything would be as it was. I deduced that from now on, I would have a more focused purpose to my life, but for what I did not know.

For the fourth jolt, the doctor went to full power and hit me with all that technology could muster. I remember nothing till the next day. I was transported to the CCU (Cardiac Care Unit). It was there that I learned from various nurses and doctors of my incessant rants after the last jolt that finally brought me back to the living. Many asked why I had said over and over, "They said I could stay," and "I don't have to go, they said I could stay!" It must have been moments that filled those people with their own "pure adrenaline." It turns out the adrenaline rush I was given translated into a short but scary wrestling match with the attending doctor. Upon being jolted that last time, I had quickly latched both arms in a kind of "bear hug death grip" around my lifesaver. Because of the adrenaline administered previously to revive me, it took almost five long minutes for those in the room to separate my arms from the doctor's scapula and neck area. The whole time I was letting everyone know how happy I was—"They said I could stay!"

A week later, when I was of sound mind, I went back to see the doctor who saved my life to thank him properly. As I entered the operating room area, I caught sight of the doctor who, in my memory, I hadn't even talked to yet. My wife insisted I had thanked him on at least ten occasions the first night. I remembered none of it, since I was heavily sedated after the episode. For whatever reason, I began to shake inside, and all those feelings from the previous week started rushing in uncontrollably. I couldn't even speak.

The doctor sprung up from his chair like he was seeing a long-lost friend for the first time in years. It was totally surreal. I simply broke down and cried like a newborn baby. He hugged me like no other human being had done before, saying, "Wow, man, it's so *good* to see you—you had us all worried."

Barely audibly, I said the words "thank you," then I lost it all again.

"It's OK, Bob—that's what it's all about, man!"

While still hugging him, I noticed the fading black and blue hues of his neck and shoulder. Seems like our first "hug" a week ago had been enough to inflict some heavy bruising. I felt terrible and suddenly very apologetic. "Hey, Doc, I am *so sorry*, I didn't know..."

He quickly replied, and most solemnly, "Bob, don't worry, I got two days on the beach for that—I know you didn't mean it, but tell me the meaning of what you said that day."

Still in shock over the sight of his bruised neck, I asked him to repeat the question.

"Bob, why did you say 'they said I could stay'?"

It sounded to me like a foreign language I could not understand. Again, he repeated, with increasing curiosity, "Bob, why did you say those things?"

To this day, it seems almost impossible to convey to anyone how I felt. Did I get a glimpse of what happens after we leave this earth? I know one thing for sure: I was very pleasantly surprised regarding how I felt about Mr. Death's visit. Before this occurred, my expectations of death were of fear and sadness, and *not* the calmness and euphoria I had experienced.

Many people believe that we come to this earth alone and leave it the same way. I *believe* the people who have been a part of our life *stay* a part of our life till the day we die. I never felt alone during my journey to "the other side," because "They" were there for me. Can it be any simpler than that? I think not. I hope you can understand.

No one ever said life was easy, and I must admit that over the past 48 years, I have learned much and retained little. But in just a span of five minutes, my whole life was changed *forever*. To advance far in one's life and then be thrown back to a new starting point can be quite frustrating, but very therapeutic as well. My own personal go-around had become a reality. The journey leading to my experience has been profound, fun, and a story I want to share. Many people "live" their lives, but forget what brought them to the present day. *"Smelling the roses"* is not a cliché; it is the *essence* of our lives.

Breathe, breathe, breathe... *God, it feels good when you know!*

Chapter 1

The Dawning of Air Traffic Control

DEAD RECKONING: *the navigation of an airplane solely by means of computation based on airspeed, course, heading, wind direction, speed, elapsed time, or simply looking out the window.*

Staring out the O'Hare Air Traffic Control (ATC) Tower windows—almost 17 stories above the terminal—in the present day, the last 48 years seem like one big blur. Like everyone else on this planet, I wonder what it was that took me to this place in time and space. People on the ground below appear to walk aimlessly from one place to another, like ants on a sidewalk. I wonder if anyone outside my glass enclosure actually knows where they're *really* going and what their lot in life truly is.

In the Tower, the radio is blaring "All Along the Watchtower" by Jimi Hendrix. Listening to Jimi reminds me of my own viewing of the outside world:

"No reason to get excited
The thief he kindly spoke…

There are many here among us
Who feel that life is but a joke, but uh…
But you and I we've been through that
And this is not our fate…
So let us not talk falsely now
The hour's getting late…
Hey… Hey…
All along the watchtower…"

Is life but a joke? Not if we have purpose. Many will say that being a goal-oriented person has its advantages. Heck, you always have a sense of direction in life. No goals and you might end up lost for the rest of your life. Having a specified path to follow in life gives everything meaning and purpose. As I've grown older, however, I began to realize these roads meant little unless I could enjoy the ride. So many people I've known became so obsessed with trying to get somewhere that they never noticed the beautiful sights along the way.

That's why people who are so-called "successful," who truly understand life, don't talk about their material wealth, but instead reflect on the trials and tribulations they faced along the way. Ironically, it is also why people *without* a multitude of earthly riches also often know that same vast wealth of spirit, love, and contentment.

It's hard to stay focused looking down on the world from the Tower above. The frantic pace outside our windows is the same day after day. People at O'Hare Airport spend each day hurrying from terminal to terminal with a single purpose. *Connecting flight. I'm late. Get there.* So how did I get *here*?! It seems that as we grow older, we look back on that precious time known as childhood and never really understand how it influenced our adult or "grown-up" life. My road to becoming an air traffic controller at the world's *busiest* airport was full of many strange twists and turns.

As long as I can remember, I never dreamed of being in the aviation field. It was the brief but meaningful experiences in my early years that made a difference. Chances are, if you weren't paying attention, you've missed the clues that often point to your future. *My* clues came early on in my life, somewhere in the year 1971.

The road to our *future* is just one road. Our *life* is like a jigsaw puzzle in

which we find the time

to put all

the pieces

together.

Chapter 2

Look Out for the Nuns

FLIGHT PLAN: *specified information relating to the intended flight of an aircraft or human being, which is orally or in writing with an Air Traffic Control (ATC) facility.*

I t was a crisp, cold fall October morning in the year of 1971. On my daily walk to school, it seemed that my life had barely started. The summer green was gradually giving way to the tannic hues of autumn. Being in the eighth grade had its advantages. I had no job to be at, nor any appointments to keep. No worrying about being anywhere but at St. Mary of Celle grammar school. My biggest worry was how I was going to make the "big" tackle football game after school with all the homework I had.

My brother, Billy, who was in the fifth grade, had even less to worry about. High school for my brother was still four years away. I didn't ever want to leave eighth grade. Most of the kids I knew who went to high school never came back to the playground. (They had lots of homework.) Walking with my brother to school, we were both plodding along, day-dreaming, when seemingly out of nowhere screamed a giant jet airplane, barely a few thousand feet above us. Our house in Berwyn, Illinois, was right below the flight path for the air traffic landing runway three-two left (the longest runway at O'Hare). While we had been shaken many times by the almost unbearable noise, it was hard not to be curious about how these giant pieces of metal could stay airborne carrying such massive weight.

In the classroom, the nuns were in rare form. Taking out the meter stick, Sister Roberta Ann had Russ Bagnuolo right where she wanted him. With a swift swing of her right hand, Sister hit dead center on the rear end of the bent-over, grimacing Bagnuolo. As Russ screamed out in pain, those same large jets flew overhead, drowning out any possibility of anyone in the other classrooms hearing Russ' cry of pain. Did Sister know the flight schedule? Or did she coincidentally know when to whip backward and forward that instrument of childhood pain? Nobody really cared, though, because it was almost time for school to let out and another big game was at hand.

Once out of school, *all* the guys rushed home, made a quick change into tattered clothes, and were ready for kick-off just 20 minutes after school ended. The field adjacent to the school was world class. From the day he entered our parish, our pastor, Fr. Robert Mastny, made sure all the kids had a place to go for sports after school by building the largest grammar school baseball field in the Chicago area. We simply converted it into a football stadium every fall. Fr. Bob, as he was affectionately called, had played football with the legendary Knute Rockne, was buddies with Bob Hope and, at six foot four and 200 pounds, was an intimidating yet very gentle man who always had a smile and a joke for us all. He spent many a day strolling out from the rectory to see the "big games."

In a chilly, fall overcast, we had almost all the eighth grade eagerly awaiting the game time kickoff. There was so much testosterone on the field we couldn't wait to start the game. Many of the guys played because they knew the girls would be watching. The class beauties, such as Eden, Renee, Pam, and Vickie, often kept my distraction to such heights that I would be blind-sided during the game while gazing at them. As a pre-pubescent adolescent, I was torn between sports, the girls who watched them, and those damned airplanes that seemed like they would fall out of the sky at any minute.

In choosing sides, it rarely deviated from the toughest to the fastest. The aforementioned Russ was a kid who would fight anyone (more often older kids) and lose convincingly. He was like our pack leader. Often wearing bloodstained shirts, Russ was always the logical first pick. Not to be outdone, Mike Johnson always challenged Russ for the tough-man competition. Being one of the shortest human beings in our class never bothered Mike much. He just kept coming at you till you acknowledged he was the toughest.

In the background, someone's transistor radio was playing "Peace Frog" by the Doors. On the football field we could hear the words,

"There's blood in the streets, it's up to my ankles... She came...

Blood on the streets in the town of Chicago... She came...
Blood on the rise, it's following me...
Think about the break of day..."

The world around us was in some kind of revolution. We were just too young to notice it. All we knew about was having fun and being with friends. Our lives were simple and free of all the hardships that would come later. It was time to play ball.

While picking teams, we would often stop, quite unconsciously, because the roars of Boeing 747s and DC10s made it totally impossible to speak to someone as close as a foot away. We had heard the noise for so long we didn't even blink an eye when they passed as low as 1000 feet above our sacred field of dreams. Low-flying airplanes were a constant in our childhood experience. Every event growing up, whether it was birthdays, communions, or sports, all had one thing in common: low-flying big jets. So, like a Pavlovian response, I always associate airplanes with the remarkable simplicity of my childhood.

I often wondered who was guiding those big jets and were those same people behind a long-standing plot to interrupt our games. Well, my friends at the time, Jim Mugavero and Danny Kuligoski, thought so. One of the contestants in the neighborhood "I have the strongest 12-year-old arm in the world" competition, Danny liked to brag that he could take a small ball and throw it so high and fast that it could hit one of the flying "pieces of tin." At the time, it certainly seemed possible. Jim just laughed, took his turn, and as we mocked Danny that Jim's throw was much closer, Danny stood ready to "kick the ass" of the next person to hold the view opposite his.

We must have looked pretty funny to anyone watching us, as we spent hours trying to throw small balls a distance of about 100 feet in the air while the planes were thousands of feet up. Even Fr. Bob would come over and, in a serious but mocking tone, tell a story of how, as a kid our age, he could have thrown the ball high enough for any pilot to see. We believed the whole story, hook, line and sinker. Heck, this guy

An O'Hare air traffic controller's personal stories of life and aviation

had played at Notre Dame with Rockne. It kept our little game of "hit the airplane" going for a long time.

Being late October, it was only a matter of time before the sun went down and utter darkness set in. But that didn't stop us. We were going to finish the game no matter what. Just like the old postman—neither rain, nor sleet, or even snow would stop us. We played until many of our parents screamed our names from houses and cars driving past the field. The faint light of the adjacent streetlights was just enough for us to see the ball and each other. However, if a player was at least 40 yards away, you probably lost him fading into the darkness.

When the dusk was lit up by a bright full moon, it might as well have been daylight. Some games lasted until late into the moonlit nights. Sometimes, we were so caught up in the excitement of playing that we forgot to keep score. My friends and I rarely came home without ripped shirts and someone else's blood on our persons. Gary Grzywacz prided himself on having the most bodily fluids on his clothes. We were all impressed. (We didn't worry much about communicable diseases at that time, and as far as I remember, Gary may have been a virgin till he was 18.)

My parents probably even forgot I lived in their house, I was at the field so much. We always used the airplanes as excuses whenever we wanted to continue to play and our parents were calling us. It was "Sorry, Ma, I didn't hear you with those planes going over," and with them flying over every minute, who could doubt our excuse?

But it was in the school itself that the most important of life's lessons were learned. Yes, the nuns at St. Mary of Celle grammar school were rough, but they often kept us pointed in the right direction. (End justifies the means?) Even the few lay teachers were no pushovers. Tom Hodina, our eighth grade

15

teacher, was a little too big to mix it up with us in football. We wouldn't let him play, anyway. Occasionally, Tom would come out to the adjacent basketball court for hours of pickup games, much to the chagrin of the "crazed" penguins (our pet name for our favorite nuns).

Being only about nine years older, Tom was at times "one of us." On our playgrounds, everyone was equal. Because of his ferociously competitive nature, Tom helped instill a zest for life in all of us by his examples about "giving it your best" at *all* times. Our court games were a war that, when ended, were followed by a few sodas and talks about our life's ambitions at the S & G food shop, the local Ma and Pa grocery store a block away. As we walked to the store for liquid replenishment in our sweat-drenched tee shirts, we all knew Mr. Hodina was buying, since he had a job and we didn't.

We were sports legends in our own minds, and everybody catered to us. On other days, Mike Celer and I would go out and buy a whole watermelon, bring it home, and watch while Mike's mother sat watching in horror, never believing we could possibly eat the whole oblong sphere. But ate we did, and till we puked our guts out, if necessary. We were decadent and childhood lushes. We had it all as kids in this one square city block, and it seemed like it would never end, but we soon began to realize it would.

Every so often, the real world would creep into our otherwise carefree lives. In the sixth grade, it was the death of my best friend Jim Mugavero's older brother, Mike. Only two years older than Jim and I, it was impossible to comprehend at the time that this seemingly healthy, stocky boy could die of leukemia. When he was taken away from us, I simply rationalized the Catholic ideal of the time taught to us by the nuns and priests: that Mike was up there "somewhere." Could it be possible he was flying some of those big jet airplanes? This little Catholic fairy tale made me feel better, until I went to Mike's wake—my first ever.

It was there at the Nosek Funeral Home that my life changed forever. In the old Italian tradition, the older women wailed as they had in times gone by. Inside the funeral home, my football friends and I were brought in, with our parents leading us. Not being prepared for what was going on, I became numb when I saw Mike lying there, his full body visible right down to his brown leisure sandals.

Only weeks before, this vibrant kid had been running, playing, and beating us up. I never thought that kids could die. The eerie cries of many in the room went right through me and were unlike anything I had ever heard. It always seemed that when someone talked about death, it was in reference to someone much older. Looking at Mike, it appeared that all I had to do was walk over and tap him to wake him up. But Mike, like many people I came to know over the years, would never awaken. He had simply gone somewhere else. It's a childhood moment I haven't forgotten to this day, even though I've been to a multitude of wakes since then.

It was then I plotted a course for my life. My human flight plan had been initiated. If God saw fit to take me anytime, as he had Mike, I wanted to taste life to its fullest. My biggest fear became lying on my deathbed, saying, "If only I had done that..."

Chapter 3

My Dad Will Kick Your Ass

WAKE TURBULENCE: *a phenomenon resulting from the passage of an aircraft or father through the atmosphere. The term includes jet blast, jet wash, propeller wash, and parents.*

Many things happen throughout our lives that shape who we are and who we are to become. Unbeknownst to many in my immediate family, I knew which occurrences formed the primary source of who I would become. My father was the main catalyst. Being a high-school dropout, my dad had a very strict work ethic. He often worked from dusk to dawn, fixing cars and trucks at his business, and then again when he got home, for all his friends and neighbors.

My father was five foot eleven and about 220 pounds, and my brother, who was three years younger, and I were always dwarfed by his stature and persona. And as dwarfs, my brother and I acted accordingly. To say my dad was very strict would be a gross understatement. Anytime my brother and I got out of line, we knew we were in *big* trouble.

Very often, it was the use of a thick, black belt, particularly when we were smaller, but as we got older, it became an open hand with an extra fist thrown in. My brother and I became good defensive fighters throughout the years, and by the time we were teenagers, we had learned how to avoid and even block good jabs and uppercuts. My younger sister of four years, Kathy, was exempt from Dad's wrath for simply being female.

My mom stayed out of father-son matters most of the time and was only questioned one time that I can remember, by her mother, about the possible severity of such punishment. Most of the time, my mom was very caring and loving about us, but discipline for the boys was Dad's "job." At the time, when confronted by my grandma, my mother could only shrug as if to say, "What should I do?"

The only reason my grandma said something to my mom was because I had come over the day before to cut her grass, wearing a bloodstained sweatshirt. I tried to lie and give the macho excuse that I had gotten into a fight with a bully on the way over, but my grandma had me figured out as an 11-year-old. I always looked forward to cutting my grandmother's lawn, not just for the great home-baked brownies, but also the nice, personable conversations. When I was feeling anxious about things at home, I could always count on my grandmother to make me feel good with some sweets or a gentle reassuring voice.

Just about every Christmas when my grandma was alive, I waited till Christmas Eve to do all my Christmas shopping with her. She worked at J.C. Penney so I had to wait till she got off work to start my last-minute shopping frenzy. Every year, my grandma would pretend that I was out of my mind to wait so late to shop, but then would follow me around the store, help me pick things out, and then even wrap everything with a smile on her face. I guess the lady was ahead of her time when it came to observing children in distress.

I'm not going to complain and play the child abuse card the rest of my life, because that was the accepted discipline method in the 1970s, not just in my house but with many of my friends as well. If my dad or any of my friends' parents were reported in today's social climate, I would have been fatherless, with my dad in jail. My brother and I quickly learned to be independent, and so much so that we figured we probably didn't need anybody's help at all.

One might argue that teaching independence is a good thing, but my brother and I had taken it to such a negative extreme and were *so* independent that, later in our lives, we had little or no tolerance in relationships for women who we perceived as mostly co-dependent or too needy. Our father, who showed my brother and me little or no public displays of affection, also dictated our emotional core. I honestly can't ever remember being hugged by my father, and that's why it sometimes doesn't come easy with my own sons. So how do you get your father's attention for love and understanding? Answer: you compete for it!

For as long as I could remember, my brother, Bill, and I would always be thrust into some kind of unconscious competition. The competition was to see if the younger sibling could outperform the older sibling. If that younger sibling was not able to compete in such things as academics, athletics, and good behavior, then a "conflict" would be created between the two siblings. Very often my parents were not even aware they were causing this problem. My brother and I would fight constantly while my parents would look at each other, puzzled as to why.

For example, good report cards were rewarded financially by my parents, such as so many dollars for an A, so many for a B, etc. Since good grades came easy for my sister and me, we reaped the cash harvest. My brother, however, did not find good grades easily, and so frustration would often set in, particularly with little or no monetary awards possible. As the older brother received praise, the younger brother would be rebuked. With rebukes come frustration, and with that frustration there must be a place to unleash it. The older brother was that outlet.

Our biggest competition was in the area of sports. Our fights were legendary. It was not unusual, during our alley pickup basketball games, to argue about a play or foul, and then go right to fisticuffs. When we weren't playing one-on-one and had to pick teams, we would purposely find a way not to be on the same team. Whenever our dad came around the alley, thinking he heard some commotion, any in-fighting ended instantly, because we knew if he caught us, he would show us what fighting was really all about.

One time, because of the intensity of our fight, we were oblivious to our dad's sudden presence and ended up getting kicked back into our shared bedroom and "next week." Not only did we have bloody lips from each other's punches, but a nice red ass from where our dad rarely missed the mark with his size 11 shoe.

Winning was everything and we would do anything, short of murder, to win. As long as I could remember, my brother and I imagined our backyard as a baseball stadium, such as Comiskey Park or even Wrigley Field. We substituted a wiffle ball for the real major league baseball. It was mostly me against my brother, and very often, the results were the same as basketball. Thank God that when our game became competitive, we could only hit each other with wiffle bats, and not the hard, wooden Louisville slugger bats of the 1970s. Very often, our games would experience a delay, or even end, when a foul ball made its way to our next-door neighbor's yard.

The old senior couple who lived next door was Alex and Gladys Vashinko, who prided themselves on having the finest manicured lawn in the neighborhood, and probably the world. Whenever a foul ball found its way into their yard, either my brother or I would immediately scale the fence, knowing if we didn't grab our game ball at the speed of light, it would be confiscated by the waiting Alex or Gladys. (The backyard lawn, we had deduced, was some kind of holy ground to our neighbors.) Very often, we didn't make it in time because out of nowhere came Alex, who would grab the ball and scare us to the point that we barely got one foot on the fence before he was screaming at us in his native Czech language. Other times, while we were playing, we could see the outline of Alex and Gladys in their kitchen window, just waiting for us to make the ultimate mistake of hitting that foul ball.

The Vashinkos would always scold my brother and me: "You're killing our grass—stop playing these games!" Now, being just 12 and nine respectively, my brother and I simply assumed that maybe it was possible that our wiffle ball, with all the holes in it, could actually kill a blade or two of grass. Because of this fact, we never tried to get our dad to get our balls back, figuring he might take the side of the Vashinkos and then punish us back into next week again. Then one day all that changed.

During one of our brother-only games, Billy hit a foul ball right into the middle of the weedless, perfectly green, trimmed lawn next door. In a split second, we were both scaling the fence and had reached the top, about to go over, when we heard, out of nowhere, our dad screaming, "Hey! What the hell are you two guys doing?" My brother and I both froze like solid ice on top of the five-foot fence, as if we could maybe camouflage ourselves so our father couldn't see us. As our dad stared at us menacingly, he got distracted watching Alex grab the ball and start back into the house. As my brother and I were still iced to the fence, my dad, in one swoop, pulled himself over the fence and went right towards Alex. The force of my dad's 200-pound "fence tremor" knocked my brother and me straight to the ground. I figured my dad was on his way to apologize, and so did my brother, who ran like a jackrabbit into the house, probably fearing corporal punishment when my dad came back.

Cornering Alex before he could reach the back stairs, my dad asked, somewhat politely, "Vashinko, where you going with that ball?"

Totally taken aback by my dad, Alex mumbled, "These balls keep coming in my yard and are killing my grass.... your boys are *bad*. I tell them all the time...I keep the ball."

Now I was scared. Not for me, but for Alex. With only faint politeness, my dad said, "Please hand me the ball." As Alex turned away, I knew it was all over. My dad, with just one hand, had Alex about a foot off the ground with a death grip around his neck. As the ball dropped, my dad, with Alex still suspended, whispered something I could not hear. Usually when my dad was this angry, he would be quite loud, but instead he dropped Alex like a rock. He then walked calmly back to the fence, grabbed the top, pulled himself over in one motion and stood staring at me.

Again, I froze in total fear, but in the back of my mind I was curious about what my dad had whispered. For an agonizing two minutes, I was like a statue while my dad just stared in my direction, but now I sensed it wasn't me he was staring at, but maybe looking into himself. I could barely hear Gladys next door, screaming in Czech at my dad, as she tried to help up her stunned and collapsed husband.

In my mind came the music my dad played over and over. Being a big Johnny Cash fan, Dad liked to play his favorite songs over and over till finally they had become a part of me. As I stood motionless, all I could hear was Johnny Cash singing,

> "I fell into a burning ring of fire,
> I went down, down, down, and the flames went higher,
> and it burns, burns, burns,
> the ring of fire, the ring of fire..."

There was a "ring of fire" in my own back yard and I was in it. Then my dad looked back at me and, in words barely audible, said, "They're not bad boys..." and then loudly, "Bobby, get back in the house."

As I walked past my dad, for the first time, I felt bad for him, but could not understand why. As I went into the house, I looked out the back window long enough to see Alex throw into the yard almost 20 wiffle balls! That was when I knew what my dad had whispered.

My dad despised the fact that my brother and I fought so much. What I came to find out from my dad's mother later was that my dad and his brother were very much the same when it came to sibling rivalry. It was clear that my dad didn't want to see history repeating itself. His only brother, Lowell, died in the Korean War, and I think not only did he feel horrible about his death but guilty because he never got the chance to make amends for years of misunderstood hate and jealousy. As people get older, very often they come to realize how ridiculous they behaved as children and adolescents. Unfortunately, when that realization comes, it is often too late to repair the relationship with the object of that conflict.

From that day on, my dad was still a very strict disciplinarian, but very protective of my brother and me as well. To prove this last point, along came the Vashinkos again. Convinced that my brother and I were the products of the devil himself (meaning my dad), Alex and Gladys went after my brother and our family on a Saturday for the last time. The scene was the local Catholic Church, St. Mary of Celle, which was directly across the street from our house. My brother was the altar boy at the 5:30 p.m. mass, and in the church at the same time were the Vashinkos. Yes, it was time for gas and fire.

Near the end of the Catholic Mass service, there is the time when communion is given. It is the job of the altar boy to hold a round, metal plate under the neck of those receiving communion while the priest simply places the holy one-inch diameter wafer into the open mouths of the faithful. I'm sure my brother was a little taken aback when he saw his favorite neighbors standing up at the altar. True to his job, my brother steadily held the plate under Alex's neck when all hell broke loose. In an act of sacrilege, unrivaled to anything seen in our Catholic Church, Alex stripped the plate from my brother, held it under his own neck, took communion, then held it under his wife's neck, and before the priest could figure it out, handed the plate back to the priest, keeping it away from my brother.

I don't remember when my brother first started to cry from the shame of the experience, but leaving church, I could see him running and whimpering as loud as I had ever heard him. As I stood outside talking to my friends, my brother dashed into the house, went right up to our dad, who bolted upright from his couch to hear what his distraught kid had to say. While I could barely hear the conversation because of my friends, I noticed Alex and Gladys not walking, but shuttling themselves quickly into their house.

As they got through the screen door, they quickly slammed the inside door. It was all a bit peculiar because with the weather being so nice, with temperatures in the 70's, the Vashinkos usually left the inside door open like everyone else, to get the fresh summer air through the screen door.

Then, suddenly, I felt a gust of wind and *turbulence* and there was my dad climbing the neighbors' steps like his life depended on it. Initially, my dad decided to bypass the doorbell and instead was banging as hard as he could on the screen door. Next came the continuous doorbell-pressing motion for about 30 seconds. He had their attention and I knew it, because there they were, staring at him through the big picture window, like scared little pigs seeing Mr. Wolf.

My dad was screaming, "Come out here, you sons-of-bitches, *now!*" Like statues, the Vashinkos stood motionless.

In a moment of total clarity, my dad realized the Vashinkos were not coming out. Therefore, he was going in. Grasping part of the door with one hand by ripping through the screen and then grabbing the doorknob with the other hand, my dad successfully yanked the door off its metal hinges and then tossed it into the street—about 30 feet. My friends were in awe. Now it was time for the solid core wood door to come off, but by this time the squad cars were coming up the street. Dad was about to be saved from himself.

As the cop casually walked from his car, no one made a sound. I say "no one" because by this time, about every neighbor had gathered outside, expecting a possible lynching. As the officer confronted Dad and asked what the problem was, my dad went into an immediate, loud, and long explanation of how the Vashinkos had disgraced my brother at the church. At one point during my dad's sermon, the Vashinkos tried to come out the front door, when my dad commanded, "Get your asses back in the house!"

I thought at that point the cop would be upset, but instead he maintained his interest in my dad's story and didn't even flinch when the Vashinkos scurried back into their house. After listening to my dad's side of the story, the officer went into the house next door to hear the Vashinko's version.

As he exited from next door, the officer again calmly walked up to my dad and said he understood what my dad had done, because he also had kids. It turns out the officer was Catholic as well—small world. He told my dad he would have to make restitution for the door, but as far as I know, the Vashinkos never came looking for reimbursement.

As weeks passed, the attitudes of our neighbors changed remarkably. Often, when my brother and I were playing backyard baseball, not only would Alex throw back the foul ball but even go so far as to say, "Hey, nice hit...how are you doing?"

I'm inclined to believe that Alex and Gladys had finally figured out that a less-than-one-ounce wiffle ball was much easier to take than a 220-pound protective father. Love you, Dad.

Chapter 4

Eden

MAYDAY: *the international radiotelephony distress signal. When repeated three times in flight or adolescence, it indicates imminent and grave danger and that immediate assistance is requested.*

My parents had been instrumental in setting me on a childhood flight path of self-learning and discovery. I was always curious about the world anyway, so the drive to experience that world was ingrained in me by the time I made it to eighth grade. My exploits with my father taught me that I would have to grab all life had to offer on my own, and not rely on anyone else. But something was missing. I was like an airline captain in position on the runway, waiting to take off without a co-pilot. Everyone has a co-pilot in life, such as a significant other, wife, girlfriend, friend, etc. I knew back in the seventh grade how important the co-pilot would become. That co-pilot was Eden Mae McMahon.

Eden was a short, petite, gorgeous, green-eyed blond girl whose incredibly sweet smile would always cause me to feel good all over. I could never understand the feeling I felt when I was in her presence, but I knew it was the most special feeling any human being could imagine. Even to this day, when I think about her, I think of how lucky I was to experience her presence. The only other time I felt that similar aura was during my revival back to this earthly life from the dead in August 2005. While I was unconscious and floating aimlessly that day came that same wonderful feeling I had also experienced with Eden. I was consumed and I don't know that I could have been happier about it.

Could Eden have been there with the "others"? My feeling for Eden was very simple—I just wanted to be around her. We might have had the most mundane and superficial seventh-grade conversations, but to me it was like talking to an angel. Our favorite song at the time was "Sugar, Sugar" by the Archies. By today's standards, it is probably as corny a song as you can imagine. But in 1970, it summarized how most of the guys at St. Mary of Celle felt about their girl classmates. It went something like

You are my candy girl and you got me wanting you.

It was a simple, melodic, and innocent song, with not a care in the world. We were both still young and free of all the problems and sorrows that life would send us later. If I could freeze various childhood moments in time, it would be any of the occasions Eden and I spent together, talking and laughing.

Eden so powerfully overwhelmed me that I talked the local newspaper, the *Chicago American*, into hiring me to do their paper route on the two streets just two blocks west of our grammar school. One of those streets was significant, because it was at the corner of 15th and Oak Park Ave., the location where Eden had to catch the bus after school to go home.

Eden was usually at the bus stop by herself, since it was public transportation and not just a regular school bus. Most of my classmates lived in the neighborhood and walked home, but Eden lived on the south side of Berwyn on Riverside Drive, which at that time was considered the "rich" side of town. While we weren't exactly poverty stricken on the north side of town, it was clearly not as opulent as the south side.

I knew the bus schedule by heart and always had about 30 minutes after school before the bus would actually stop to pick up Eden. It was in that time, under the disguise of my paper route, that I would "bump into" Eden. I'm sure at some point she must have thought that our "chance meetings" could not have been a day-after-day coincidence, but never did she protest or be anything but amicable. It became such a routine that my boss, Homer Brown, always made kidding remarks when I went to his office to get paid, such as "I was driving down Oak Park and saw you with that pretty girl you're always talking to—how is that going?" Still being very shy about the whole thing (and not knowing why), I simply said, "She's just a girl I know from school—no big deal." No big deal? I was lying through my teeth, of course. I guess it was still just too hard to come out and express my real feelings, which was something that would take years. I simply kept it *all* to myself. I wouldn't have it any other way.

In all my after-school conversations with Eden, time stood still. It was a banner day when the bus was late—I could have stayed for hours. As the school year proceeded, our dialogue became more profound. Eden knew I was infatuated with her and, after a while, I could sense the same. The problem with me, however, was not having the courage to tell her how I really felt. Hell, I couldn't tell anyone, and I didn't understand why. I even rationalized how hard it would be to have a "long-distance" relationship. How stupid was that? So, up to graduation, I maintained this close but distant relationship with Eden, and figured I'd just have to wait till high school to see her again.

As the innocence of grammar school gave way to the intense academia of high school, my life took off like the afterburners of a fighter jet. For the next four years, I was buried in books, homework, and basketball. I had been accepted into Fenwick High School, an all-male Catholic institution and one of the most prestigious high schools in the Chicago area. Fenwick alumni included many CEOs, Olympians, lawyers, doctors, and even an astronaut. I spent most of my time studying, without much playing. Eden was attending the all-girls Trinity High School, which was right up the street and considered our "sister school," but just as intense academically.

Periodically throughout high school, I would run into Eden at school dances and local parties, but each time we tried to reconnect, she would instead introduce me to her latest boyfriend, who was usually one of my classmates. Besides, how could any woman look at me, anyway? I was hideous, with my thick, dark-framed glasses and my short, skinny build. Most of my classmates had cars, while I was still bumming rides from friends.

I could tell that high school was wearing her down the same way it was taking me down. The pressure to succeed at a private Catholic school would sometimes outweigh one's ability to live a normal, fun life.

As time went by, I just about gave up hope that Eden and I would ever find one another again, until one Sunday just before Christmas in 1974. It was a cold, snowy day when I found myself walking alone just outside the Cermak Shopping Plaza in Berwyn. To my utter amazement, there was Eden, standing outside a clothing store, wearing a cute beret and looking as if she might be lost. At that point, I locked my radar directly to her area.

As I suddenly jumped in front of her, a surprised but happy smile came across her face as she said, "Oh my God, I almost didn't recognize you."

I came back, "Yes, it's just contact lenses, but I *did* recognize you, and you look spectacular and as cute as ever."

Eden smiled again and then, with deeper thought, remarked, "God, you look great, too. How have you been?"

The next portion of our conversation involved her talking about her future plans as some kind of fashion designer. I wasn't paying attention to her words as much as the fact that, at that moment in time, I was as happy as I had been in a long time. Before she could continue talking too much further about her future career, I interrupted, "Eden, I have been in love with you since the seventh grade—I've always wanted to tell you that. I think you're a very special person and I didn't want another minute of my life to go by without you knowing that." The next 30 seconds, she just stared into my eyes, and then my soul. For the next few minutes we were reconnected.

She next took her right hand and touched ever so softly my right cheek and calmly, but very slowly, said, "You don't know how nice it is to have someone tell you you are special. I always thought of you in the same way. Many guys have called me special, but I know *you* mean it." As tears formed in her eyes, I knew she was hurting, and now all I could feel was helpless. Her life was clearly in some kind of upheaval. She then gave me a hug that, while only lasting for 60 seconds, was so full of life and tenderness that I can still remember it to this day. That was the last time I saw Eden.

On March 6th, 1975, I received a phone call that literally ripped a part of my heart from my being. It was the ultimate distress call. Eden had been found dead in her garage the night before. I really didn't want to know the details, because to me, it didn't matter. The one person on this earth I had connected with was gone.

In my mind all I could hear was the Doors song, "Blue Sunday." In perfect sweet harmony, Jim Morrison sang,

> *"I found my own true love was... on a blue Sunday...*
> *She looked at me and told me...*
> *I was the only... one in the world...*
> *Now I have found my girl...*
> *My girl awaits for me in tender time...*
> *My girl is mine, she is the world...*
> *She is my girl."*

She had filled that part of my life where all the feel-good inside lived. I would spend the rest of my life trying to find that same connection with every woman I met. It would be a lifetime quest that would be impossible to achieve, since there is no substitution for the original. It took me 30 years to figure that out. Love you, Eden.

Chapter 5

First Flight

CLEARED FOR TAKEOFF: *Air Traffic Control (ATC) authorization for an aircraft to depart.*

After Eden's death, I was left with more questions than answers. I was like a plane flying in bad weather, looking for someone to take me to the safety of calmer skies. My co-pilot had died in flight. I still could not talk to anyone about how I felt. I was restless on a daily basis, worrying if there was going to be someone or something that could fill the void in life that made everything special.

Since I had childhood asthma, I actually started taking extra medicine to dull the emotional pain. Instead of taking one Primatene tablet for my asthma, I would take as many as three or four. Loaded up on ephedrine, I was so hyped up I never stayed home or even slept. I drove my brother insane by staying up all night in our shared bedroom. I'd spend weeks at my friend Danny's house in Antioch, or with my other friend, Jim, in a room above his garage Like a lot of kids my age, I had no idea where my life was headed, didn't give a shit, and all I

knew was that I was running constantly. I had to get away—
but where?

My first instinct was to talk to someone. But there was
no one I felt comfortable with, other than my best friend, Jim,
and we seldom talked about death since he had lost his older
brother only years earlier. Since the age of four, Jim and I never
spent much time in serious conversations, nor in our teenage
life, because Jim was trying to find his way as well. I was pop-
ping asthma pills while he was smoking "Mary Jane," and I
don't mean the next-door neighbor.

Our life became all about rock and roll. We spent much
of our time headed to one rock concert after another. Jim and
I loved music and saw just about everyone from Steppenwolf
to the Rolling Stones. When we were making money at part-
time jobs, we thought nothing of spending money to see Led
Zeppelin, Yes and, of course, Bad Company. Jethro Tull, whose
music I felt bordered on everything I felt about my life, personally consumed me. The Tull classic "Life is a Long Song"
simply chronicled the old adage that life is short—so short, in
fact, that it might last only as long as a song; metaphorically,
of course. This song reminded me of Jim's brother, Mike, and
of course Eden, two people who left the earth way too early.

When Ian Anderson of Jethro Tull wrote and put out
the album-long song "Thick as a Brick," a parody about life, I
must have played it over a thousand times, beginning to end.
It was an album that satirized all the hypocrisies of people,
governments, and religion. It was Jethro Tull that gave me the
courage later on to expose people or cut them down to size
when they thought they were better than the rest of the human race.

It always amazed me that Jethro Tull was mostly recognized for their hit song "Aqualung," a song about a brazen

homeless person. While it was a good song, I felt there were many far more meaningful Tull tunes about life that were overlooked by the world and extremely relevant. All that mattered at that time, and even to this day, is that *I* knew their relevance.

And then there were the rebel bands, including The Who, Ozzie Osborne, and the Rolling Stones. "Won't Get Fooled Again," by The Who, was the anthem of the 1970s in my neighborhood. The most recognized verse—"Meet the new boss, same as the old boss"—was about any of the people in our lives who have betrayed us. Ozzie Osborne's "Iron Man" made my friends and I feel invincible—even though we weren't, of course. The Rolling Stones were everybody's favorite, and if you listened closely, you could learn a lot. It wasn't just about the drugs.

Years later, in whatever tower I worked, when the music of these great bands and songs came screaming out of boom boxes, I became so uplifted inside that air traffic control became fun, even orgasmic. There was nothing like grooving to the music and working a mess of airplanes at the same time. It was pure motivation.

After graduation from high school in the summer of 1975, it was time to make a decision about where I was headed. Was it college, or ? It turns out initially I chose ? I headed back up to Antioch to hang out with my friend Danny Kuligoski and discuss our future. You have to appreciate the Kuligoski family letting me stay weeks at a time with their family. Danny was one of nine kids, seven boys and two girls. The two children out of the house and older than Danny were Linda, who was married, and Joe, Jr., who was away in the Air Force. Only one of the girls, Patty, was still at home while the other boys were.

The last thing Danny's mom needed was another boy in her four-bedroom house. But since I had blond hair and blue eyes like the rest of the family and bore a striking resemblance, I was always accepted as one of the family. The family even nicknamed me "Wheaties," after the cereal. Danny's dad, Joe, remembered a famous Olympian with the same name as mine, Bob Richards. *That* particular Bob Richards was fêted on the Wheaties cereal box for winning the decathlon.

So that summer, Danny and I made a pact that we would work some part-time jobs and bring home some food and money for the family until we would join the United States Air Force by the end of the summer.

The summer of 1975 was a big turning point in my life. For the first time, I learned an extensive lesson about the traditional birds and the bees. On a bright, sunny, hot summer day while Danny was working, I was playing catch football out in the back yard open field with Jimmy, Danny's younger brother by a few years. As we were running back and forth, throwing the "bombs," as we called them, I inadvertently landed in the yard next door, where a girl was hanging up wet clothes to be air-dried. Caught by surprise, I noticed the girl had dark, curly hair, a cute face, and an incredible womanly body with all the curves in the right places. She couldn't have been more than a few years older. I was totally fixated on her.

Before she could speak, I quickly apologized. "Sorry, Ma'am, I hope I didn't scare you."

She replied, "Not at all. Are you one of the Kuligoski boys?"

Sheepishly I replied, "No, Ma'am, I'm just a friend. I think they're going to adopt me."

As she laughed, she then introduced herself: "Well, my name is Sharon. What's yours?"

Since I was so busy gawking at her body and overall splendor, I could only say, "What... what did you say?"

Then, with concern, Sharon asked, "Are you OK? What is your name?"

At this point I noticed my body was shaking and I felt flushed from head to toe. What in God's name was happening to me? As Sharon walked closer to me, Jimmy was getting impatient: "Hey, Wheaties, c'mon—throw the ball!" So I took one step and threw Jimmy the ball. It rolled 50 feet short of the mark.

Then, quickly, I turned back to Sharon. "My name is Wheaties; well, not really... oh, what the heck, call me Wheaties. What's your name?"

Sharon started to laugh again and then replied, "I told you my name. It's Sharon. Maybe you have heat stroke—why don't you sit down?"

Still shaking, I agreed, "Yeah, it's gotta be in the 90s."

Jimmy still hadn't moved from his spot and finally, in anger, capitulated, "Hey, Wheaties, I'm going inside—let me know when you wanna play!"

As I sat down on one of the lawn chairs, Sharon pulled up a chair right next to me. As she stroked my sweaty and sunburned right arm, she said, "Man, you're real hot. Do you want something to drink?"

Again I paused because that crazy feeling of goose bumps overcame me the second she touched me. I said, "Sure, how about some ice water?"

Then Sharon came back with, "Hey, Wheaties, how about we go into my house, where it's cooler? In my basement I have a pool table—do you like playing pool?"

As I turned with her to go into her house, I noticed an angry-looking Jimmy across the way, outside his back door with his hands on his hips, probably wondering what the hell I was doing. Well, Jimmy and I were even, because even I didn't know what the hell I was doing. Maybe in a couple of years from then I would have known, but at that moment I was clueless.

As I was led into the basement, I inquired if anyone else was at home. She simply said, "No, they're all at work. Probably be back in a few hours." I had no idea why I asked that question, but I was more assuredly nervous, waiting for Sharon to bring down the cold drinks. As she made her way downstairs, I couldn't help but notice her shorts were almost up to her pelvis. In fact, she had actually changed from blue jean shorts to some kind of cute pink hippie color. As she made it down to the bottom of the stairs with two glasses of ice water, I could feel my heart moving faster than I had ever felt it.

In the background downstairs, playing on a spinning 45 record, was the song "You're Sixteen" by Ringo Starr. I truly thought I was suffering from some kind of heatstroke. Ringo was taunting me with,

You touched my hand, my heart went pop...

Ooh, when we kissed, I could not stop...

I next grabbed a cue stick to maybe loosen myself up by hitting a few balls. As I hit the first ball, I felt Sharon's arm reach around me from behind. As I slowly turned around, I noticed Sharon's long, black curly hair just barely covering her now-exposed and perfectly rounded breasts. It was clear I was not aborting this takeoff. I spent the next hour practicing my newly discovered talent.

As I left her house, I felt like Columbus after discovering America. When I got back to the Kuligoski homestead, I entered the kitchen, and there were Danny, Jimmy, his mother, and most of the brothers.

Jimmy immediately started in like a parrot, "Wheaties was playing hide the weeny... Wheaties was playing hide the weeny!" By about the fifth repeat of Jimmy's diatribe, Danny whacked him right in the back of his head. Jimmy cried for a second, called Danny an asshole, and fled the scene. I simply didn't know what to say.

Neither did Danny's mom, who said, "Did you have a nice afternoon?"

"I think so," I said.

Danny quickly changed the subject and said, "Hey, Marilynn, what we having for dinner?" When I was around, Danny rarely called his mother "Mom," thinking it was kind of funny to call her by her first name when he was in a funny mood, which was quite a lot.

Just when I thought the subject was dropped, in came Danny's dad, who had been briefed by Jimmy. "Hey, Wheaties, come here for a second," came the voice from the family room.

As I approached Danny's dad, I noticed a big smile waiting for me. "So how's it going, Wheaties? I heard you had a lot of fun today... well, did ya?"

Answering almost politely, I came back with, "Yes, AJ, I do think I had some fun today." The AJ reference stood for "Antioch Joe," which was a nickname Danny and his brothers had given him, again all to be funny and cute. "Well, good for you, Wheaties. Now what's for dinner, Marilynn?"

I guess it was just another day in the Kuligoski household.

Chapter 6

Get a Life

INSTRUMENT FLIGHT RULES (IFR): *a set of rules governing the conduct of flight under instrument meteorological conditions.*

The summer of 1975 was the point at which I would climb to new heights. My new flight plan for my life was to abandon college temporarily in the hopes of getting away to see the world. I was tired of school and needed a break. There had to be more to life than just the standard chronology of school, new job, retirement, death, etc. The more I traveled, the more I wanted to see.

My experience with Sharon taught me that life could be very exciting, to say the least. After a few subsequent landings and takeoffs with Sharon, we parted ways. We both never looked back but simply realized we had been a part of something special, virginity notwithstanding. It was time to set a new course.

Danny and I had discussed the Air Force many times and, after talking extensively with a recruiter in Antioch,

Illinois, we signed up together. Then our flight plan got diverted. Danny wasn't able to pass his medical due to high blood pressure and would eventually end up in the Army. I stayed with my plan, and in November was regular Air Force, stationed at Eglin Air Force Base in Florida, working in the Operations Area and Air Traffic Control of the 33rd Tactical Fighter Wing.

While most people might consider the military restrictive, I was fortunate to do some traveling, since our squadron was always on the move with temporary duty assignments (TDY) to attend military exercises. Most of the squadron support people at Eglin were allowed to volunteer for such exercises, since it was not always necessary to have the whole squadron anchoring home base. The most senior support people (and often people with immediate families) were given the first shot at TDYs and often declined to the more junior people like myself, since many didn't want to leave home and their families if they didn't have to.

The exception: whenever the TDY destination was Hickam Air Base in Hawaii, or some other exotic location, then, mysteriously, everyone above me would abandon their families. Because someone had to stay behind, it was usually me.

No one pulled rank or seniority when volunteers were needed for exercises in Alaska in January. I was the first to go then. One day I found myself on the streets of Fairbanks, Alaska, alone in January, wearing my ten-pound Air Force-issued parka. Peering through the small opening of my hood, I spotted a bank sign that was flashing a temperature of -45 Fahrenheit. So much for traveling and seeing the world.

While I was initially trained to be an air traffic controller, most of my time was spent in operations at a desk, overseeing flight scheduling in and out of Eglin, including all flights relating to my unit and various cargo operations. The few controlling opportunities I was given were hemmed in by the fact that in our unit, there was an overabundance of air traffic controllers and I was, of course, the low man. The possibility existed that years could go by without getting more experience, since the little I received made me hungrier to work with the big jets. I was fast growing impatient about what to do with my life. Since the Air Force couldn't accommodate my request to be more involved with airplanes, I decided to try and get back to college while I figured out another plan to get back to air traffic.

In just two years after joining the Air Force in May of 1977, I was given an honorable discharge to join the Air National Guard of Illinois at O'Hare Airport. I could have stayed two more years, but the Air Force at the time had a program called "Palace Chase," which allowed a G.I. to use his/her G.I. Bill, which was basically a college stipend under the condition that for every one year of active service commitment remaining, the G.I. would give two years. So now, even though I was committed to the Air Force for the next *four* years, it was only for one weekend per month and two weeks in the summer.

Best of all, Illinois provided all veterans with the "Illinois Veterans Scholarship," which gave any veteran free tuition to any state school. I could now go to school for free and receive a bonus of almost $700 per month from my good Uncle Sam. I next bought an MGB sports convertible and, since I was living at home with minimal rent, there was but one thing left to do: meet people and see more of the world. I could now delay my future plans for a few more years while I tried to "figure it all out."

I spent the next year making up for lost time. My friend Jim and I hit every lounge, bar, and rock concert, meeting gobs of human beings and just having fun by being incredibly stupid. We had spent far too much of our lives by this time "hitting the books" and "preparing for our future." It was time for a break, and Jim and I knew it was long overdue. When we were in school, we studied hard, but when we were dismissed, we turned into "party people." When we weren't meeting new people, we could always call some of Jim's neighbors, including Cheryl and Karen, who, like us, were only interested in having fun and getting stoned.

Almost unconsciously, I would size up every woman I met. I was still looking for that special woman I had only found once before in my life. My "quest" was a daily fixation. The energy level that drove me was totally unexplainable. It was that same drive that brought me to Air Traffic Control later on in life. I'd meet girls at the local watering holes and at school, talk a few minutes, smile, and away I'd go, interviewing them as if they were a part of some bad reality television show. I was so fearful of rejection that I usually ended the relationship first.

When I was playing basketball at Morton Junior College, I was dating two of the cheerleaders, named Joyce and Eileen. Unfortunately, though, it was at the same time. I wasn't proud of myself, but I simply couldn't make up my mind. On a road trip up to Wisconsin with the Morton College basketball team in January 1979, I was finally exposed. As part of a two-day road trip, the team and I encountered a snowstorm and ended up stranded in a small town just outside Madison. With over a foot of snow at our hotel and twice as much in Chicago, it was decided by school officials that we should stay put. So now it was not only the players stranded, but the cheerleaders as well. After checking into the same hotel, it was obvious both girls knew the other's secret. I could see and hear them in the lobby, using my name in ways I was not used to.

So on a snowy, blustery, Saturday night, there was nothing left to do but open up our hotel rooms and take advantage of the 18-years-and-older-drinking-state status. My teammate, Eddie Sailer, and I had started drinking early in the afternoon, long before the real party began. Eddie was the most mild-mannered, six-foot-six guy you'd ever want to meet. He was always fun to be around, thoughtful, and jokingly self-intro-spective. By the time the cheerleaders walked into our room that night for more revelry, Eddie and I were totally shit-faced. I had even clued Eddie in to the fact that I was probably going to catch a lecture from some angry women. My drunkenness was always timely to avoid conflict.

As we offered beers to the girls, I could see the stares of Joyce and Eileen growing more pronounced, and just before all hell could break loose, Eddie shouted, "Free Bird, Free Bird, hey, we need more beer—Slick," my given basketball nickname, after "Slick" Watts, the basketball player, "and I are going out for some more to keep this party going." Eddie's timing was impeccable. By the time we hit the school van, we were laughing uncontrollably.

Eddie was so drunk all he wanted was to hear his favorite song, "Free Bird" by Lynyrd Skynyrd, on the cassette player in the van. He had no intention of getting more beer. Neither did I. As I swiped the keys from Eddie, we simply took off into the snowy night with no sense of direction. We didn't have a care in the world. As Eddie gingerly pulled the sacred cassette out of his pocket, he yelled out, "Free Bird is here!" Eddie's eyes were mesmerized beyond anything I had ever seen in all my experiences with him.

For the next two hours, we were high on Old Style while singing "Free Bird" over and over. All of Wisconsin could hear,

> *"If I leave here tomorrow, would you still remember me?...*
> *For I must be traveling on, now,*
> *'Cause there's too many places I've got to see..."*

I remember trying to turn the volume knob past the point where it would go—it just wasn't loud enough. The experience was as if we had become part of an MTV music video.

The visibility because of the snow was probably about ten feet at the most. Once in a while we would see a person at an intersection, and it was all Eddie and I could do not to roll down the window and scream "Free Bird" at the top of our lungs.

> *"Cause I'm free as a bird now,*
> *And this bird you cannot change...*
> *Lord knows, I can't change..."*

Occasionally, a few people would clench their fist up in the air as if to agree with us. There were more affirmations to the song than we could have imagined. The whole world wanted to be free and we knew it.

"Won't you fly... high... free bird, ya..."

"Free Bird" was a song special to a lot of people, not just because of its high-intensity rock and roll, but also because of what it meant to anyone who heard it. Everyone had their own interpretation, but to Eddie and me it was about freedom from life's conflicts and problems. For just two hours, we were flying high above the clouds, without a care in the world. It's an experience that can only take place at a certain time and place in our lives. We had lucked out and found that moment to remember. Anytime I saw Eddie after that, his smile would tell the story—he never forgot it.

As much as I wanted to continue the "Free Bird" life, I knew circumstances in life would eventually change how I would look at the world. In May 1978, while I was up in Minneapolis for the week on a summer job with a window-washing company, I received a disturbing phone call from my Uncle Mike back in Chicago. It was early Monday evening when I received his call telling me to "come home, your mom needs you." As I inquired further, "What's up, is it Dad?" Uncle Mike replied, "Yes, Bob, it is. We need you to get home as soon as possible—let me know if you can get a flight."

At that point, I hadn't even considered the seriousness of my dad's condition, since he was in need of a heart bypass and had just been diagnosed with testicular cancer. I knew he was sick, but I was hoping it was just another setback and not anything else. The doctors were putting off the bypass to instead treat what they thought was a fast-moving cancer.

Finding a flight out of Minneapolis airport was next to impossible, since it was late at night and the primary carrier, Northwest Airlines, was on strike. It was already after nine o'clock and I was shaking in the fear that I would never find a way home. I had driven up with the company and six other guys, so I knew having them drive me back was not an option and, besides, I had to get home quick and find out what was going on. I found myself wandering around the tarmac at Minneapolis near the cargo area. My thought at the time was to find some pilot who might be heading towards Chicago. I spent hours endlessly strolling, talking to various cargo companies, trying to hitch a ride.

Just as I was about to give up, I spotted two young pilots wearing brown leather jackets with old-fashioned Snoopy

World War II pilot caps. They were overseeing the loading of their large, single-engine propeller airplane. I was never quite sure what kind of airplane it was, because at the time I only saw it as my last hope.

As I approached the two pilots, I was barely able to speak, but finally it came, "Hey, guys, can you help me out—I'm totally desperate."

The pilot responded piercingly, "What are you doing here—how did you get here?" I just broke down crying—the thoughts in my head were thinking the worst both in Minneapolis and Chicago.

As I started to walk away, one of the pilots came up behind me and said softly, "Sorry, pal, we're not used to seeing someone out here this time of night—what can we do for you?"

Angrily, and with a number of tears, I answered, "I need to get home—my dad is very sick and I don't know how I'm going to get back home!"

As the pilot handed me a handkerchief, he inquired, "Where are you trying to go?"

I had now barely enough energy to talk, but out it came, "Chicago or anywhere close by. Can you help me? Please, dear God."

As I fell down to a crouch on the tarmac, I was spent. Before I could feel sorry for myself, the one pilot's uplifting voice came through. "My friend, you are very lucky tonight. We're going to Chicago and we have just enough room for you." As he said that, I noticed his partner nodding his head up and down, in total agreement. They might as well have been two angels. I was ecstatic.

The ride, however, was a different story.

As I boarded the airplane, I noticed there were only the two seats in the front of the plane. There were no seats in the back for me, just a bunch of boxes tied together. It was clear my seat was somewhere near the boxes on the floor, but I wasn't going to complain since these guys were doing me a *huge* favor.

The flight was noisy and cold. Throughout the flight, the pilots apologized for the lack of heat, but I was too busy being squeezed into the fetal position on the floor to say anything. I was in total amazement at the fact that I had found a way back home—what were the odds? By the time we landed at O'Hare, the sun was just coming up.

As I disembarked and thanked both pilots at least ten times, I asked if they could give me their names so I could send them money for the gas. The one pilot simply answered, "Just go home and good luck—maybe we'll talk later."

To this day, I have no idea who these two pilots were, or the company they worked for. It's always possible that I would or did talk later to them. They were "angels" without an identity.

I wasted no time calling my Uncle Mike and, just as quickly, he was there with my brother riding in the front seat, pulling over next to me at the curb in front of Butler Aviation. I was extremely tired, but now, as I opened the back door and let myself in, I could notice nothing but the uncustomary stoic looks on the faces of both my brother and uncle.

As I sat down and closed the door, my brother just looked straight ahead and said not a word. I could tell from his bloodshot eyes he had been crying. As I looked towards my uncle, he slowly turned around, put his right hand on my left thigh and quietly whispered, "I'm sorry, Bobby, your dad passed away last night."

Even though I heard him, it didn't register in my brain. I clenched the now-moist handkerchief I had received from the angels. I had known my dad was sick, but he had been the picture of health when I left just a few days earlier. At first I cried tears of sorrow, but then came anger. Why? How could God allow this to happen? It was, of course, an answer I would not receive till some time later.

Chapter 7

Say Hi to God

PROGRESSIVE TAXI: *precise taxi instructions given to a pilot unfamiliar with the airport, or issued in stages as the aircraft proceeds along the taxi route, or in life.*

After my dad's funeral, I retreated back to the world of school and partying insanely. I was self-sufficient with the G.I. Bill, and was enjoying school and playing basketball at Roosevelt University. There was still that emptiness inside that I could never pinpoint. I was traveling down a road in life with no destination in sight. Rather than try to deal with my future (and even the present), I found it was better to simply not ponder anything. Having been recruited by Roosevelt University to play basketball, I moved out of my house and into the downtown Chicago dorm on an athletic scholarship.

My roommate was Julius. At six foot eight, with a Marine haircut, he was one of the best ballplayers I ever played with. He was loaded with potential, but short on the ability to find it. Scouts from numerous NBA teams periodically appeared at our games to see Julius, but most were suspicious of his on-court behavior, which ranged from comical to out-of-control anger. Julius was the original trash-talker and had the ability to back it up. Many of our opponents were so intimidated after the first few minutes of Julius talking to them that they either put up or shut up. Most of the time, it was complete silence.

My first few months as Julius' roommate were fun and interesting. We hung out together, ate together, and partied to all hours of the night. Julius was always upbeat and telling jokes—the life of the party. I soon began to realize, however, that if I didn't get back to my studies, I wouldn't be at the university for very long. Julius didn't feel the same, though, and continued to party day and night. I couldn't understand how any human being could maintain that energy level 24 hours a day.

Every one of us seems to have a dark side, and Julius was no exception. One evening after coming back from dinner, I walked in on him to see him with a friend, sniffing a powdery white substance through a short straw. My first reaction was to be angry, since the last thing I wanted was to get arrested on coke charges.

As I started my drug and bust lecture, Julius held his hand up in my face and said, "Quiet, man, and be cool, you'll get us all in trouble."

"No kidding?" I mockingly replied.

Julius then handed me his little mirror with the lines of cocaine on it. "C'mon, Bob, just try a little—it won't hurt you."

I confess curiosity at this point, since I had never seen cocaine up close, much less tried it. As soon as I sniffed the line, I knew I had made a big mistake. My sinuous cavity exploded as if all the internal contents had been ejected. My heart then went into high gear, beating at easily twice its normal rate. It was hours later and I was still wide awake at three in the morning.

Julius had left right after feeding me the mother lode dose, so my guess was I wouldn't see him until the next day. I just wanted to go to sleep and be done with this nightmare called "coke." I made a promise to myself the next day that I would stay clear of any drugs—with the exception of alcohol, of course. Well, at least I was trying.

I started spending more time at home and away from the dorm by commuting to the suburbs. Julius was out of control and rarely saw his bed before two in the morning. He would always keep me awake with his tales about life and how tough it was living in Michigan City, Indiana. I had no idea when he actually did his homework. Occasionally, I would help him with his homework, but he had so much trouble trying to focus that he would usually end up walking away in disgust.

As I spent more time at my home, I began to reconnect with my old friend, Jim. Just as we got caught up on old times, Jim's life took a detour of its own. Jim had found the love of his life and was spending so much time with her he'd forget some days that I was coming over to pick him up to hang out.

On one occasion, he was in his bedroom at five in the afternoon, with his girlfriend, Dale, just taking a nap. When I asked his brother, John, why was he so tired, he just rolled his eyes and said, "I think he's in love and quite busy at it." Since his back bedroom door was closed, I knew it was best to come back another time. I have to admit I envied Jim because I could see the grin on his face was as wide as I had ever seen it. Jim's parents, who were also in the house most of the time, seemed to take it all in stride—they just wanted to see their kids happy.

Then one day, Jim hit me with a big "secret." As I picked him up from Dale's house, I noticed a more dejected Jim walking from the back door to the street where I was parked. As he hurried into the car and sat down, I knew he was upset about something. I had known Jim since the time we were four years old, so gauging his facial expressions was quite easy.

Without hesitation, he deadpanned, "My dad is going to be so disappointed. I'm telling you, he's going to be disappointed."

"Jim, what the hell you talking about?" I inquired.

"Dale is pregnant, man. We're gonna have to get married," Jim replied. I was stunned.

Measuring my words, I knew this was a key moment in our lives. It was as if all the pressure he was feeling was now also in me. The first thing that came to mind was Jim's dad. I *knew* Jim's dad extremely well—he treated me like one of his own sons.

The first part was easy, and out it came: "Jim, your dad will never be disappointed in any of his kids, including you. Wake up, man, you know your dad better than that—he's a great guy. I love him like my own dad."

Jim just stared ahead for a few seconds before answering, "I guess...."

Now it was time for the second point, and again I proceeded cautiously. "I don't know much about marriage, Jim, but the real question is, do you love her?"

Jim paused for only a second, swallowed a lump in his throat and proceeded, "Yes and ..." It was at that point that he pounded my car dashboard in frustration.

I knew he was still trying to figure it all out, so I came back with my last bit of advice: "Don't worry, Jim, this will all work itself out—you *can* talk to your parents."

Jim just looked straight ahead and meekly proclaimed, "Let's get outta here."

A month later, on April 5, 1980, Jim got married, and stayed that way till present day. Jim's marriage was a feat unto itself and also a tribute to his family, who rallied around him and his new wife with all the love a family could hope for. I was envious.

Life was changing all around me at a furious pace. My friends were getting married and having kids. Others were getting out of school and into their dream jobs. It was time to ponder. Where was I heading? On the two-year anniversary of my dad's death, in May of 1980, I decided God and I needed to talk.

Since I was still a little intimidated by the Almighty (having been raised in private Catholic grammar and high schools), I stopped at a liquor store around four in the afternoon and loaded up a cooler in the back seat with two six packs of Old Style. For the next two hours, I simply drove anywhere in the Chicago area with the top down on my MGB and the Doors music blasting so everyone in traffic could hear. I had decided to talk to Jim Morrison before meeting up with God.

I knew my meeting wasn't going to be easy. Jim was singing,

"I live uptown...I live downtown...I live all around...

I had money, and I had none...I had money, and I had none...

But I never been so broke that I couldn't leave town...

I'm a Changeling... See me change..."

Jim was good conversation but did not have the answers I was looking for. I guess I was left with God.

God had decided our meeting would be at the Mary Queen of Heaven Cemetery just outside Chicago, around eight o'clock, by my father's grave. God knew where the best meeting places were. What God didn't tell me was that the outdoor gates would be locked, since the cemetery closed at around seven. No problem, though. I simply parked outside the north gate in the grass and carefully scaled the fence. God likes to test us once in a while.

When my shirt got caught on the fence, I asked God to "free me, please." At that second, my shirt ripped to the point where I fell feet up onto the cemetery grass. Nice catch, God.

My faith told me where to go, and with my now four-pack in hand, I made my way to meet up with God and my dad. God drank beer too, I thought—why not?

After stumbling for a few hundred feet, I came across my dad's gravestone. Our meeting started out rather slow—I think God was feeling me out. For the next hour, none of us spoke. I think everyone else was waiting for me to speak first.

It was now dark, and all I could see were a few cars driving by along the road in the distance, where I had parked. The sky was clear, so I knew God was looking in and hadn't left yet. There were so many stars I had to ask God, "Hey, God, how do you do it, being everywhere and in everything—what's the point to all this, and what do you want from me, anyway?" When God didn't answer right away, I became angry and screamed at the top of my lungs, "What did you do with Eden and my dad—was it their choice?"

Before I could get a response from God, a Boeing 747 Jumbo Jet came right overhead from O'Hare. I laughed and proclaimed, "So that's your answer—that they took a flight somewhere and aren't coming back!?" I admit I was a little over the top, and God was most patient. He gently instructed me to get back into the car and keep driving. I was taken aback by these *"progressive"* instructions, since I figured God was way out of line, condoning drinking and driving.

So I decided to drive, as God had instructed, and I wouldn't stop until *He* brought me to where I was supposed to go. After another six-pack and two gas station stops, it was now approaching three in the morning.

I was still full of energy and even decided to challenge God. "Hey, God, how long are we going to play this game?" I think I heard God chuckle a little bit, so I decided to kick my MGB into fourth gear, down a residential neighborhood street at about 50 miles an hour. This got God's attention. Without warning, I seemingly lost control of my car and then begged God, "OK, God, you win—let's bring this thing to a stop."

As my car came to a screeching halt, I ended up over the curb in the grass, right in front of a church. "OK, God, what's next?"

Without thinking, I got out of the car and walked towards the rectory by the church. The light in the window and a large swing on the porch fixated me. As I proceeded up the stairs, I made myself comfortable on the swing. It was apparent to me that God had called someone for me. But who? Curiosity now had the best of me, so I rang the doorbell. When the door opened, I went into shock. My Uncle Ray, who was a Catholic priest and the pastor of the church, gazed curiously at me through the screen door.

Nearly anyone else in the world would have been angry and not very understanding of someone who drove a car onto their lawn and then proceeded to wake them up at three in the morning. Not my uncle, though, and God knew this.

The irony of this whole incident was this was the first time I had ever been at my uncle's parish at St. Barnabas. I had never been anywhere near there till that night, and my uncle had been the pastor there for almost seven years. Clearly, God was using GPS (Global Positioning System) long before it was invented.

Of all the people I knew in the world, my uncle, Father Ray, was the most kind, trustworthy, and humble human being I ever knew. Even if he hadn't been a priest, I would without hesitation trust my life with this man. His demeanor was gentle and clear. I told him of my experience with Eden and my dad. He already knew about my dad, but Eden was someone new to him, as were all my questions that I initially gave to God earlier that night.

For the next hour, my uncle spoke and I listened. Anyone who knows me can tell you I'm not always a good listener, but that night I was at my best. By the time my uncle was done with me, I realized it was time to get my life back under control and not let everyone else's actions dictate my own. It wasn't a selfish act, but instead one born out of love.

As my uncle turned away to head back to bed, I told God, "Man, you sure *do* work in mysterious ways—now get me home."

Chapter 8

Growing Up Fast

CLEARANCE LIMIT: *the fix, point, or location to which an aircraft is cleared when issued an air traffic clearance.*

Did you ever get to the fork in life's road and not know which way to go? The summer of 1980 presented itself with all the challenges that would determine which way I was headed. Since it was the last few months before my last year of college, I decided on a new course for my journey. So on a sunny, hot day in June, I got into my car, put the top down, the music up, and waited for a revelation. I didn't have to drive for very long or very far before I came upon someone I had noticed many times but never acted upon.

Anytime I came home, I would pass the house of one of my sister's friends who lived on the next block over. Her name was Debbie and, while she was four years younger, she was cute, with long brown hair and beautiful brown eyes. As long as I had known her, she'd always had a boyfriend and was considered mature beyond her years. As many times as

I hoped to ask her out, it seemed every time I saw her in the neighborhood, she was with another guy.

Throughout her teen years, I would see her walking by my house with one of these guys or just girlfriends, simply hanging out. When my brother and I were playing our at-war basketball games with our friends in the alley, she would often casually walk by. Often our game would be suspended for a few minutes so my brother and I could talk to Debbie and her girlfriends. If she was with a boyfriend, however, we would just keep playing.

I must have caught a break in Debbie's life that summer, because on a lot of warm, sunny days, I started to notice her sitting in the front of her house on the brick stairs, all by herself. That in itself was unusual. All Debbie knew about me was that I was her friend Kathy's big brother. One day after dinner, I decided to head out aimlessly into the heat of the summer dusk before the sun went down. As I drove around the block, I saw Debbie once again sitting on her porch alone, but looking more mature than I had ever remembered. I wanted to see her again, if only to be sure I wasn't hallucinating. Rather than stop and look too obvious, I circled the block again. It was probably hard not to notice my continuous driving around the block a third and fourth time with the top of the car down, but by the sixth time, I figured out a good line to break the ice. On my seventh time around the block, I stopped in the middle of the street, a mere 75 feet from Debbie's front stairs.

"Hey, Debbie, you want to go out for some ice cream?" I astonishingly said. I loved ice cream. It seemed like the right thing to say.

Upon my invitation, Debbie strolled down the brick stairs, past the sidewalk and into my car, which was still sitting in the middle of the street. Politely she said, "Sure, where do you want to go?"

As I pulled away, I had no answer, mostly because I was stunned she was even considering going anywhere with me. I stumbled to answer her important question. I couldn't help but notice her long, brown hair flopping all over the place. She was actually more attractive in person and up close than I had previously thought. It seemed I had always observed her from a distance. What a difference.

As I was trying to think of a good ice cream place, I found myself getting onto the highway that leads into downtown Chicago. Again, Debbie casually asked, "So where we going?"

Quickly I came up with, "I thought we'd go downtown for a ride. It's a great night, don't you think?"

Then Deb cleverly asked her own question, "How many more times were you going to drive around the neighborhood before stopping?" At that comment, we just laughed, because now the ice was broken.

We talked about our common friends, the neighborhood, and most of all what we really wanted to do that night—drink beer. So instead of searching out a downtown ice cream parlor, we decided we were going to do the "adult" drinking experience. I found an out-of-the-way liquor store downtown and picked up a six-pack of Old Style with the last three dollars I had in my pocket. We drove straight to the lakefront and set up a blanket on the grass next to a boat harbor by the Adler Planetarium.

For the next few hours, we talked about each other's lives with keen interest. We shared common issues when it came to our fathers, mothers, and siblings. The conversation flowed like the lazy Lake Michigan, peaceful yet satisfying. It was already past ten o'clock, and by this time we were pretty much alone. At that point, there was nothing left to do but catch up on the years we had both missed out on.

When I finally brought Debbie back home, around midnight, there was a man waiting patiently outside her house. No, it wasn't one of her old boyfriends, but her dad. He didn't seem too appreciative that his 18-year-old daughter had been out late with an older guy. After I kissed Debbie on the cheek goodnight and let her out of the car, her father jumped off the stairs and immediately motioned her to get in the house. I could see that the look in this man's eyes wasn't very different from my own dad's when he had been poised to attack.

As I stood in the street, the father came right up to me, nose-to-nose, and in a quiet but very firm voice commanded, "You will always treat my daughter with respect—do you get me?"

It was as if my own dad had said it. I nodded my head in the affirmative. He simply turned and walked away, but in just those few short seconds he made a very strong argument that left a lasting impression on me.

For the next two years, Debbie and I dated, looking forward to the future when I would finish college and then other plans could be made. Since I loved working with kids, I was leaning to a career in teaching, but in the back of my mind, I was still attached to the Air Force and, more importantly, those airplanes that flew directly overhead every day of my life.

When the air traffic controllers strike occurred in August of 1981, I was totally oblivious. I had just graduated a few months earlier and was lining up various teaching jobs at some area high schools. I had received a phone call from my Air Force Reserve Unit saying that, due to the controllers' strike, it was possible the government could change my reserve status back to full time Air Force, to help staff the crippled civilian workforce fired by then president, Ronald Reagan. Just as today's reserve units were activated to go to Iraq full time, the possibility existed that I would be thrust into the civilian workforce as an enlisted military person.

Before Uncle Sam could put me back in the United States Air Force, I hooked up with the government civil service and took the federal exam for air traffic controllers. I knew that the civil service air traffic controllers were making at least twice the salary of the military. It was a real "no-brainer" decision.

After scoring well on the federal exam and then being given a five-point veteran preference, I was guaranteed a slot in the Federal Aviation Administration (FAA) Air Traffic Academy 16-week course in the dust bowl of Oklahoma City, Oklahoma. The next decision was to state my preference, between either a center or tower option. Air traffic controllers are like apples and oranges when it comes to these two functions. To understand the two options, one only has to go to the FAA. gov website. The FAA describes the center option as follows:

En Route Center Controller - Air traffic control specialists at FAA Air Route Traffic Control Centers (ARTCCs) give aircraft instructions, air traffic clearances, and advice regarding flight conditions while en route between airports. They provide separation between aircraft flying along the Federal airways or operating into or out of airports. Center controllers use radar, or in some cases, manual procedures to track the progress of all flights within the center's airspace. Where radar coverage is available en route, controllers also provide radar service to pilots who are not on instrument flight plans, alerting them to potential traffic conflicts.

Translated, the "center" option controllers are the people who work in a dark radar room, staring at a radar screen throughout their eight-hour shift. The only time these controllers see the outside world is when they are on a break and can walk outside the building. The airplanes controlled by the center controllers around most major airports are typically high altitude, above Flight Level 230 (23,000 feet).

The FAA describes the tower option as follows:

Terminal (Tower) Controller - Terminal controllers control air traffic at airports and give pilots taxiing and takeoff instructions, air traffic clearances, and advice based on their own observations and information from the National Weather Service, Air Route Traffic Control Centers (ARTCCs), flight service stations, pilots, and other sources. They transfer control of aircraft to the ARTCC controller when the aircraft leaves their airspace, and they receive control of aircraft coming into their airspace.

Translated, the "tower" option controllers are the people who work in the tall control towers that are present at virtually every major airport across the country and the world. Typically, these controllers work the ground traffic at the airports, clear aircraft to land and take off, and even work some radar, typically within five miles of the airport to an altitude of 5000 feet. Tower controllers get the best of both worlds. Not only can these controllers work aircraft on the radar but also, weather permitting, can actually see and control the aircraft out the window.

The third option not specifically mentioned on the website is the TRACONs, which are the Terminal Radar Approach Control Facilities. Typically, these controllers are the go-betweens for the Tower and the Center. TRACONs vector aircraft received at high altitude from the center to land at airports to a point about five miles from the runway, known as the outer marker. The outer marker is the place where transfer of responsibility occurs from the TRACON to the Tower. Conversely, when aircraft take off from the airport, the Tower transfers responsibility, usually within five miles of the airport to the TRACON. From that point, the TRACON separates the departures from the arrivals before transferring responsibility to the Center, usually somewhere at a specified high altitude. Like the center controllers, the TRACON controllers spend their eight-hour shifts in dark radar rooms. Some TRACONs are located at the airport, just underneath the Towers, while others may be located as far as 40 to 100 miles from the airport they are responsible for.

Since I always wanted to have an outside job without necessarily being exposed to the elements, I elected for the tower option. The wildest thing about being in a tower is that you could be in the middle of every kind of weather, from a lightning-filled thunderstorm to watching a major snowstorm, surrounded by nothing but eight large panes of glass. On July 4th, for instance, tower controllers would have the best vantage point to watch fireworks in communities surrounding the airport. The variety of the tower experiences made my decision simple.

So with part of my life decided in terms of vocation, it was time to make a life decision on Debbie. The FAA not only granted my request to be in the tower option, but also agreed to let me start in California. It was my request to start my career in a new place, far from Chicago, in keeping with the idea of "seeing the world." Leaving Chicago also represented a new start to our life. I knew it would be hard at first for Debbie to leave her family, but the more we discussed it, the more she relented.

I was so caught up in my excitement about leaving Chicago that I almost forgot my wedding proposal. As it was, I took it for granted that since I loved Debbie and she me, there would be no protest on her part to move 2000 miles to the west. Debbie often put aside her own feelings. It wasn't a conscious act, but one born out of our youth—she was still only 20 and had always lived in the same house, while I was 25 and always dreaming about a better life in other places. When I presented her with an engagement ring, my proposal was more in the order of "Will you go to California with me?" instead of "Will you be my wife?" I simply wasn't in tune with what was the most important part of anyone's life: the romantic relationship with my soon-to-be-new wife.

Leaving in January of 1982 for Oklahoma City and the FAA Academy, Debbie and I seemingly had our lives mapped out. She would spend the first ten weeks of my 16-week course with me and then head back to Chicago to plan our wedding in May.

After four months of intensive study, I passed the course that would allow me to become a fledgling air traffic controller at a small tower in Fullerton, California—the start of a career that would dominate and, in some respects, control the rest of my life. Within two days of our wedding in May, Debbie and I had packed up our belongings and were driving cross-country to start an adventure that neither of us could have ever imagined. Our lives were moving so fast it seemed our past was just a blur.

As we got in our car to leave the Midwest, the FM radio foretold the future with the Mamas and the Papas singing,

"I've been for a walk on a winter's day…
If I didn't tell her, I could leave today…"

It's amazing that the innocence of childhood simply seems to disappear without our ever noticing it. It was too late to go back. California, here we come.

Chapter 9

The Minor Leagues

VISUAL FLIGHT RULES (VFR): *Rules that govern the procedures for conducting flight under visual conditions.*

It was a sunny, bright early morning in Fullerton, California, in the summer of 1982.

The airport at Fullerton Municipal Airport was abuzz with the sounds of propellers in all directions. Like the start of the Indianapolis 500, all the pilots, both student and private, were awaiting the opening of the Air Traffic Control Tower promptly at 7:00 a.m. There were no really big airplanes at Fullerton, since the longest (and only) runway was only about 4500 feet. Jet aircraft were not even allowed. This was where it all began. My journey to O'Hare Tower started in a small airport 2000 miles to the west of my hometown.

As I arrived in the parking lot just below the Tower during my first month of training, I spotted the other controllers I was opening up with that day. One was Ron, a typical ex-Marine with a standard jarhead crew cut, bad Marine-issue sunglasses, and an attitude that said "go ahead and knock this battery off my shoulder." In contrast to Ron was Jim, who was very handsome, with long, flowing brown hair, and a look that said "happy days were here again." Jim's appearance, hopping off his motorcycle, was more relaxed. Sporting old, beat-up blue jeans, Jim almost always had a smile or joke to tell when you first saw him. Jim despised Ron because he felt Ron was wound way too tight. Ron hated Jim because he was funny and well liked.

As we took our positions in the Tower, Ron plugged into the "Local" position, the position that is responsible for separating traffic in the air and clearing aircraft for take-offs and landings at the runway. I plugged into the ground control position, which is responsible for taxiing aircraft to and from the runway, as well as issuing ATC clearances to pilots. Jim and I were plugged into the same position because, as my trainer, Jim was responsible for everything I said. If any of my commands were incorrect, Jim could override my transmissions by keying his microphone. This was on-the-job training to its fullest.

As we awaited the opening of the Tower, at two minutes to seven in strolled the Tower supervisor, Bob Starkey. Bob was a crusty older man in his 50's whose only goal at that point in his career was to coast into retirement and into a boat in the Pacific Ocean. Totally gray at the temples and sporting the typical "beer gut," Bob had been in just about every other Tower in the L.A. Basin. A totally "hands-off" supervisor, he acknowledged our presence with a passing caveman grunt of "hello" and headed back down the stairs to read his daily newspaper.

My first job this morning was to complete the ATIS (Automated Terminal Information System). This is a recording that goes out on the air every hour on the hour, repeating over and over the hourly weather, as well as any other important current information a pilot needs to know about our airport. The ATIS is so important that every pilot has to let us know he/she has that information (usually titled by the phonetic alphabet, alpha for A information, bravo for B information, Charlie for C information, etc.) on initial contact before they can receive our services.

Besides the normal L.A. Basin weather that morning ("Fullerton Airport Information Alpha, visibility three miles, haze, smoke"), we added on a special NOTAM (Notice to Airmen). NOTAMs are put into the ATIS to warn pilots of special closures or unusual conditions in the airport traffic area. This day I broadcasted information on a toxic waste area known as the McColl dumpsite, one of the top ten most toxic sites in the country. The Environmental Protection Agency (EPA) issued this warning to us specifically, to have us instruct aircraft not to fly within a one-mile radius lateral or within 2000 feet airborne vertical. Toxic cleanup was ongoing, by environmental specialists in full body suits.

It was Ron's job to keep all the aircraft from flying over this area. We never knew the exact reason, but I guess if the EPA had wanted us to know why, they would have told us. Well, it was about time for Murphy's Law. Ron was doing a good job of keeping his traffic patterns away from the dumpsite when "Copter 2LA" called. Copter 2LA was the local Channel Two news copter in L.A. On initial contact with Ron, Copter 2LA requested permission to fly over the dumpsite to take a few pictures for their newscast. At first, Ron performed his job like a true Marine, telling 2LA he was "unable to approve his request at this time."

Copter 2LA persisted—"Tower, 2LA, we'll only be over the site for a few minutes."

And then the ego in the jarhead came to the surface. Ron looked over at Jim and me and queried Jim, "Hey, Jim, aren't we the controlling authority for this NOTAM? Heck, we put it out..."

Without hesitation, Jim shot back forcefully, "I don't *think so, Ron!*" With that exchange came an awkward silence. And then...

The Marine felt he'd become in charge. "Hey, Copter 2LA, I can approve that—proceed as requested. Plan about two minutes, then I'll have to depart you. Is that OK?"

Well, Jim and I just about fell off our chairs in total amazement. In the distance, looking two miles north out the Tower window, we could see the bright red 2LA circling over the site. In equal astonishment and horror, we could also see some kind of spray and smoke being kicked up by the rotor blades. Within a Marine minute (approximately five minutes), supervisor Starkey had ascended to the Tower with a scowl that was "ready to kill." Apparently, the EPA supervisor at the site had called Bob personally with a severe tongue-lashing.

Watching Bob move amazingly fast toward Ron, I was certain that Ron's life and career were coming to an end. Government officials told us later that when the copter flew directly over the site, it came down so low that many of the contaminants were launched upward in every direction. With many of the toxins making their way into workers' necks where the two suits came together, many of the EPA personnel were affected. Channel Two News had created their own story which, you might imagine, never made it to the five, six, or even ten o'clock news. While this wasn't the first time Ron had found himself in deep with the bosses, it certainly was one of his best.

Air Traffic Control is not unlike professional sports, in that to become the best in your profession, you have to pay your dues and spend some time in the minor leagues (Fullerton) before you can hope to make the big leagues (O'Hare, LAX, Atlanta, JFK, etc.) There are exceptions, of course, but I am not one of them. Fullerton was the first stop on my way to the major leagues. I was always in awe of the fact that I was getting paid very well for something I truly enjoyed and had loads of fun doing.

Periodically, pilots who flew in and out of Fullerton would find time to have casual conversations on the frequencies with us in the Tower. Since most of the pilots were students and instructors in small, lightweight aircraft, the atmosphere on the radio frequencies was often casual and jocular. These little "chats" often led to friendships, debates, and free airplane rides. These "communicative diversions" would drive some of my peers crazy (even to this day), since to them it seemed unprofessional. To me it was as natural as talking to a friend standing right next to me. Many of the local pilots recognized controllers' voices, and mine was no exception. Most aviators knew that if they heard my voice, they could say just about anything, professional or not. The pilots were my friends.

One of the best friends of the Tower was an Air California pilot named Mike Blackstone. While he was an airline pilot full time around the surrounding big airports such as LAX, San Diego, and San Francisco, Mike managed to find time to fly his glowing red Pitt Special biplane at our small airport in his free time. Nicknamed the "Red Baron," Mike was always fascinating to watch, so much so that I and the other controllers would often let him try some of his aerobatic maneuvers in the local airport traffic pattern (a practice often frowned

upon by management, since it at times delayed other aircraft).
I very rarely let Mike land without showing us a break out to
the right or left, followed by a full rollover. Eventually, Mike
asked me if I wanted to go up with him. Not wanting to say
later "I wish I had done that," I got instant permission from
Starkey, who often needed a break from my turning the Tower
upside down with my, as he called it, "air traffic nonsense."

As I walked out from the Tower to the flight line, my
body shook with both fear and excitement at the thought of
flying in this machine that looked like a novel roller coaster
car. Mike was about as nice a guy as you could meet, never
talking in anything but a soothing and calm voice. As he started to talk in his quiet voice, however, I could barely hear him
with the "hard rock" noise blaring from another plane just a
few feet away.

Next to Mike's airplane, a young man was prepping
his small Cessna. On top of the hood was his boom box, blasting out Robin Trower's "Day of the Eagle." It seemed very
inspiring:

"It's like a weight that brings me down...
If I don't move, I'm on the ground...
Living in the day of the eagle,
Eagle, not the dove."

I couldn't wait to be airborne like the eagle.

Mike initially equipped me with the familiar "Snoopy"
headgear. Looking up to the Tower, I could see the amusement
on everyone's faces. I must have looked absolutely ridiculous. I
felt like a World War One flying ace lost in the '80s. One of the
flying instructors walking nearby upon seeing me, said, "Good
luck, Ace, hope you make it back alive."

Then it dawned on me. "Make it back alive" must have
referred to what could be a fun ride or one that would end up

with puke everywhere. Upon taking my place in the open-air rear seat, I could tell there was plenty of room to leave my recently eaten breakfast. Mike took his spot in the front seat while my heart felt like it was coming out of my chest.

As Mike started the engine, his voice came booming through my headset, almost flipping me out on to the tarmac. "OK, Bob, are you ready?"

Promptly I replied, and in my cocky air traffic controller voice: "Yeah, Mike, let's see what this thing can do!"

How stupid could I be, challenging a pilot in his own special airplane to "show me"? As we taxied to the runway for departure, I could hear Jim on the frequency, telling Mike to "Give him both barrels" (as in barrel rolls). Instead of Jim issuing the words "cleared for takeoff," it was "Pitts-four-mike-bravo cleared for extreme aerobatics. Good luck, Bob." It was now obvious that Jim had flown with Mike before, and somewhere inside the Pitts, there was probably some of Jim's breakfast residue.

As we lifted off the runway and then almost straight up, it didn't seem possible that the flying harness holding me would keep me from falling out of the cockpit. After leveling off, Mike asked me where I wanted to go. Without hesitation, I replied "straight to the ocean." It was only ten nautical miles to the ocean from Fullerton, and in no time at all, with one big engine blaring over our voices, it seemed like we could see forever. To see the ocean in all its splendor, reflecting the bright sunlight just a few thousand feet above the ground, was as if in a dream. This was the childhood image I had imagined of how God must view the earth.

My fascination soon ended abruptly with a sharp upside-down maneuver and then back level again. "Whoa, Mike, what the heck was that?"

Mike replied, "You wanna try that?"

Like a simulator, I grabbed the stick in front of me, still able to tell Mike was in control of my stick and the airplane. When he let go, I was in total control. The neatest thing about a bi-plane is its ability to almost never stall out, since it is like two giant wings floating through the sky. Pulling back on the stick with Mike's help, we went straight vertical and then all the way over. I thought I had died and gone to heaven. *We* had become more flexible in flight than all the seagulls around us.

Watching the setting sun glistening off the waves reminded me how insignificant I really was. Having spent many nights looking into the dark, starlight skies and the immense distances, I was in total awe of this seemingly endless view of the Pacific. As we made our way from the ocean back to land, the new reality set in. Below us, the Long Beach and Riverside freeways were one big parking lot. For just one hour we had become one with the sky, while the rest of the world was lost in traffic.

Just when I thought I had made it back in good shape, a sudden nauseating feeling overcame my whole spirit and spread itself throughout the inside of the cockpit. I was just a mere three miles from the airport. So close, yet so far. Mike, I'm sure, had seen this many times before and just pretended it was just "another passenger." Best of all, though, I had come back alive.

Chapter 10

Pumping at Palwaukee

FORMATION FLIGHT: *More than one aircraft that, by prior arrangement between the pilots, operate as a single aircraft with regard to navigation and position reporting.*

My journey to the O'Hare Tower was not by accident. I was very anal about what I would do next in my life. I planned my every next move with the precision of pilots doing a preflight checklist. I would go over and over in my mind every detail, until I knew it so well I had totally memorized it. I listened to my supervisor at Fullerton. Big Bob would tell stories about how he was from Chicago and had worked at O'Hare back in the '60s (Bob was well past retirement at this time already). His stories included colorful terms like moving the "'heavy metal' while I was at the 'Big O.'" At times, Fullerton was "just like the Big O, only on a smaller scale," Bob would say.

Moving a large number of airplanes, even at Fullerton, was quite a thrill, and at times like drinking ten cups of coffee. Very often, after working an hour of busy traffic, I could not contain my euphoria, much like a long-distance runner who experiences the "runner's high." For many reasons, my endorphin level was sky high whenever I worked a lot of airplanes. Most times, I felt like a kid playing video games for the first time. Many of my fellow controllers stayed out of my way when I got off position, because I was so hyped up I would say and do such off-the-wall things as run up and hug them because I was so happy to be there.

Very often, I would sneak up behind another controller before I went on break and make some colorful remarks in their background transmissions so I could be heard by whomever the other controller was talking to. I would say things like "Hey, you, get off my airport!" or "Oh my God, I've made a terrible mistake!" To the layman, this would have sounded crude and rude, but to the controllers in the Tower, this was live comedy for free. I was so obnoxious and off-the-wall I could get away with it because it was hilarious, and since it didn't hurt anyone, it became standard practice. On top of it all, they were paying me to perform this service—unbelievable!

Money was never the major issue, working as an air traffic controller. I wanted to work at the big places like LAX or O'Hare, and to get there I would have to "bid" out, a process at the time that could be more politics than how well you presented yourself. And as I would find out later, being terribly obnoxious has it advantages. So with my bid paperwork in hand, I ventured to the O'Hare Tower to personally present my bid and talk (politicize) with Chester "Andy" Anderson, the Tower Chief.

Andy was a mild-mannered, soft-spoken gentleman who made you feel at home in his office, and at such ease that I just blurted out conversation. Not able to contain myself, I came straight to the point. "Andy, it's my lifelong goal to be here at O'Hare. I'll do whatever it takes to get here. Please, sir, please." At this time I clasped my hands and said, "Please, Andy, please, all I want is to move the heavy metal—and by the way, do you need your house painted?"

Finally, a smile stretched across his stern face. I had got to him. "Well, Bob, *slow* down now, your supervisor already called me yesterday."

My mouth dropped right there. My supervisor had never told me he was going to call ahead about me.

"Your supervisor had nothing but great things to say about you, Bob."

I was startled at first, but then remembered he must have been trying to get rid of me and this was his out.

It was at this time that Andy gave me my new game plan. "You know, Bob, air traffic is like the big leagues."

"But, Andy," I chimed in, "I'm ready, big fellow!"

One of my pet colloquial terms had slipped out once again, much to the amusement of the chief.

"OK, Bob, here's the deal. You spend some time at the Tower [Palwaukee Airport] just up the road so you can familiarize yourself with the local geography, and as soon as you get certified there, I'll pick you up here."

So now, and without Andy's help, I had to go and talk to the Tower Chief up at Palwaukee, a woman named Linda Brown. Since Andy didn't know me from Adam, he wanted me to jump through his hoops to see if I could pull it off.

On my ten-mile drive north to Palwaukee Airport, billed as the "world's busiest private airport," since it was privately owned at the time, I couldn't get out of my mind the first poem I memorized when I was about five years old. It went something like this:

I went downtown to see Mrs. Brown

She gave me a nickel to buy a pickle,
The pickle was sour so I bought a flower,
The flower was dead so I bought some thread,
The thread was thin so I bought a pin,
The pin was sharp so I bought a harp,
The harp wouldn't play so I gave it away
Then I went back downtown to see Mrs. Brown.
Oh well, forget the poem.

I knew I had to concoct another plan to sway the Palwaukee Tower Chief. I figured, what the heck, I'd stop at the local florist along the way, pick up a dozen roses, and then simply charm the living hell out of her. What a mistake.

When I first met Linda, I noticed her stone-faced, blank expression. Her first question in a very solemn tone was, "Who are the flowers for?"

So, without hesitation I said, "Well, for the Tower and you, of course."

Not impressed, Linda looked at me and said, "Well, Bob, you can stop trying so hard—I've already talked to Andy at O'Hare."

Wow, in the span of my half-hour trip to Palwaukee, Andy had given Linda my complete story. Linda continued jokingly, "Oh, and by the way, good luck, big fellow."

I felt totally exposed, but was glad the ordeal was over. Everyone has a humorous side to him or herself, and I was happy to have found Linda's. I now knew that my stay at Palwaukee, however long, would be fun with Linda as the boss.

My plan was simple. I would get checked out on all the positions at Palwaukee Tower and go straight to O'Hare, as Andy had promised.

Working at Palwaukee was like working at a mini-O'Hare Airport. While the number of airplanes was great, it was only a small warm-up to the big house at O'Hare, just ten miles to the south. The main traffic at Palwaukee was small, single-propeller airplanes, with occasional business jets. It was an interesting mix of airplanes. Trying to separate one airplane that was three times slower or faster than another was quite a challenge. Traffic periods ran in streaks.

At times, there might be 20 to 30 airplanes you could be handling within ten miles of the airport, and at other times, not a one. Weather was the determining factor for how many planes would fly on a given day. The better the weather, the more planes per cubic airspace. The majority of pilots were students, with or without their instructors. If the weather turned bad, such as high winds, thunderstorms, low ceilings, etc., most everyone but the most experienced stayed on the ground. Most student pilots flew after work during the week, and then again on the weekends, when most were either out of school or on days off from their regular jobs. Consequently, if any Saturday or Sunday featured nice weather, it was a good bet that the sky would be full of airplanes. And where did all these airplanes come from?

The bigger airplanes, such as the jets, mostly belonged to big companies and celebrities. The companies included Baxter Travenol, International Harvester, etc. The main celebrity based at Palwaukee was the owner of the Baltimore Colts, Bob Irsay, who on subtle requests from other controllers in the Tower, occasionally gave us tickets for various Sunday games, and even flew a few of us out to the games.

The other, and more fun, celebrity was none other than John Travolta. He flew his Citation in and out of Palwaukee, usually to visit his sister or, at other times, he'd have Marilu

Henner in tow. Being celebrity awestruck, we would often take out our binoculars to see all the beautiful people around John's airplane. John was an excellent pilot and thought nothing of making short visual approaches in his Citation jet to help us out when we needed it. He looked like he was living the life of a fighter pilot. It was always fun to talk on the frequency with someone who's enjoying his job just as much as you are. Every once in a while I would try to get John to give a line from one of his movies before I cleared him to land. Very often he obliged, but it was hard to tell if it was actually John, or his first officer having fun with us. One time, however, when he proclaimed, "Summer Lovin'," from *Grease*, I knew I had a winner.

While having seen movie stars might have provided entertainment to an already fun job, one of the biggest thrills of my life came along on October 6th, of 1983. My first child and son, Adam, came into the world seemingly out of nowhere. During my wife's pregnancy, the reality of actually having and experiencing a child was totally imaginary. You never know what having a kid is all about until they are actually right in front of you. We had no desire to know ahead of time the gender of the baby. It didn't matter to us. All that mattered was a healthy baby. We had been through all the Lamaze classes hoping for a routine childbirth where I could be present to witness the grand event of our lives. But having a baby is anything but routine.

As my wife's labor approached the 20th hour, it was obvious to the doctor that a cesarean section would have to be performed due to the breached position of the baby. Debbie had already been through so much pain and anguish that the doctor had been expressing concerns about her well-being. He even insisted that Debbie would have to have general anesthesia. I couldn't believe that he was actually talking about knocking out my wife to have a baby. It seemed all too surreal. What had started out at as a joyous event when we entered the hospital had become a life-threatening event for my wife and the baby. When the crusty, old doctor told me I had to leave the birthing room and that my wife would have to be taken up to the operating room, my heart sank. I was shaking with fear and, with no other family members present, I was banished to a waiting room, thinking the worst.

I was as lost as a pilot flying in the clouds with no instruments. I was so afraid I didn't even think to call family for support. I had told relatives I would call as soon as there was news since they all lived nearby. After about an hour, the doctor came into the waiting room with his surgical mask still around his neck. It was almost as if he couldn't wait to talk to me. As he started to talk, I thought I was going to faint. All the emotions since I left the birthing room had totally consumed me. When I saw the doctor coming through the door it re-minded me of what it must have been like for other families to get bad news about their loved ones. I confessed I feared the worst and told God to please help Debbie and the baby. I sim-ply could not bear to witness the pain of those close to me.

Thankfully, the first thing out of the doctor's mouth was a faint smile and the words "congratulations, it's a baby boy – mom is doing OK but will be unconscious for a little while yet." I was so elated I hugged the doctor, who awkwardly returned the favor. I was told I could then go back upstairs to see and hold the baby as he and Debbie were leaving the oper-ating room. I just about knocked over the doctor as I made my way to the entrance of the operating room. As the gurney with Deb passed through the doors, a nurse was holding our new-born son and smiling at me. As I attended to Deb, I noticed she was still in a sound sleep. When I questioned the nurse she said that Deb would awaken in few minutes. As she said that she handed me Adam. I felt guilty about seeing Adam before Debbie but, unfortunately or not, that guilt lasted only a few seconds.

When I looked down at this small baby it would have been hard to imagine that this seven pound, 20 inch long baby would eventually be six feet two and over 200 pounds. His extremely light blond hair and blue eyes were like looking in a mirror to my own past. It was obvious to me that the nurse had given me the correct baby. He was the perfect combination of his mom and dad. I could not have been more proud. I couldn't spend enough time with Adam after that. To me, he was the "champ" and for his first few years that's how I referred to him. I knew though I would have to go back to work and spend time with the "baby" pilots at Palwaukee. I, of course, mean the word "baby" in the positive sense since most of the pilots were only recently "born" into the aviation world.

Most of the Palwaukee traffic was composed of people learning to fly for the first time, known as the "student pilots." Very often, these students would come and visit the Tower with their instructors, to become familiar with how the aviation system really worked. On these visits, I got to know two young instructors named Mike McClellan and Jim Johnson. We all became good friends, both on and off the airport.

Our conversations, at first, were very professional and not very revealing about each other's jobs, but as time went by, we would very often share our private stories and laugh endlessly. When Mike and Jim were flying, I knew I could count on them to keep the students from driving everyone in the Tower crazy. If I needed some kind of unusual flying to make my job easier, I knew I could count on Mike and Jim. But even they could not imagine how wild it could get when the sky was literally full of novice pilots.

On any nice, sunny weekend, you could count on coming to work and guiding more airplanes than you could handle. As the weekends went by, controllers became more competitive to see who could work the most airplanes at one time. This "competition" to work several airplanes at one time was always a fun time for me and my fellow Tower controllers. The reason I think that is because it *was* like trying to win at the video arcade. Everyone's abilities were tested far beyond what you might be capable of, thereby forcing you to learn new techniques quite by accident.

During one busy Saturday afternoon, I was inundated with a sky full of student pilots and other weekend joy riders. Without a cloud in the sky and temperatures in the 70s, the weather could not have been better for flying. In the immediate vicinity of the airport, I was working about ten airplanes (the estimated maximum number of aircraft for the airspace within one mile of the Tower). There were another 20 or so outside the airport traffic area that were requesting to land at the airport after making their local area joy rides.

Like a waiter taking walk-in reservations, I simply annotated on a notepad the flight names of those who called outside the traffic area and worked them all in as soon as I could, on a first-come, first serve basis. However, as my waiting list began to grow, so did my impatience. I now had to work more airplanes than I was comfortable with, simply because there was a real potential for a lot of people to run out of fuel. Even student pilots and their instructors who didn't mind spending extra time in the air were starting to get a little testy.

Finally, one of the impatient pilots started a chain re-action that would define most of my career. One of the flying club's patrons outside the traffic area insisted that he wanted to fly as a formation with another plane that belonged to the same flying club. While somewhat unusual and mostly par-ticular to military aircraft, formation flying was something I could not find as a violation of the rules with non-military aircraft. But like a chain reaction, other pilots saw this as their way to get back to the airport in record time.

After talking amongst themselves on other company and club radio frequencies, the requests came anew. "Hey, Tower, Cessna Three-alpha-golf, Cessna Five-bravo-foxtrot and Cherokee One-alpha-november would like to come in as a flight of three." Then, before I could speak, came another transmis-sion: "Ah, Tower, Tomahawk Three-niner-five, Cherokee Six-oh-two, Cherokee Five-eight-foxtrot, *and* Champ Six-oh-four are six miles north, requesting landing as a flight of four." As long as the aircraft involved similar aircraft, such as all single-engine propellers or dissimilar aircraft in a group that had the fastest as the lead aircraft, I could not see or remember any-thing in the air traffic manuals that would not allow this con-trived air show. Well, I had been in the Air Force for two years, so anything seemed possible.

By coincidence, just below our Tower were some air-plane hangars, where one of the FAA's finest regional office persons was shining his airplane on this beautiful Saturday afternoon. Doug was his name and he was one of those bu-reaucrats who dictated FAA policy from a remote office just five miles from O'Hare and Palwaukee. With Doug's hangar lo-cated right next to the landing runway, from the Tower above I could see the absolute horror on his face. Probably without any kind of military experience, he must have been shocked to suddenly see groups of civilian airplanes landing two, three, four, and sometimes even five at a time. Maybe he thought the airport was under some kind of attack. This was not the norm at Palwaukee or any other airport, for that matter, since typically most airplanes normally land one at a time and have to be clear of the runway for the next arrival to land.

To make my air show even a little more complicated, and since it was getting close to dusk, I decided to tell everyone who could hear me to turn on their landing lights. At certain times, I would ask for certain groups of pilots to blink them as a form of verification of their locations. I simply made up this whole plan on the spur of the moment. I sensed that I was going to be bombarded with an insane amount of airplanes coming back to land, because most student pilots at the time preferred to be on the ground before it got dark and many were still flying.

Sensing the imminent rush of airplanes, Jim and Mike, in different airplanes, rushed back so fast that they ended up landing without even talking to me. They said later that they knew if they didn't get in right away, they might have to end up at another airport or in the middle of one giant hornets' nest of airplanes. I was talking so much that barely anyone could answer, and too often the wrong aircraft was answering, anyway. So, unbeknownst to me, Jim and Mike, with a few other experienced pilots, slid in on runway six-right, which was seldom used by anyone, anyway, since it was the shortest of the five runways at Palwaukee. What a beautiful sight around Palwaukee Airport, to see at least 20 to 30 airplanes in little packs with their landing lights blinking on and off—this would make anyone watching from the ground nervous. So along came Mr. Nervous.

Immediately sensing some kind of perceived mayhem, Doug ran to the base of the Tower, where our direct phone line to the cab was located. When he picked up the receiver, it rang next to me. At the time, there was only myself and another controller, who was also quite busy, working ground traffic and making weather observations. Having heard Doug's voice before and knowing who it was, I simply said, "Hey, sorry, we don't have time for a tour of the Tower today, come back later," and just as fast, I hung up the cab phone. Then, as quickly, the phone rang again, and again, and again, and after about twenty rings, I simply lost count. I was too busy with aircraft to explain my newly developed air traffic technique to some old man who probably hadn't talked to an airplane since the Wright Brothers. Within a half hour, my supervisor called from home and again I simply assured him all was well, not to worry, and Doug was simply being governmental. But it would not end there.

Doug had called other regional office people over the weekend, including the Regional Air Traffic head and others in the FAA, such as the medical department, to have "my head examined." To Doug, I was a snotty kid who had to be put in his place. So a meeting was called with all concerned for the following Monday morning at 8:00 a.m. My immediate supervisor, who was supposed to be off on Monday, was also called in since Linda, the chief, was on vacation. I reveled in the fact that my supervisor, Tommy "Downtown" Brown, was as brash and as "off-the-wall" as I was. In fact, Tommy enjoyed my methods of controlling traffic so much he nicknamed me his "Bullet Bob."

I hadn't slept much over that Saturday and Sunday night, fearing the worst come Monday morning. Tommy came in with his typical hangover. Tommy was a known partier and often spent his breaks from the Tower at the local racetrack. He and I were the first to arrive. Tommy had not been briefed on my "incidents," since he rarely answered his phone. All he had was a phone message to make sure he was in Chief Linda's office at 8:00 a.m. sharp, or else.

So along came Monday morning and before I could even talk to Tommy, in walked the entourage of G-Men. Leading them was Teddy Burcham, our Air Traffic Regional Head. Teddy was a tall man, about six-foot four, and spoke in a much-defined southern drawl. I had only met this man in passing and had always been intimidated by his stern demeanor. Behind him were two people from the FAA medical department. One was introduced as an FAA flight surgeon. (Later, I found out he was a doctor of gynecology. Go figure.) Next in line was my primary antagonist, Doug, followed by Tommy, who had the main recording tape in hand from Saturday's "fun time." As he placed the big, round tapes on the player for all to hear, my heart sank. Had my air traffic career come to a crashing halt? Would I be banished to some desk job— say, in Doug's office?

As the tapes were played to all, I could see the look of disgust on the faces of Doug and the medical people. My supervisor, Tommy, however, was smiling the whole time, not even sensing their dismay. It turned out later he thought they were there to give me some kind of award for moving "the metal," as he put it. The tapes were even more surreal than I could have imagined.

Never realizing at the time I was bordering on the incredulous came such pilot remarks as "Hey, Tower, this is Cessna Three-niner-golf, flight of four Cessnas, and we have the flights of two and three ahead of us and will follow." Then, from no one in particular came, "Hey, Tower, this is a *lot* of *fun*, can we do this again next Saturday?"

I don't think anyone had a real problem with my creativity, until it involved the flights of three and four, which seemed like far too many airplanes to land at once. (Only the world's biggest air show up in Oshkosh, Wisconsin, ever tried that trick, and it was encouraged there.) But land they did, and even while the inquisition was proceeding, instructors from the general aviation on the airport were calling to tell us what a "great job" we had done Saturday afternoon. I had Mike and Jim to thank for that.

As the meeting continued, all I could thing about was John "Cougar" Mellencamp playing the "Authority Song." It was the situation I was in. John would say,

"*They like to get you in a compromising position…*
Well, I think it's a total disgrace…"

About 20 minutes into the tape and with heads shaking all around, Teddy abruptly stopped the tapes and turned quickly to Tommy and bluntly stated, "What do you have to say about this?"

And with his typical smile from ear to ear, Tommy emphatically stated, "Yeah, Teddy, that's my Bullet Bob—listen to him *pump and bang* those airplanes!"

Seemingly not expecting that answer, Teddy turned to me, looked directly into my soul, and said, "Kid, you're a flake."

It was a kind of validation, and his way of saying "while I might not myself do what you did, I can't find anything terribly wrong here." Teddy, like everyone else present, grew quiet for a few seconds, and then a faint smile came across his face. "OK, Bob, what is your goal in your career as a controller?"

I immediately replied, "I simply want to go to the Big O."

Teddy confusingly replied, "The Big O, well?"

And right there, Teddy granted my wish, and within three weeks I was walking through the doors at O'Hare. I had finally made it to the big leagues. Amazing what a government agency can do when it puts its mind to it.

Chapter 11

Welcome To The Big O

AUTOMATED TERMINAL INFORMATION SERVICE (ATIS): – *the provision of current, routine information to arriving and departing aircraft by means of continuous and repetitive broadcasts throughout the day. Frenchmen make the best recordings.*

February 17th, 1985, was the day that I walked into the aviation big league training camp known as O'Hare. Ever since I first started, it had been my dream to work with the best of the best. O'Hare, at the time—as it is today—was considered not only the center of aviation for the country, but as O'Hare goes, so does the rest of the country. Delays, whether due to Mother Nature or volume at O'Hare, usually translated into delays at other airports as well. Chances are if you are a passenger on the ground at Newark or San Francisco waiting to go somewhere, you are probably waiting for a plane from O'Hare to serve your particular flight.

When I casually strolled through the front entrance at the base of the Tower, I was in complete awe of the fact that I had finally made it to a place few other controllers dream about (or have nightmares about). I felt like the Chicago White Sox or maybe even the Chicago Cubs had just signed me. Seems as a native Chicagoan, I am also a fair weather fan, having always leaned toward my godfathers' White Sox. Since my mother was the die-hard Cubs fan, I struggled between the two for years until my godfather, Uncle Bob, won out.

It was a great thing, though, since I got to go to my first World Series in 2005. The feeling I got walking into Cellular Field for Game 2 of the World Series on October 23rd, 2005, was exactly the same as walking into O'Hare for my first day at my so-called job. I say "so-called" because I have never considered what I did as work. So like Chicago baseball, O'Hare was the "Big Leagues," and *every day* there was the World Series of air traffic control. Time to have some more fun and get paid for it.

Rather than report directly for duty, I instead walked to the break room to observe a number of controllers sitting at three small tables, four abreast, engaged in some friendly games of cards. They were playing something called "tonk." While I wasn't familiar with how the game of tonk was played, I was familiar with the betting at 25 cents a point. One controller was pointing out that he was up five dollars thanks to the "dumb ass" sitting next to him, and then playfully whacked his neighbor on the back of his head. The atmosphere was very spirited and lighthearted. You sensed that everyone wanted to be there. Many were engaged in conversations about the day's shift. Others were mocking, wrestling and taunting each other while still others sat passively on a couch, scrolling through the local television channels. This place had fun and adventure written all over it. This was where I wanted to be.

Most of the controllers were fairly young, probably in their 20's and early 30's at most. It was clear that the leftover management that existed from the controllers' strike in August of 1981 was managing the workforce at O'Hare. In August of 1981 came the low water mark for labor and air traffic controllers. That year, Ronald Reagan fired over 12,000 air traffic controllers for walking off the job. Only a handful of experienced controllers were present at O'Hare from 1981, and it was clear that the number one goal of management was to train new controllers and to do it as quickly as possible.

Six-day workweeks were the norm, and since everyone was fairly young and naïve, I could sense an aura of invincibility amongst all I encountered. An older workforce might have been discouraged by the long, six-day workweeks, but not this group of controllers. It was just another challenge in all their short lives. Besides, no one was turning down the big paychecks that came with overtime pay. So it was just a bunch of young kids happy to be at the Shangri-La of Air Traffic Control.

I observed very few shy people at O'Hare. Most of the people in the break room were fairly loud and even competitive about who was controlling the conversations. This all confirmed my preconceived notion that most, if not all, controllers at O'Hare were either Type A or, as I saw it, "Type AA." My newly invented designator of AA was clear to me, since I had never observed such an abnormally high level of testosterone (the guys) and estrogen (the gals) in any social setting.

Bypassing my meeting with the new Tower Chief, I followed some controllers out of the break room to the elevators, headed for the Tower. The two controllers were Vinnie and "Tex," and as I got onto the elevator with them, they immediately inquired about my identity. Without hesitation, I introduced myself, but before I could get four words out of my mouth, Tex interrupted, "Oh, you're the new guy from Palwaukee... good luck, man. You're in for the ride of your life." And then, as quickly, he went back into his conversation with Vinnie.

As the elevator creaked its way up to the Tower, Tex pulled out a comb and started combing his moustache with simple down strokes. How weird. By the time the elevator got to the top floor, I wondered if Tex had some kind of some schizophrenic disorder. Then as the door opened at the top, Vinnie turned to me and said, "It's not too late to turn back."

As we ascended the one flight of stairs to the top of the Tower, Tex introduced me to the Tower supervisor, Bob Pywowarczuk, known as "Pork Chop." Seems "Pork Chop's" last name, of Polish descent, had so many consonants and vowels that it was shortened just enough so people could make sense of it.

As I introduced myself, a bellowing voice echoed through the loudspeaker at Pork Chop's position. "Hey, Tower, ease up on the west-bounds a little—we got weather out there!" The voice was from the radar room at the base of the Tower, from the man they called "the Mish." Bob Mischke was the manager of the TRACON and was responsible for coordinating any activity with the Tower. The urgency in his voice barely made an impression on Pork Chop who, without a flinch, shook my hand with his right and answered the phone with his left. Multi-tasking at its best.

He then calmly told me to go ahead and walk around and "plug in wherever you'd like." So as I grabbed my head-set to walk around, Pork Chop jumped up into his controller chair, put his feet onto the console and stared aimlessly into his *Car* magazine. The whole time he was as cool as a cucumber, if there is such a thing.

I couldn't help but notice a big radio in the middle of the Tower, sitting on a counter. It was pure rock and roll by the Rolling Stones, belting out "Jumping Jack Flash." As loud as it was, it appeared no one was being distracted. In fact, people were swaying back and forth as if they were Mick Jagger. Mick was screaming,

> *"But it's all right now, in fact it's a gas!...*
> *But it's all right. I'm Jumpin' Jack Flash...*
> *It's a GAS! GAS! GAS!..."*

As I walked up to the various controllers around the Tower, the nicknames started to come fast and furious. Seemed just about everyone had a nickname. The first controller on position I encountered introduced himself as "Geoff Ross," but then several other controllers chimed in and said, "No, not Geoff, that's Chumley." I have to admit Geoff did look a bit like Chumley, the Walrus from the old kids' cartoon. So Geoff just smiled as if amused, and from then on I called him by his given Tower name.

It was a strange tradition, since later on, if I had friends visit the Tower and I introduced them to some of the controllers, I would inevitably forget their real names and always make the nicknames sound like they were their real names. Chumley was a good sport, and as I plugged in at the outbound ground control position, I could see he was about to get very busy. With most busy airports across the country, it's feast or famine when it comes to the number of airplanes that taxi out for departure at one time, but at O'Hare, it was just one big feast. Chumley initially started by taxiing groups of three or four airplanes to their departure runways while giving me a detailed explanation of his every move. Chumley was the modern-day John Madden, diagramming the "plays."

As Chumley was instructing, someone turned the volume up on Mick Jagger.

"I was raised by a toothless, bearded hag...
I was schooled with a strap right across my back...
But it's all right now, in fact, it's a gas!...

I could almost feel the adrenaline rush from the Stones. I wanted to talk, but not knowing what to say, I simply waited my turn. Within a few short minutes, Chumley had around 15 aircraft waiting to taxi and still, without missing a beat, he kept them all moving. The traffic got so busy that Chumley stopped allowing *any* response from the pilots to answer his instructions. There simply was no time to wait for any pilot's reply. In the rest of the normal aviation community known as the FAA (Federal Aviation Administration), it was standard procedure to allow *each* pilot to read back controllers' instructions. But O'Hare was clearly not standard, and to spend any extra length of time on one aircraft meant delaying several others also awaiting taxi instructions. (That procedure exists to this day, and if anyone doubts that, please turn to Channel Nine at United Airlines and find out for yourselves when you're in Chicago.)

Like a policeman working a busy intersection, Chumley simply kept talking and the aircraft kept moving to their respective departure runways. To my amusement, Chumley would mockingly ask me if I was ready to take over, and all I could say was "Dah, dah..." Chumley clearly knew how to play the crowd around him, and I admit I couldn't wait to get my opportunity to do the same years later. I grew tired just watching Chumley attack as many as 20 airplanes at a time. By the time I went back downstairs for my initial orientation with the training department, I knew I was in for the battle of my ATC life.

One of the first supervisors I worked with was Dan Kuhn. Dan tried to remember my name, but since it was Bob (and there were a number of Bobs in the Tower), he settled on the name imprinted on the back of my blue jeans. So the rest of my time, to present day, everyone work-related called me "Calvin." It got so normal that when people outside work called me at the Tower, looking for "Bob Richards," people answering the phone in the Tower simply said, "There's no one here by that name. You must have the wrong number." When members of my immediate family called, they were often told, "Bob Richards? Bob Richards? No one with that name works here." Many in my family started to doubt if I even worked at O'Hare.

For the first year at the Big "O," I worked with a crew of seven people, four of whom were journeymen and the rest trainees. The main problem for me was I was the third trainee on the crew known as E. It was tough enough to find training time for one trainee per crew, much less the number three person. So, for the first year, I waited and waited.

The wait was worth it. On December 29th, 1986, my second child, a son, was born. Andrew Robert Richards was a planned cesarean section. Even though I wasn't training, it was still perfect timing since now I could spend as much time as I wanted with my new boy. I was even allowed to be present at the birth. I must confess when I saw the doctor cutting my wife down her middle with the scalpel I wanted to be back at work. More amazingly, my wife seemed like she was without a care in the world. I guess having "that area" anesthetized and not being able to see it made the whole birth almost painless.

Initially, the doctor pulled out a giant piece of tissue about the size of an extremely large football. When I calmly asked the doctor what the heck that thing was he announced "uterus." That's when I knew my wife and I were done having kids.

When he put his hand in there like a magician pulling a rabbit out of the hat, I had to look away for a second. Andy came out a little darker complexion than his brother but was just as feisty and cute. All the waiting in the Tower meant nothing compared to this moment. The magician had done his magic.

The great thing about Andy's birth was the timing. I don't mean for tax purposes but rather Andy had taken tradition into the third generation. The previous generations of me and my brother Billy, our dad and his brother Lowell, and now Adam and Andy were all equally three years apart. It was still one more chance to make brothers with more improved relationships than were exemplified by the previous generation. Adam and Andy became closer than their previous "brother" generations. My then wife and I did everything to make that happen in the following years. I was just more obsessed about it, not wishing for history to repeat a third time.

After taking a little time off to be with the boys, I finally went back to work. The first thing I did when I came back from my "vacation" was to see if the supervisors in the Tower were going to let me back in the "game" anytime soon. The answer was a solid "maybe." I was itching so badly to work airplanes, I almost wanted to scratch anyone who would listen or train me. I started to feel like my "flake" reputation was being misconstrued by the people around me.

Meanwhile, the other trainee I walked in the door with was well on his way. Kevin Winn was a controller from a small airport tower in Beverly, Massachusetts. His attitude to O'Hare was exactly the same as my own. He was excited beyond belief to get a chance to work at the world's busiest.

Kevin's large eyes made him look like a possessed man when he started training. His distinctive New England accent always stood out from the native Midwesterners at O'Hare. I was so impressed with it, I nicknamed him "JFK" and "Mr. President," since when he talked, it sounded like President John Kennedy reincarnated. Kevin spent three years at O'Hare before heading back east, where he would eventually end up at Boston Tower. He would take what he learned at O'Hare and share it with the rest of the east coast. Years later, we would compare notes.

With two trainees on my crew already training on ground control, I ended up spending most of my time in what was known as the corner. Basically, I was reading clearances to pilots and putting out the hourly weather observations known as the ATIS (Automated Terminal Information Services). Every hour, I would record the ATIS, which would be repeated over and over for the full hour, till the next hourly observation was due. I got so bored with the repetition of the position that I would often allow visitors to the Tower Cab to compose the recording, with my coaching.

One day, it was my job to familiarize a group of visiting controllers from France on the inner workings of the Tower. You could tell the FAA wasn't interested in keeping good relations with the French, as they had me show them around. While I was working the clearance delivery position, it came time to do my hourly ATIS, so I decided to put the French to work. I whispered in the ear of one of the French controllers the words that he would repeat into the microphone, which would become the hourly weather. Keep in mind the hourly weather must be listened to by every pilot before they can leave or land at O'Hare. In fact, each pilot must tell the controller they have that specific bit of information, titled with one of the letters of the alphabet. For example, "O'Hare Airport

Information Alpha," then the next hour would be "O'Hare Airport Information Bravo," etc. Each lettered hourly observation always contained the current weather, such as cloud ceilings, temperature, wind speed and direction, etc., and all the things a pilot needed to get in and out of O'Hare.

So in a heavy French accent, the hourly weather observation went out over the airwaves to pilots on the ground, and to others as far out as a hundred miles from the airport. Reviews were mixed. Many of the pilots found themselves paying more attention to the ATIS because it sounded so unusual. Sensing I had found a way to keep the pilots' awareness level up to a new high, I cleverly used other voices, including Richard Nixon, Truman Capote, Jimmy Stewart, and even Mickey Mouse.

Just as I was getting to the point of utter boredom, I was moved to another crew, where I would not have to wait in line to train. I was now about to leave one area of adventure to find another. I was just starting up the roller coaster known as O'Hare. Get ready for the ride!

Chapter 12

The Bob and Steve Show

TAXI: *the movement of an airplane under its own power on the surface of an airport or on the stage with Chuck Berry.*

By the time it was my turn to train on ground control, I had already built up quite a reputation. For my first year at O'Hare, I had taken up drinking as a new sport. I confess that before 1985, I had been a sporadic beer drinker, but by the time I had gone out on many lounge field trips with my fellow controllers, I knew about everything from home brews to Long Island Iced Teas. Having a few drinks after work was a tradition at O'Hare—a time to tell wondrous stories of the present and the past. We patronized establishments in all directions: to the west it was Fiddler's, to the north it was the Shady Rest, and to the east it was Carmichaels. When the owners of these fine watering holes saw O'Hare controllers coming through their doors, a cash smile usually followed us throughout the night.

One night I was so happy to be at O'Hare, I celebrated till I ended up in the Schaumburg, Illinois, jail. The cop didn't even wait till I put the car in drive. He followed me in the parking lot outside the Derby Street lounge while I was yelling goodbye to another controller. When I screamed "I am invincible" just a few feet from his face, I knew I had made a big mistake. Honestly though, I didn't see his face before it was too late.

"Oh, tough guy," the cop sarcastically exclaimed, "Let's see how invincible you'll be when I bring you in!"

I was like superman loaded with kryptonite. I went from invincible to "babbling idiot." It was a lesson I never forgot, particularly when I realized I had two small boys and a wife at home.

Not wanting to upset my family, I called Dave King, one of my closest friends in the Tower and about the only one I trusted to save me at two in the morning. Dave, known as King-size, stood well over six foot five but was a gentle giant. If you got him upset, he would simply ignore your presence. Dave didn't seek conflict, he avoided it like the plague. I didn't know what to expect when I called him to bail me out.

As we left the jail, Dave kindly informed me he had talked to my wife and all would be OK. Then he let me have it. "What the hell are you thinking Calvin!" All I could say was "I guess I wasn't." Lesson learned.

When we woke up the next morning, Dave prepared his "shoreline breakfast". He even woke me up early at 7a.m. I was "almost" ecstatic. Dave was the only human being I knew who stored panfish mixed with Campbell's soup in old milk cartons frozen in the refrigerator. He swore by this "home-made" breakfast. Being from the north woods of Wisconsin, Dave was the consummate "nature boy." I was the sick "city boy."

The "bluegills" were making me so nauseated, I truly had learned my lesson.

Before I left, Dave gave me the O'Hare lecture. In a joking tone, Dave explained "Calvin, you got to slow down man and take care of your family or I'll kill you." Dave was right. I wasn't ready to die.

Dave had done such a good job talking to my wife the night before she forgave me as soon as I came home. She knew I was angry and ashamed of myself. I had learned about patience and forgiveness from two caring people. It was time to be trained.

I'm sure there was a lot of behind-the-scenes jockeying as to who would train me, or possibly, who didn't want to train me. Many controllers would say mockingly, "Not me, brother—you're way out there." I guessed these were all references to the local administrator, Teddy, calling me a "flake." Finally, out of the smoke came two brave guys who probably never had a clue what they were getting into, or how many years I would eventually take off their lives.

The first was Bob Karnick. Bob was tall, lean, good-looking, and very optimistic. His training partner was Steve Colfer. Steve was short, almost lean, somewhat good-looking and cautiously pessimistic. The first time I trained with Bob, he smiled and asked, "Get the picture?" The first time I trained with Steve, he *almost* smiled and asked, "Do you know what you're doing?" I knew I had Bob sold on the idea of training me, but Steve, as best I could tell, was either in shock or felt pressured that he was somehow about to be part of a very harrowing experience.

I knew Bob had a sense of humor, but it would take some time and effort till I could find Steve's. It was my idea that *everyone* has a sense of humor. Given time and a good

effort, I hoped Steve would relax to the point of actually smiling and laughing. To my way of thinking, smiling and occasionally laughing in the Tower was also a sign of verification
from the trainer, or it could be the final days of one's training
at O'Hare. At the outset, though, Steve was very tentative and,
given the option, usually let Bob do the training.

In my first few hours of training with Bob, it was all
about sinking or swimming. Even though training at O'Hare is
like training anywhere else, in terms of starting with light traffic and eventually moving to heavy traffic, it was always prob-
lematic to find a good time for light traffic, since it really didn't
exist at O'Hare. On outbound ground control, which was responsible for getting the airplanes to the departure runway, I
attacked the problem like a homeless person at a free buffet.
Bob was patient and when I occasionally sent an aircraft to an
incorrect runway, he simply pointed to the flight strip and,
after a few good guesses, I usually came up with the proper
solution. Bob was the teacher of positive reinforcement.

In the same situation with Steve, instead of pointing at
the strip as Bob did, Steve would roll his eyes into the back of
his head. He could get those eyes so far back you couldn't even
see them. Wow, what a trick. Steve was the teacher of negative
reinforcement.

Keeping track of the airplanes on ground control at
O'Hare was very low tech at best. When working outbound
ground, an ancient computer (still used to this day) had printed out paper strips of each outbound flight that were then
mounted into a strip holder. The strip holder representing just
one flight measured about 1"x 8". The strip holder itself could
then be moved around a strip board to sequence the aircraft in
the order to the different departure runways. When the order
was established, the strips were delivered to the next controller

known as "local control" who then was responsible for clearing aircraft for takeoff. You still had to place all the strips on the local's board as well. Multiply that times around 1400+ departure flights a day and you have quite the manual labor.

All ground controllers spend a lot of time moving around the Tower to see the whole airport. It's impossible to stand in one place and work the position. As controllers walked around the Tower, they were tethered to 10 to 15 foot long cords which often got tangled with other controller's cords and inanimate objects, such as chairs and tower area managers. This can become an annoying distraction. It always amazed me that we never had cordless headsets while the employees at Burger King and many clothing stores have been using them for years.

The other ground control, known as inbound ground, was even lower tech. As aircraft landed, cleared the runway, and then contacted inbound ground, the controller had to write down the company flight numbers on a notepad. Someone had even designed an even slightly higher tech system by using small plastic chips with magnets that could also be moved around a metal strip board just like outbound ground. A grease pencil was used to write each airplane on the plastic strip. Many didn't adapt this method because they felt it too labor intensive versus simply writing down everything on one sheet of paper.

Both methods were simply used as aids to ground. If you spent too much time looking at your strip board and not out the window, chances are you would be doomed to failure. The priority for both ground controls was to avoid conflicts on the ground. The less time looking out the window, the more likely a collision could take place. Occasionally, the traffic on inbound would be so heavy that looking down at a strip board was non-existent. When traffic was that busy, it was "sink or swim" time. Most controller training failures at O'Hare Tower happened during this time.

All the information on each departure strip was hand-written, including the runway assignment, time of taxi, aircraft heading, etc. The only preprinted information was the aircraft flight number, type aircraft, and route of flight. Technology has been and still is a long way from the big Towers across the country.

The FAA for years had talked about and even designed a "stripless" board that could be worked by using a simple touch screen. While such a system would have no great impact at a small airport, O'Hare and other high volume facilities would have valued greatly from such an upgrade. But due to the budget and "government red tape," the real actual stripless environment isn't scheduled to visit O'Hare until sometime in the year 2008.

It was often hard for my trainers and particularly Steve to see what I was doing since a trainer had to watch out the window and the notepad as well. Steve was always trying to look over my shoulder and I would purposely or accidentally block his view. I knew I was making Steve crazy but I confess I was entertained watching him as well.

I figured I had to loosen up Steve a little, so I tried all sorts of bizarre tactics. One time, while Steve wasn't looking directly at me, I grabbed the hand-held radio in front of me, hidden from Steve, and got on my own ground frequency; in my fake, deep pilot voice, I said, "Hey, Tower, I'd just like to say this is United Two Sixty-nine and you guys are the best—keep up the good work there, Mr. Ground Controller." Steve, not knowing who had made the transmission, just looked out the window and exclaimed, "Oh my God, is he kidding!?"

Another time, while on my break, I ran into a Simmons pilot in the terminal. Since the Tower was located across from the terminal, it was not unusual to sit down at one of the airport restaurants and next to an airline pilot. After a long and cordial conversation and knowing he was flying out, I asked the captain to make a kind remark on the ground frequency. I told him it would be a clever joke on my trainer.

The pilot agreed, and when he came up on my frequency later in the day, he said, "Hey, Tower, this is some of the best ground-controlling I've seen in years. Keep up the good work, man."

Steve, upon hearing this, simply said, "Are all these pilots fucked up in the head? Did I hear that right?"

Not wanting to let Steve down, I quickly retorted back to the pilot, "Simmons, could you repeat your last, just a little slower and clearer."

And again the pilot said. "Aw, c'mon, we're just saying that this is some of the best ground-controlling we've heard in a long time."

Steve didn't say a word, but contorted his face in utter disbelief and then stared at me with his head on a perfect 45° angle. Steve *was* the toughest egg to crack in the sense-of-humor area.

Then, one day by accident, I finally brought the "Happy" Steve Colfer out. One of our favorite visitors to the Tower was a local television weatherman and aviation expert by the name of Jim Tilmon. Jim worked for Channel Five in Chicago but also at one time had been a pilot for American Airlines. He was frequently allowed by management to come up to the Tower to get file footage and occasionally ask questions of the supervisors in the Tower. It wasn't his being a local celebrity that impressed me, but rather his unbelievable likeness to the great Chuck Berry.

Having played guitar since I was in fifth grade, I loved music and, in particular, Chuck Berry. After a while in my mind, I believed Jim *was* Chuck Berry. It got to where when Jim came up to the Tower, I would say, "Hi, Chuck, how's it going?" As I extended this greeting, usually most of the Tower would start cracking up. With a puzzled look, Jim would reply, "Good, man, really good." Every other word out of Tilmon's mouth was usually "yeah, man" this and "yeah, man" that.

At one point, while Jim was taking some footage and talking to a supervisor, I went into that famous Chuck Berry "duck walk," where he bends his knees and glides across the floor with his guitar. I kept going from one end of the Tower Cab to the other while controllers around me could barely speak to pilots without laughing.

And then it happened—Steve smiled. Then came an actual smirk. Finally, after a year of repressed humor, came the loud guffaw. I had found in Steve what few around me had known: Steve, indeed, had a sense of humor. His partner, Bob, even reveled in the moment and patted Steve on the back, although I am not sure as to why.

Two weeks later, I checked out on ground control. I could not have been more excited. How excited was I? The day after I checked out, I had a little accident on the floor just below the Tower. On my first day of being checked out on ground, I was working with a Tower Area Manager named Dick "Shifty" Shaftic. (Honestly, you can't make up that name.) Dick had been a controller in both the Tower and TRACON for years. After watching my first "virgin" hour on ground, he jokingly offered, "Well, Calvin, looks like the airlines will have someone to blame for future delays." Dick was pure "old school," and his remark put me at ease.

Dick was so impressed he even serenaded everyone in the Tower with his favorite song, "American Pie," by Don McLean. I could remember several occasions when Dick would just blurt it out in the Tower, but this time he put more feeling in it:

"So bye-bye, Miss American Pie,
Drove my Chevy to the levee but the levee was dry,
And them good old boys were drinking whiskey and rye,
Singin' this'll be the day that I die..."

I was so happy with his positive "feedback" I *ran* down the stairs to the elevator in total euphoria. As I reached the point where I was five stairs from the landing, I jumped as high as I could to bypass the last steps. Unfortunately, my head drilled itself into the pointed section of concrete where the ceiling meets the side wall. As I fell to the ground, there was blood everywhere. My head was soaked in dripping, red clumps of hair. I immediately ran back up to the Tower for medical attention. As soon as Dick saw my bloodied head, he didn't even flinch, only calmly announcing, "C'mon, Calvin, what did you do now?"

After I explained my stupidity, everyone in the Tower got a good laugh. I, on the other hand, received ten stitches for the effort. No one ever said training on ground would be easy.

I was left with one more step to complete my O'Hare ground training. As was the O'Hare tradition, I would have to buy the entire Tower food and drinks after work on a given night the following week. Since many of the controllers lived to the west, Fiddlers was the spot chosen for my checkout party. Checkout parties at O'Hare were usually like big weddings, including all you can drink, eat, and puke. Each Tower controller had two main checkout parties. The first was for successfully finishing ground control, both inbound and outbound. The second was for checking out on the local control position (the clear to land and takeoff position), which also meant that all training had ceased and the controller was now a fully certified, bona fide O'Hare Air Traffic Journeyman Tower Controller.

Since the checkout process was grueling and could often take as long as two years, very rarely were any controllers concerned about the expense of such a party. All that mattered was the significance of the checkout, which was the equivalent of joining one of the most exclusive clubs in the world. Many controllers didn't make this club and ended up becoming higher management in the FAA. To this day, many of them still exist. I will speak about them later.

I figured I'd be able to cut down on my checkout expenses if I had my party right after one of my night shifts. Many controllers, I thought, might want to go home, having not gotten off work until 10:00 or 11:00 p.m. Some of those leaving the night shift had day shifts the next day, so it seemed logical that certainly they wouldn't make it. I couldn't have been more wrong.

Controllers are like vampires and love the late night. Alcohol was their blood and I was soon caught up with the whole idea that Count Dracula was everywhere. The Tower supervisor let me take off a few hours before the shift ended so I could "set up" my little party. I made it to Fiddlers just after 7:00 p.m.

After I introduced myself to the bartender and told him what kind of party it was, he shot back with, "Holy shit, guy, this is going to be a long night for me, isn't it. Do you have money? How about a credit card for the tab? I was hoping to go home early tonight. Oh, well."

I was just starting to get a feel for what was about to happen. I knew the possibility of a big turnout existed, since everyone not just in the Tower but the TRACON, as well, was inquiring about the location and time. Since the Tower and TRACON were located in the same building, going to each other's checkout parties was the norm. The relationship between the two entities was like a family, since the Tower depended on the TRACON to receive landing airplanes while the TRACON depended on the Tower to receive departing airplanes.

I made friends with just as many people in the TRACON who I didn't directly work with as the Tower personnel, who I stood next to through an eight-hour shift. The reason was simple. The one break room at the base of the Tower was the common meeting point for *all* the controllers. It was the only break room. If you had to go to the bathroom, chances are you'd run into someone from the TRACON, because that was their bathroom as well. Any disagreements between controllers in the Tower and TRACON could usually be resolved with a few harsh words, a game of cards, or a simple drink at the hotel sports bar, located just outside the Tower entrance. The team concept at O'Hare became a positive reality, due to the simple fact we had to be with each other on a day-to-day basis.

As I waited for my party to start, I struck up a conversation with the three other patrons present who happened to be off-duty mechanics at American Airlines. When I explained why I was there, they kindly bought me a drink. That was the last drink anyone bought me that night. It was almost eight o'clock and still at least an hour before any of the night shifts would get out when I noticed the first few people from the Tower and the TRACON walking in.

Apparently, the kindly supervisors in both the TRACON and Tower let people leave early just for me. What a cool tradition, I thought. In no time, there were at least 15 to 20 controllers buying me drinks with my money. The first hour I drank every type of mixed drink, beer, and variety of shots known to Fiddlers. The rest of the night was a total mystery to me, due to the fact that my brain was spinning at an uncontrollable rate. I knew Bob and Steve had made it, since I probably thanked them about 30 times in my drunken state, and Steve repeated 20 times jokingly, "You're welcome, now get the hell out of here!"

As fate would have it, the jukebox was playing "Johnny B. Goode" by Chuck Berry:

"Go!

Go! Go! Johnny!... Go! Go! Go! Johnny!... Go! Go! Johnny B. Goode!"

The energy level was high at the party, and not just because of Chuck Berry. Everyone was having the time of their "O'Hare" lives.

Most of the controllers from the TRACON and the Tower at the party had all just been checked out in the last few years, and knew what the party represented. It was a new, young aviation family coming together, which would be a force to be reckoned with for many years to come. Working at the world's busiest airport was a daily struggle that everyone had only recently become familiar with. Most of the controllers, with the exception of the supervisors, were still in their 20's, with their whole career ahead of them. Pride was everywhere. There was no pride, however, when my credit card was swiped at about two in the morning. A mere $900.

One of the controllers, Ralph "Bub" Gehrig, , also known as Baba Louie, simply looked at the tab and said matter-of-factly, "Looks like you got off easy, man."

Looking back at Ralph, I proclaimed, "Maybe, but what about the next ten years? Let's see how easy that's going to be."

Ralph just shook his head and pondered, "Who cares, let's just have fun."

And in that short answer, Ralph had summarized what I would adopt as my new attitude for the rest of my career. Ralph was predicting the future and didn't even know it.

Chapter 13

Fun with Fieweger

STANDARD INSTRUMENT DEPARTURE (SID): *A preplanned instrument flight rule (IFR) air traffic control departure procedure printed in graphic form for pilot/controller use to provide obstacle clearance and a transition from the terminal area to the appropriate en route structure. E.g., "Fly the Pete Rose departure."*

One of the most memorable characters early on in my O'Hare career was a supervisor by the name of Jon Fieweger. Jon was a personality unlike any other and totally born out of the "old school" way of conducting business. "Old school" meant Jon wanted everyone to learn on his or her own—totally through self-discovery. If you made mistakes of any kind in the Tower, Jon didn't just let you know, he would ride you for hours, thereby making you never forget your miscues or repeat them again. New people coming to O'Hare at this time probably had a 50/50 chance of making it at O'Hare. The training was tough and such that supervisors wouldn't ever call you by your correct name, but by ones invented by the other certified controllers and supervisors.

There were a lot of controllers I worked whose real names I barely knew. But I knew their nicknames, such as "Goose," "Sparky," "Volcano Man," "Newt," "Chumley," "Mr. President," "Kingsize," "Loser Boy," "Opie," "Craw Daddy," "Howard Sprague," "the Butcher," "Sabutosaurous," "Mudcat," "the Mayor," "Rosie Palms," "Angry Squirrel," "Harpo," "Scare-os," "Cocoa," "Soldier," "Loafpinch," "Shakes the Clown," "Buttercup," "Fred Flintstone," "Mr. Peepers," "the Waz," "Kuze," "Boozer," "Johnny B," "Sweet Roy," "Genius," "Bruno," etc. Even our supervisors had their own nicknames, including "Pork Chop," "Dancing Bear," "Big Ears," "the Baron," "Da Fuhrer," "Shiny Pants," "Baba Louie," "the Ficker," "T-Bone," "McGarrett," "Fat Bastard," "Minnie Me," "Shifty," etc. As long as I could remember, nicknames were terms of endearment and a part of acceptance. Most of the time, you had a good chance of making it through training if your new nickname became a part of everyday conversation in the Tower.

So that's how I knew Jon would be a friend for life, since it was *"Hey, Calvin"* this and *"Get your head out of your ass, Calvin!"* It was this type of focused attention that let me know I had a chance of making it. Jon was usually very out-spoken and took crap from no one, including upper manage-ment. He simply knew more about the operation than just about everyone above him, and since Jon got results, he was rarely questioned. What kind of results, you ask? Well, when Jon was the supervisor in the Tower, delays were usually at a minimum, and *not one* airplane on the taxiways was allowed to stop. "Keep *my* inner and outer moving grounds," Jon would often say out loud to everyone in the Tower. The inner and outer taxiways were the two main plane arteries circling the terminals. They were the lifelines of the airport.

At the weekly controller meetings, I joked to our Tower Chief, Chester (Andy) Anderson, (and it was true at the time), "Hey, Andy, we haven't seen you up in the Tower for months. Is Jon still in charge?"

Well, wouldn't you know it, the next day I plugged into ground control and I could feel someone's breath coming down the back of my neck.

"Hello, Calvin, look who's here."

For the next two days, Andy came up behind me with the same playful, clever lines, such as, "Bet you didn't expect to see me here," or "Hey, Calvin, if you're keeping score— that's two days in a row now." And then I didn't see him for months.

Andy was one of those nice, happy, jolly, almost quasi-Santa Claus people you always enjoy being around. He knew the controller's job as well as anyone, having gone through the ranks at O'Hare, both in the Tower and the TRACON. It was that understanding of the job that let Andy give free rein to people like Jon. Most air traffic facilities across the country stressed the importance of "phraseology," or how controllers should talk to pilots. O'Hare had only one goal (as it does to this day), and that's *move* the airplanes and *move* them as safely and as *quickly* as possible. In December of 1987, it was with deepest regret that the regional office "relieved" Andy of his duties to give him a desk job at their field office.

Mostly politics, of course (Andy simply wasn't a good politician, and we all loved him for it). In tough situations, Andy always backed up the controllers and told the regional office to back off. Many at the regional office resented O'Hare controllers and Andy because they perceived us as "snotty, overpaid, immature children." Most of the resentment resided in the fact that many of the controllers at O'Hare were paid quite well. In fact, most of the controllers with ten or more years of experience were making as much or more money than regional office personnel, who were considered upper management in the FAA.

Andy was totally devastated at being removed from O'Hare. O'Hare was Andy's whole life. At one point, after having been at the regional office for only a few months, Andy hadn't even told his family of his new job. It was when his daughter Kelly came over to the Tower from the terminal before catching a flight that his secret was out. Andy couldn't even tell his own family about his transfer. He was that proud. When told her dad had been gone for almost two months, Andy's daughter was also devastated. She knew how much it meant to her dad.

It was that same pride in his job that made Jon the strong taskmaster. When Jon spoke, it was as if God himself had spoken. (This, of course, was Jon's own analogy.) When the weather got bad and airplanes were coming out of our ears, we would ask Jon, "Hey, Jon, can't you do something about these thunderstorms?" Even Jon believed he could change the weather. Everyone in the Tower would stop what he or she was doing whenever Jon spoke. To ignore Jon at times would be to provoke a sure verbal "ass whipping."

Jon's gruff appearance most resembled the Popeye cartoon character, with an unfiltered cigarette dangling from the side of his mouth and hair balding on the top. But most of all, Jon was loyal to the troops. Like General George Patton, as long as you fought the fight to keep airplanes moving, Jon would play the part of cheerleader and encourage you with phrases such as, "kick 'em in the ass," and "let's keep my airport moving," and "who the hell taught you how to move airplanes?" This was how you knew Jon liked you.

I was always impressed with Jon's knowledge of the entire O'Hare operation. He ate, smoked, and drank the O'Hare air traffic controller experience. His dedication to the Tower was beyond reproach.

While most of us in the Tower knew Jon's stern manner was mostly an act (and often a funny one, at that), there were a few people who genuinely feared Jon. People who didn't like to work with Jon would often trade work shifts or even call in sick.

As a newcomer to O'Hare in 1985, I was quite intimidated by Jon at first. When he first looked at you, he didn't look at you, he looked right through you. Gradually, though, other controllers would come up to me and tell me that if I just gave 110% to my job, Jon would be there to help.

Not giving 110% all the time at O'Hare often translated into less than stellar air traffic controlling which in turn meant a *safe* but not so expeditious flow of traffic. If you reduced your speed of clearing aircraft for takeoff by as little as 20%, it would only be a matter of time before delays set in. Remember, a plane delayed at O'Hare will be the same plane delayed when it takes off again at its next destination and even the next destination after that. The human factor is tough to measure but most supervisors could tell quite easily if someone was "dogging" it.

It was also a known fact that if you ever came to work to give less than 110%, you would probably drown in the flood of O'Hare airplanes. You had to stay on top of your ground airplanes at all times. Training was the key.

On-the-job training of air traffic controllers consisted of plugging in to two jacks, one for the instructor and one for the trainee. If the trainee was talking to the pilots and said something that was incorrect or inappropriate, the instructor, by keying in his mike, could override an errant transmission. Jon's method of OJT training was simple. He would plug in with you, ready to train, and as soon as it got a little busy, he would remove his earpiece, walk away, and amuse himself with some other Tower activity. Now it was sink or swim with no lifeline. While I was fighting to keep the airplanes moving in an organized, almost balletic manner, Jon was in the background, humming to one of his favorite cassettes I had brought in.

It was "The Animals," blaring out their hit song "It's My Life." (Eric Burden, I figured, had to be Jon's hero, without ever knowing it.) Music has always been a great source of comfort and motivation for controllers when working traffic in the Tower, so having the radio or cassette playing was standard procedure on every shift. Very often, the radio was turned off or down whenever visitors came to the Tower, but as everyone got used to it, we simply stopped turning it off. Even Jon got into the music, singing out loud,

"*It's my life and I'll do what I want... girl, there's a better place for me and you."*

Jon despised lazy people and there was no time to be lackadaisical at O'Hare when you were trying to move 2200 planes a day. Like Coach Bobby Knight yelling instructions to one of his players, Jon would systematically walk around the Tower and give on-the-spot corrections, such as, "Hey, who's stopping my inner and outer taxiways?" or "What the hell you doing with that guy?" Most often the responses to Jon's antics were quick and with youthful enthusiasm. If the responses were not at Mach One, then Jon would say, "Get 'em [him or her] outta here!" and immediately another controller would fill in. If you argued with Jon on the position, he would sometimes grab his own headset and do the talking. This to me was the most entertaining and, I confess, I sometimes baited Jon into doing just that.

One time, I had an American flight that was taxiing from the runway to the gate. After giving the flight crew the most precise of instructions, I sat back and watched as the plane turned in all the wrong directions. As I corrected the pilot's mistakes, I wondered aloud in the Tower, saying such things as "can you believe this guy?" and "this pilot is killing me!" By this time, Jon was breathing over my shoulder and fuming, just waiting for his turn.

Eventually, Jon pushed me aside, plugged in his headset, and screamed to the pilot, "Hey, American! Hey, American Three-oh-five, we don't have all day to baby-sit you to the gate—get out your taxiway charts and use them!"

The response was even quicker: "Hey, Tower," angrily, "we want the phone number to the Tower supervisor, now!"

Jon obliged with the phone number and said, "I would be happy to talk with you." After that, there was dead silence on the frequency.

Jon was a big believer in every person being innovative when necessary. Everyone was expected to creatively deal with the problems that arose on the frequency. There really is no possible way during on-the-job training to simulate every possible trouble situation that could arise in the Tower.

One day, after a thunderstorm moved through the airport and left about 60 flights grounded at the runways, awaiting departure, it was clear we would become very busy when the weather cleared. At least 30 arrivals had been circling for a half-hour, poised within 50 miles of O'Hare, waiting for the green light to proceed to the airport. When the all-clear was given, the quiet Tower gave way to controlled chaos and confusion. I was working inbound ground at the time.

My task was to talk to the airplanes after they landed and taxi them via the most appropriate routing to their gates. This was no easy chore by itself, since after storms it was not unusual to be talking to ten or 20 flights at one time. Combine that with the fact that there were gate holds and you had to find areas to hold aircraft until their gates became available, and it was one big mess. And if that weren't enough to start an ulcer, other, bigger problems would come up.

Because of the bad weather, the back-up frequencies would be used up to read other alternate weather clearances and more ground controls. The only frequency this day that wasn't being used was 121.5. This frequency in aviation is the most sacred and not to be used except by aircraft in an emergency situation. It is constantly monitored by other facilities, the communications center at the airport and regional office, and just about every law enforcement agency around the area.

During a flurry of transmissions that day, someone had a stuck mike, on *my* frequency. This was when true panic set in, because here I was, moving around as many as 25 arrival airplanes on inbound ground, trying to get them from their landing runways to the gates. Because of the stuck mike, all the pilots were having a hard time understanding two simultaneous transmissions. One was mine and the other was the idiot holding down the mike button (accidentally, of course) talking about his layover in New York and what he was "going to do to that buxom flight attendant." While entertaining to many pilots, it was quite a dangerous distraction.

I immediately looked down at my console for one of the back-up frequencies. I first selected 119.25 (a back-up frequency), but soon realized someone else in the Tower was using it. When I saw all the other back-up frequencies being used, I went to select the only frequency not being used. By this time, the situation is known as "going down the crapper" (in controller lingo) and it's a sinking feeling you have, knowing things are not going to get better for some time. Some airplanes were stopped on the taxiway, some were making wrong turns, and all the flights on the concrete tarmac looked like a bunch of ants, all lost with nowhere to go. So I did what almost any controller would do in this impossible situation. Yes, I selected the emergency frequency, 121.5, and told all who could hear me on the stuck mike frequency to come up on 121.5. I told the controllers who were handing off landing airplanes to me to make sure they sent them to me on 121.5. My devious plan worked great for about ten to 15 minutes, and then the phone calls started coming in.

"Hey, Tower, this is Charlie Fox Dog [Chicago Fire Department]. What's going on—you have some kind of emergency?" bellowed CFD. From the Communications Center came, "Hey, Tower, someone *is* transmitting on 121.5." Even the airlines called in, saying, "Hey, Tower, there must be some kind of situation on 121.5—you need to check it out ASAP!"

While all this was going on, I noticed Jon, who was taking the phone calls, scratching his head. Suddenly I made eye contact with him. What a mistake.

After I gave Jon one of my patented silly grins, Jon looked back at me and screamed just one word—"*Calvin!*" I had unleashed the sleeping giant. In an O'Hare minute, Jon's mouth was two centimeters from my ear, whispering "Calvin, don't tell me you're using the emergency for inbound ground."

The reply was short but sweet and just as quiet: "Yes, Jon... I am."

Jon's reply was the famous quote from the old "Get Smart" television sitcom: "Calvin, I asked you not to tell me that."

During that whole summer of 1986, I kept Fieweger on his toes. There are many things in air traffic control that can slow down arrivals and departures, such as fog, snow, rain, etc. Summer is the time of thunderstorms, and no pilot wants any part of lightning and the turbulence associated with the tall, ominous cumulonimbus clouds. Shaped like an anvil, these storms can rip the wings off an airplane in seconds.

One morning, a thunderstorm descended over O'Hare just as one of the big daily rushes of airplanes was outbound to the runway. Jon made the decision to send just about every departure up to runway one-four left until the storm abated. Meanwhile, the line at the runway grew from a few to ten then 20 and then 40, and soon just about every gate in the terminals looked like a ghost town. At the runway, like sleeping giants, all the airplanes shut down their engines, waiting for the green light to start up. This time always reminded me of the eye of the hurricane. Everyone is relaxed, while just about 50 miles in all directions from the airport, arrivals are in holding patterns, cascading in circles at increments of 1000 feet, anxiously waiting.

As the storm began to subside, I could feel the adrenaline inside my body starting to pump at an uncontrollable rate. Overlooking the tranquil north side of the airport, I knew that soon the arrivals would come screaming in simultaneously and across intersecting runways, as many departures would attempt to get out with my help. This, in air traffic, is known as the "gap shot." There is little room for error as controllers must get out one, and sometimes two, departures between arrivals landing at an intersection (at a 90° angle) halfway down the departing runway. If the words "clear for takeoff" don't come at a precise time, the end result is hundreds of tons of twisting metal and bodies at the intersection of departure runway 14 left and landing runway 22 right. O'Hare is very unique in this respect, as virtually all of its operations involve landing and takeoffs across intersecting runways.

At most other big airports, such as Los Angeles and Atlanta, the runway configurations are mostly parallel. And, as we know from high school geometry, parallel lines do not intersect. While controllers at O'Hare constantly throw airplanes at each other at these intersecting crossroads, the controllers at other places are departing one runway and landing the parallel runway, never worrying whether an imminent situation might develop. This is a point not lost by many experienced pilots flying into O'Hare who, by an almost unanimous vote, consider O'Hare controllers the best in the world, and often spend parts of their flying time just looking out their windows in childlike amazement at the maze of airplanes all around them.

Finally, the word came through the speakers in the Tower from the TRACON located beneath the Tower. "Hey, Tower, here come the arrivals, pucker up!" An ongoing game between the Tower and the TRACON is to see who can throw more traffic at the other at one time. Since the Tower is responsible for airspace starting at the runway to an airport radius of five miles and 5000 feet high, once a departing flight leaves that airspace, it becomes the responsibility of the TRACON, which handles flights from an airport radius of 40 miles and as high as Flight Level 230 (23,000 feet high).

The TRACON, on the other hand, transfers the arrival flights to us (known as the handoff) just inside the five-mile airport radius at a place known as the outer marker. This marker (about five or six miles from the airport) is the location where all flights landing at O'Hare must first contact the Tower, requesting clearance to land. O'Hare typically lands a minimum of two runways, up to a maximum of four. It normally uses a minimum of two runways for departure but can use up to four, depending on the runway configuration. The potential to land and depart large numbers of airplanes is constant from seven in the morning to ten at night. If weather becomes a factor, then the volume can easily persist past ten o'clock, and even well past midnight.

As I saw the first arrival approaching the outer marker, Jon slapped me in the butt and to everyone in the Tower said, "Let's get the departures moving." As the menacing Jon walked towards me, I knew what was coming. In his typical mocking, comedic tone, Jon said, "OK, Calvin, are you going to move some metal or what? If you can't do it, I'll get someone who can."

Having only been recently certified as a full performance journeyman for a few weeks, I proceeded with total and reckless abandon. The first thing to disappear when working busy "O'Hare" traffic is the book phraseology. (Jon had written his own book in his mind, anyway, and dumped the FAA version years ago.) My phraseology was short and simple. To the departures, it was, "taxi into position and hold runway one-four left, traffic landing the crossing runway (22 right) and be ready for an immediate departure." To the arrivals, it was, "clear to land runway two-two right, no delay through the intersection of runway one-four left, traffic departing right behind you, keep your speed up."

As pilots sensed my enthusiasm and immediacy, they became caught up in the excitement. But now as I looked out the window to see how well the next departure was moving, his slow rate to position and hold on the runway told me I might lose a departure gap. "United Four-oh-five, you're next. Are you ready to go or what?"

The immediate reply: "Yes, Tower, sorry—we'll move a little faster!"

The next blanket broadcast is just as quick. "Come on, guys, you're moving like molasses in January!"

The next departure, an even slower taxiing American, upon hearing United's rebuke, still didn't understand the big picture. Upon seeing this, I knew I had to find another way to motivate the departures, as the gaps they had to depart in were barely three miles (the minimum for such an operation). "Hey, American Fifty-one Heavy," a DC10, "*hustle* into position and hold." It's then you realize you must change your plan of attack to make your arrival-departure gap shot work more efficiently.

Most air traffic control is about having a good plan. Every pilot, in every intersecting runway operation, must know all the information you know to make the arrival-departure conflict work out. It was essential and mandatory that every plane at O'Hare abide by controllers, as an orchestra follows its conductor. So it was, "Hey, American, I need you to roll as soon as you get the clearance [for takeoff]. The final [airplanes lined up for the landing runway] is a little tight. Be ready."

We would even work ourselves into the cockpit and instruct pilots to "Come up on the power," "Put the pedal to the metal," and "Hey, wake up, Skippy." It always seemed a little strange to have to tell pilots to be ready at O'Hare, but occasionally, you could tell by the way an aircraft was taxiing, or the way a pilot was answering instructions, that maybe this flight crew was going to make my job a little slower and way too interesting. You could often tell by the delay in the read back of clearances that some pilots needed a little more *help* and prompting than others.

So here I was working the position known as Local control ("Tower" to pilots) and it was my job to say "clear to land," "clear for takeoff," and anything else I could say to give pilots the general idea that at O'Hare, our pace was faster than anyone in the country (or the world, for that matter). Transmissions to pilots are usually short and brief, since to spend any length of time with any flight would be tantamount to a back-up on a major interstate.

If just *one* plane stops on any taxiway or makes a wrong turn, then the ripple effect is felt instantly with all the other flights. Unfortunately, during certain times of the day, the traffic jams are so large that no matter how well or how fast we move air traffic, there is little we can do to stop John Q. Public from sitting on the ground from as long as 30 minutes, on nice weather days, to hours when bad weather approaches.

It's when traffic starts coming out of your ears that the standard FAA phraseology heads "south."

Clearing flights to land runway 22 right, I quickly turned them over to ground control as they exited the runway. With two and sometimes three Local controllers "feeding" only one inbound ground controller, the ground position can get busy in a hurry. There are only two (rarely ever enough staffing for three) ground controllers at a time in O'Hare Tower, and one is the outbound ground, who taxies aircraft for takeoff to the runway and then hands them off to one of the Local controllers responsible for the landings and takeoffs.

The other ground is known as inbound ground, who taxies aircraft from the runways to the gates. The inbound ground has one of the toughest jobs in the air traffic world, as he or she must talk to aircraft coming off two or even three runways every 40 to 50 seconds. Also, inbound must work the hangar aircraft, which are the planes that go up and down from the maintenance hangars to be fixed and returned to service.

Often, emergency vehicles are controlled by inbound ground during an emergency. On an average of once every eight-hour shift, emergency vehicles were called upon to answer such calls as loss of hydraulics, smoke in the cockpit, medical emergencies, etc. Thankfully, however, most emergencies are low profile and simply precautionary, such as when an aircraft loses a hydraulic system. Most aircraft have several back-up and redundant systems, but still have to declare an emergency when any of the main systems fail. That is why most declared emergencies are precautionary in nature.

Meanwhile, back on inbound ground, there was Jim working feverishly, trying to talk to as many as twenty flights that have landed and need his constant attention. Jim was the quintessential rough-around-the-edges, spiky-haired, world's oldest punk rocker. Having worked airplanes for over twelve years at O'Hare, Jim was nearing burnout by losing patience more readily and not willing to tolerate pilots' perceived incompetence as easily. Jim not only told pilots how to get to their companies' gates but also had to make traffic calls at intersections all over the airport.

With only a handful of airplanes, he could easily memorize company and flight numbers, but with over ten planes taxiing, it can become almost impossible without looking down at your notepad (used as a visual aid to copy and remember flight numbers). Then, add the fact you have to find parking spots for flights that don't have gates because they're occupied by outbound airplanes, and patience starts to run thin.

As fate would have it (and this was a daily occurrence), a pilot made a wrong turn on the taxiway. At this point, Jim looked down at his notepad to find the errant pilot's flight number. Since his pad looked like something in Arabian script, he quickly went to his back-up plan. Throwing the pad in the garbage can nearby, it now became survival time or, as they say in air traffic, "trying to keep your head above water." The ground radio frequency was now abuzz with as many as four and five pilots talking at once. To anyone listening to the frequency, all you heard was the loud squeals of people talking over each other.

Jim quickly screamed out a few words about someone's mother and then took charge. "Hey, that United Seven-twenty-seven off of runway two-two right, turn right on the outer [taxiway] and give way to that Northwest D-C-9." And, "Hey, Continental at the stub [taxiway], where are you going?!" Finally, Jim, like everyone else in the Tower at one time or another, lost his patience with another wayward pilot, saying, "Who's the *jag off* making the wrong turn at the bypass [taxiway]?"

The sheepish answer came back, surprisingly, instantly: "That would be United Seven Fifteen, sir."

Only at O'Hare could you get away with calling someone a "jag off" on the frequency. The reason is very few pilots want to risk confrontation with a government agency (FAA), which can unleash punitive action for mistakes on the ground and air in a Chicago minute. When you're a pilot making as much as $200,000 a year working for a major airline carrier, you'll probably eat a little crow from the government to maintain a low profile.

Very rarely, and not unless it caused an accident, did people in the Tower write up pilot mistakes. Most pilot errors in the 1980s were dealt with by a simple phone call from the flight crew to the supervisor in the Tower. Jon was the *master* of the phone call. All pilots respected this method of "government supervision." Everyone in the Tower realized that at some point, a controller could make a similar mistake and might appreciate that same courtesy from a pilot or his company—that was why the system worked so well at O'Hare. Everyone, from the flight crews, the controllers, and all listening to the radios, was always focused on the task at hand. To not be focused would be tantamount to certain catastrophe.

It was when bureaucrats from the regional office decided to listen in on the frequencies and write pilots up on such small mistakes as missing a turn or controllers not identifying themselves as "ground" did the system take a turn to paranoia. Everyone makes mistakes. These controller wannabes at the regional office never understood this simple fact. As the government wrote up more pilots, sometimes issuing extreme measures such as fines and suspensions, the whole system became defensive. Pilots who had once enjoyed flying into O'Hare now became worried that if they made the smallest mistake, Big Brother would take them down, job and all.

In the defense of pilots, O'Hare is probably one of the toughest places to fly into and out of if you don't do it regularly. As controllers, at times we tend to talk as fast as an auctioneer and about half as clearly. To the pilots who fly in and out of O'Hare, communication is a finely tuned art, but to those unfamiliar with it, we might as well be speaking Greek.

While Jim was fighting for his air traffic life on inbound ground, I had to depart airplanes between arrivals on the intersecting runway halfway down the departing runway. As the pace picked up and the adrenaline kicked in, then so did my unique phraseology. Because of the long wait for takeoffs due to the storms, many of the planes were only casually moving both to ground taxi and roll for takeoff.

This was totally unacceptable at O'Hare, and the "Ayatollah of air traffic controlla," Jon, knew it. Jon's instruction was simple: "Calvin, you need to start motivating these departures!"

Just as Jon issued his proclamations, I could hear the radio blaring "Born to Be Wild" by Steppenwolf:

"Get your motor running…

Head out on the highway…

Looking for adventure

And whatever comes our way…

We can climb so high

I never wanna die…

Born to be wild…"

Now I was fully motivated. So now the tone and speed of my voice needed to switch up to the next gear: "Hey, people, we need to start hustling onto the runways or we're going to miss the gaps between arrivals, so Delta Two Ninety-four, *hustle* into position and hold now!"

Delta replies at attention, "Yes, *sir*!" also abandoning standard phraseology (by FAA protocol, Delta was supposed to identify himself by saying "Delta Two Ninety four, roger").

Next, to the arrivals, *"Hey,* Simmons Two-seventy, clear to land runway two-two right and *no* delay through the intersection of one-four left, as I'm rolling Delta right behind you."

Simmons replies, "Roger, Tower, we'll keep it up" (speed).

After I repeated these same transmissions, the next few pilots in line, who had been paying close attention, tried to help me out by answering my "position and hold" (for takeoff) and then adding, "And Tower, we're going to hustle into position and hold runway one-four left." While this kind of help is sometimes appreciated, it often leads to digressions with other pilots. It was about when the tenth flight in line (who'd had almost 20 minutes to think up something clever) reached the front of the departure line that the phraseologies took a bizarre turn.

"OK, Tower, United Forty-two Heavy, we're hustling into position and hold just like *Pete Rose*."

Not making the "Pete Rose" connection, my curiosity got the best of me, and I inquired, "Hey, United Forty-two Heavy, what is the reference to Pete Rose?"

The response, without hesitation, was, "Hey, Tower, you're asking everyone to hustle…. Pete Rose is number one-four, just like our departure runway…and isn't Pete Mister Charlie Hustle?"

It was then the light in my brain switched to high intensity. I had discovered the "Pete Rose" departure. So the next plane in line, *even without* my prompting said, "Hey, Tower, we're ready for the Pete Rose departure!" (The controller and pilot minds can sometimes think eerily alike). With the Pete Rose departure intact, the next ten to 12 departures, which had been paying attention to the previous transmissions, were hustling and using the same phrase religiously, as if it was standard FAA phraseology: "Yes, Tower, we have that Pete Rose departure—let's do it!"

Eventually, however, we got down to the flights near the end of the departure line, which hadn't been paying attention, and what had once been magic in motion became a frequency *nightmare*.

"Britt Air Five Seventy, Pete Rose departure, position and hold…"

"Ah...sorry, Tower," in a defeated tone, "but we don't have the Pete Rose departure anywhere in our manuals."

And then the flight behind Britt Air chimed in, "Yeah, Tower, American Five-oh-seven can't find the Pete Rose departure in our manuals, either."

While normally the supervisor (yes, it was Jon again) would be watching me work this somewhat complex and fast operation, Jon was too busy answering phone calls he could barely understand or keep up with.

It seemed operations at United, American, and a host of others were upset at the Tower, asking why they hadn't been briefed concerning the new departure procedure known as the "Pete Rose." There are actually published departure procedures known as SIDS (Standard Instrument Departures) for all airports, which all the pilots have in their manuals. As Jon's phone began to ring off the hook from airlines trying to get more information on the Pete Rose, Jon caught my goofy smile out of the corner of his eye. And then it came.

"Calvin! Calvin!" Jon shrieked.

Even though he was quite angry, I knew he was also mildly amused. No FAA punitive action was taken for my use of this new phraseology since, like other supervisors before him, Jon knew that in the O'Hare Tower, unique situations required creative solutions often born out of sheer craziness.

It was from that point that the "Calvin" name became emblazoned throughout all of management. It was like I was out of the old Chipmunks cartoon. Those a little older might remember an angry David Seville screaming at the three chipmunks, "Simon... Theodore..." and, loudest, "...*Calvin!*" Well, it was "Alvin" in the cartoon, but at O'Hare Tower, it was the chipmunks and *Calvin*. The chipmunk routine would be repeated for the rest of my career at O'Hare.

Despite the unorthodox solutions, I very rarely received anything but a laugh and an exclamatory *"Calvin!"* I guess even the government has a sense of humor.

Chapter 14

Merry Christmas to the Contras

FULL ROUTE CLEARANCE (FRC): *used by pilots to request that the entire route flight be read verbatim in an ATC clearance or any "covert" operation.*

ack in the mid 1980s, Nicaragua and Panama's leader, General Manuel Noriega, was a hot topic. O'Hare Chicago Airport and I were there to experience the heat firsthand. The issue was that the United States government (CIA) was aiding the rebel Contras in Nicaragua with guns, ammo, and supplies in the hope of overthrowing the "Sandinista" government that controlled Nicaragua at the time. General Noriega covertly funneled US aid to the Contras in exchange for a better relationship with the United States. The US aid was obtained from money received from Iran in exchange for US weapons. This was where the Iran-Contra scandal was born.

Oliver North was the purported dealmaker at the time and thought to be the main sympathizer with the Contras. Our government, of course, denied it by saying that there were no such covert operations proceeding. But on a warm summer night, Jim Brabec and I, working the Tower together, would see things differently.

Military cargo operations were common at O'Hare during the day and took place along the northeast side of the airport. Nighttime activity was generally restricted to air refuelers, such as the Air Force KC-135s, and *not* cargo operations. Well, Jim and I got our first clue concerning the clever "covert" operation when a Southern Air cargo plane asked if he could "taxi practice" from the south side to the north side of the airport (where the Air Force Ramp was located). While not known to the layman, most of us in air traffic knew, from talking to various pilots, that Southern Air was one of the primary civilian contractors for the CIA.

We gave permission for Southern Air to taxi its airplane to the north side, and generally assumed that the plane would not go into the actual military ramp. With a range of warning signs marking its entrance, any unauthorized airplanes wandering into the ramp were considered to be on military property and, as such, were subject to immediate search. Very often, whenever any civilian plane accidentally taxied into the ramp, the military police, like bees on honey, would surround the plane, pull the passengers and crew out of the airplane, plant their faces on the ground and search the whole airplane piece by piece. Military personnel at the ramp treated any wayward airplane as a possible enemy.

So it was with complete surprise that Jim and I watched as the Southern Air made an abrupt turn into the military ramp. We called to them, "Hey, Southern Air, you know you don't want to turn there, that's the military ramp."

After a pause came the response, "That's OK, Tower, we know these guys."

As we looked out the windows, we could see the Southern Air Electra (one of the largest civilian cargo planes) back up right next to an Air Force C-141 cargo plane. The C-141 was quite an uncommon sight at O'Hare (particularly at two in the morning), since the Guard Base was primarily a refueling base. It was surrounded by military vehicles, and we watched a seemingly endless unloading and loading process of materials from the Electra into the C-141. It became obvious to us that we were watching the local and national news unfold before our very eyes. Jim remarked, "Look at these sons-of-bitches. It's two in the morning and they think no one will know what they're doing."

As the Southern Air plane left the Guard Ramp unimpeded by the military police, the roaring of the C-141 jet engines starting up broke the night silence. Within minutes, the printers came out with the flight plan strip for "MAC2" (Military Airlift Command and flight number). It would be my job to read this clearance to the Air Force pilot. It included the airport destination and route of flight. What was very unusual about this particular flight plan was that it showed no destination, but rather simply an abbreviated routing over a small town south of O'Hare known as Roberts, Illinois. Having Roberts as the first point to fly over heading south was not unusual, but that was where the flight plan ended. Jim and I deduced, quite brilliantly, that Illinois was not the destination.

Within minutes of pulling the flight plan strip out of the printer, a stern and professional-sounding voice resounded on my frequency from the C141: "Tower, this is MAC Two requesting clearance to Roberts."

How unusual. Virtually every other flight Jim and I worked had a bona fide destination airport. So I asked, "Hey,

MAC Two, I didn't know there was an airport in Roberts, Illinois, you could land at."

After a few seconds came back the response, "Tower, just *give* us the clearance to Roberts."

I was beginning to feel like I was some kind of "secret agent" man. Johnny Rivers was in my head, singing,

"There's a man who leads a life of danger...
To everyone he meets he stays a stranger...
With every move he makes another chance he takes...
Odds are he won't live to see tomorrow..."

I was putting myself in a dangerous situation and didn't even know it. Now that I knew I was in a verbal sparring match, I asked the questions with total FAA by-the-book phraseology. "Hey, MAC Two... per our procedure, you know I have to clear you to a particular airport in case of radio failure or equipment malfunction, and Roberts isn't making it."

Confused by my remarks, the pilot timidly replied, "We're going to Texas."

I said, "OK, MAC Two, that's great, now simply tell me which airport or Air Force base in Texas so we can get the proper clearance and I can keep you out of trouble with the rest of the controllers across the country and along your route of flight."

A long pause ensued, and after a few minutes, the MAC pilot sheepishly retorted, "OK, Tower, put us on request.... err, oh, request clearance to Nicaragua."

Bingo—this was the answer Jim and I had been expecting. Probably sensing that two highly placed government controllers with security clearances wouldn't cause problems, the pilot felt time was a-wasting and we should be trusted. Also, if anyone else was listening to the frequency, they probably wouldn't have been able to put two plus two together, and certainly not at two in the morning.

I was having too much fun at this point and Jim was laughing uncontrollably at the irony of the whole incident. Just that day, Illinois' own governor, James Thompson, in head-lines across the *Chicago Sun-Times*, had denied that the military at O'Hare had anything to do with "aid to the Contras." The newspaper was right in front of us. Go figure.

So now I went in for the knockout punch. "Hey, MAC Two, Nicaragua is a country. I need a specific airport where you are landing."

After another dramatic and awkward pause came the defining answer. "Hey, Tower," exasperated, "we're landing in Managua! *Now can we have our clearance?*"

Having been in the Air Force, I replied with prompt military courtesy, "Yes, *sir*, MAC Two is cleared to Managua, Nicaragua, via radar vectors to Roberts, rest of route as filed, maintain five thousand…"

By this time, Jim and I were so proud of ourselves we decided to find a way to show them we understood what they were doing, even though we knew we couldn't say anything publicly for fear of losing our jobs. So, in the remarks section of the flight progress strip (which goes to every controller in the country that MAC Two would talk to), I typed "Merry Xmas to the Contras." Now any controller across the country, while talking to MAC Two, would also see this message and be able to relay to the MAC Two crew my personal holiday greetings.

Very often controllers would type their own personal greetings, such as birthdays, congratulations for the captain's last flight (due to retirement), "happy anniversary" to relatives, etc., in the remarks section. And just as often, it became pro-fessional courtesy for all controllers to mention the remarks section whenever a flight checked on to their frequency. So after the flight departed, Jim and I went back about our normal ATC business, not realizing until early that same morning how appreciative the Air Force brass would be of our efforts.

The first sign of appreciation came about 8:00 a.m., just two hours after my shift had ended. Top officials at the Air Force had conveyed their dismay regarding the "wise-guy" controller, and there would be a meeting later that afternoon between O'Hare management, Air Force officials and, of course, myself. Since it was my voice on the frequency, I was the main target of this Air Force "Inquisition."

As I drove back into work that afternoon, the realization set in that maybe I had violated some kind of top-secret operation. Would I be tortured for information? Flogged for inappropriate behavior? Maybe given a nice vacation to a place called Leavenworth in Kansas?

It was quite an array of government officials, including Chester (Andy) Anderson, Jon, various military officials including a two-star general, his military entourage and civilian guys who just sat quietly, saying nothing but looking officially agitated.

It was apparent to me that the meeting had proceeded without me initially. As I walked into the large conference room that was Andy's office, I could tell there was a heated discussion going on, both positive and negative, concerning my actions. When I entered the crowded room of 12, a dramatic silence came over the room.

Andy looked at me quite uncharacteristically sternly and said, "Well, Bob, you probably know why you're here, don't you?"

Now I knew I was in trouble, since no one at the Tower called me by my real name except when they were upset at something I had done. In good times, it was, "Hey, Calvin, how's it going?" or "Hey, Calvin, how's it hangin'?" In troubled situations, though, it was "OK, *Bob*, now what did you do?"

I answered Andy back calmly. "Well, Andy, could it have anything to do with my heartfelt greetings to the Contras?"

Upon that response, I noticed some of our O'Hare people with smiles that masked their ability to laugh hysterically. The military persons did not even flinch.

At that revelation, Andy pointed to his desk, to the written transcripts he had obtained from other facilities across the country. "Well, Bob, I want you to listen to what was said last night from conversations involving MAC Two and various other air traffic facilities across our fair country." Andy continued, "Bob, from Kansas City Center came MAC Two radar contact, maintain flight level three-three-zero (30,000 feet) and hey, by the way, merry Christmas to the Contras! From Dallas Center came MAC Two radar contact, and don't forget to say a hearty merry Christmas to the Contras from the guys and gals at Dallas–Fort Worth Center!"

No controllers across the country knew, of course, they were giving away government secrets along the airwaves, because, at that time, not many people even knew what a Contra was. As the icy stares from the O'Hare base commander descended upon me, I simply looked back at the General like a parent looks back at their baby making a funny face. Just great—here was another guy thinking I was just some punk kid. As I looked over to my right, there was Jon with his hands over his face, cleverly hiding his laughter by making grunting noises to camouflage his obvious thoughts about what was happening. Many of our operations people could only look the other way and hold back their amusement.

It was clear to me that the only persons in that meeting who understood the whole situation were our people. The military had never met a "Calvin" before, nor experienced years of my antics. To the people in that room who knew me, this was just another in a long line of harmless practical jokes that I had orchestrated, designed to expose governmental hypocrisy.

I could tell at this point that Andy was simply having this meeting to appease the military for giving away their "top secret operation," which wasn't supposed to be happening, anyway. I knew at this point that a slap of my hand was on its way.

"Well, *Bob*," Andy quizzed, "are we going to continue to have this kind of unprofessional behavior on the frequency? You know, Bob, there is a time for levity and a time to be professional. Can we count on you not to do this again?"

I stared at Andy dead center in the eyes, and after a dramatic five-second silence, I mustered up all the fake sincerity I could find and said "Sir, yes, sir!" I had inadvertently become transported back to my days in the Air Force. The military guys were impressed, but our people knew I was faking it. Jon, over on the other side of the room, simply shook his head, cupped his hands back over his head and let out a laugh that gave away his true feelings to everyone.

The General immediately looked over at Jon and said very sternly, "You think this is *real comical*, don't you?"
Jon replied as quickly, "No, sir, I think this is extremely *hilarious*! I doubt Calvin even knows what a Contra is, much less the controllers across the country."

A more agitated General turned to Andy and replied, "Mr. Anderson, are you going to do anything about this incident?"

Andy, in a soft tone, calmly answered, "What would you have us do, General? I will speak with Mr. Richards in detail when you leave. We can handle our own people—I assure you this will never happen again, but I don't think we can convict him of any war crimes at this point for wishing people a merry Christmas."

The angry General looked to his entourage and exploded. "OK, Mr. Anderson, we are out of here! This cannot happen again, or we will hold you personally responsible!"

As Andy walked the Air Force out the door, he simply nodded his head gently, with the words, "Yes, sure, General, no problem, you bet, I got it, oh and by the way, have a wonderful day."

Have a *wonderful day?* Have a *wonderful day?*

Andy had plagiarized my most frequent saying on the air traffic frequency. My signature transmission, when sending pilots to the next controller, was to say, "Have a *wonderful* day" or *"wunnerful* day," depending on what kind of mood I was in. Andy knew this (from listening to several tapes of my many previous incidents) and it was his way of condoning what I had done.

As the angry, fuming flyboys walked out our front entrance, Andy turned to everyone left in his office and said, "Will everyone here, including you, *Calvin*, please have a wonderful day?"

I guess Calvin was back.

Andy then put his arm around me, looked me straight in the eyes and said, "Yes, kid, you're still a flake."

I love vindication.

Chapter 15

The Fix Is In

CLEARED AS FILED: *Means the aircraft is cleared to proceed in accordance with the route of flight filed in the flight plan, whenever it may take effect.*

Gambling has always been a distraction for many people I have known. Having a sister who moved to Las Vegas after high school always made it easy for my mother to decide where to go on her vacation. My sister spent most of her time working inside the big Vegas casinos, learning all the ins and outs. Since my mother enjoyed gambling, it was often with my sister's assistance that my mother made a killing by winning at the slots, in games such as draw poker.

She is the only human being I know to get almost 50 "natural" royal flushes in her lifetime. (I've never even met another human being who got more than one.) Knowing the inside workings of the casinos, my sister, Kathy, had a sense of which progressive poker machine might be due to pay out next. With that information in hand, my mom would play those machines "endorsed" by my sister. Although many times my mom did not win, her losses were far outweighed with the winnings from those royal flushes. Having the inside track can be a great financial benefit.

Throughout the late 1980s, I came across a type of gambling that would reveal the reality of how intense people's desire to win could be, and the extent to which they might go to improve the odds. Gambling on sports was always prevalent wherever I went. Wherever I worked, including the Air Force, Fullerton Airport, Palwaukee (now Chicago Regional), or O'Hare, there was always someone initiating some kind of football pool, baseball pool, basketball pool, etc. Many times, it was the air traffic controllers who acted as bookies for the real bookies. The amount of money involved throughout the years varied, but when I first started out, all betting was fairly low key and involved small amounts of money.

At Fullerton, for instance, the Super Bowl squares might cost as little as 50 cents per square, but as the years went by and I ended up at O'Hare, where all my co-workers made six-figure salaries, the squares went up to $100 per square, and then as high as $1000. I point this out to demonstrate that although most of the sports pools were initiated outside the Tower facility, many of them had far-reaching hands into the people at the Tower.

It was not uncommon to know fellow controllers who ended up in extreme debt due to bad bets. And it didn't end there. Even the controllers in management, such as a supervisor I'll call Jack, owed so much money to a controller acting as a bookie that he had to cancel his retirement to keep working to pay off his debt. So it was not hard to understand how desperate people might become to pay their debts or simply find a way to make a quick buck. It was the desperation aspect of gambling that totally blew me away.

Anyone who worked at O'Hare was keenly aware that the major sports teams in Chicago, and their opponents, flew in and out of our airport. By simply matching their game schedules with flight plans, we usually knew when and where the flights would take off from. The Chicago Blackhawks hockey team, for instance, frequently flew with United, while a visiting team such as the St. Louis Blues used Trans World Airlines (TWA), because at the time, the hub for TWA was St. Louis. A logical pick of airlines for any sports team in St. Louis was TWA, since almost all the flights out of St. Louis were run by TWA. In Minneapolis, the airline of choice for the Minnesota North Stars was the home-based airline, Northwest Airlines. Sports teams like to keep the hometown airline happy.

So it was on a cold December night, following a game between the Chicago Blackhawks and the Minnesota North Stars at the old Chicago Stadium, when I found out what real desperate gambling was all about. The Hawks had played the North Stars hard, but fell on the short end of a six-four score. Having worked the day shift, I was to come back eight hours later to work the midnight shift—a common practice at O'Hare when working the last two days of the workweek. As I slumped into work and happened upon the break room before heading up to the Tower, I noticed a handful of controllers engaged in a heated conversation. Some of the controllers present were about to leave, having finished their night shifts (3:00 p.m.– 11:00 p.m.), while the other half were the controllers about to get started on the midnight shifts (11:00 p.m.–7:00 a.m.).

What struck me about this group of guys was that some were the big gamblers, taking bets, and regulars at the casinos. They seemed very intense about their conversation, and when I approached them, they shifted their serious talk into something much lighter (or so it seemed to me).

"Hey, Calvin," one of the controllers blurted, "don't the Hawks suck! They took it up their asses again." I knew the Hawks had lost that night, but I was too tired from the day shift, besides having not gotten any sleep. I simply didn't care. Then, in an offbeat tone, the same controller exclaimed, "But you know what, Calvin, things will be different tomorrow— we'll see to that."

Clueless about this last statement, I would soon find out the deep, dark meaning of his last outburst.

As I was riding up the elevator to the Tower with two other controllers, I overheard one telling the other that the "Hawks were going to kick ass tomorrow night and it will be just like with the Blues." The reference to the Blues, as I was later to find out, was the St. Louis Blues hockey team. The controller also stated, and this was the most telling of all, "We're going to make it all happen when we get upstairs." So how was this controller going to make it happen, and what was he going to make happen?

As smart as I had always thought I was, in fact I was quite naïve. One of my fellow controllers had devised a system that, although not 100%, was certainly designed to create an advantage. He had deduced that when any athlete, and particularly professional sports athletes, compete on back-to-back nights, a certain fatigue factor sets in. Professional athletes typically fly several times a week, and often late at night. Chances are the longer the flight, the more fatigue one might experience, which is what some believed. Many of the hockey athletes were big people, often crouched in small airplane seats so that the longer they were airborne or even just sitting on the ground, the more likely they might be a little more tired for the next day's game.

As I strolled into the Tower cab to relieve the night shift, I went right over to ground control to start the relief briefing. As I was about to assume the position, the midnight supervisor tapped me on the back and told me to take a short break because he wanted to work the position for a few minutes. As odd as this request was, I simply unplugged my headset and slouched back into a chair, awaiting further orders.

To help out the supervisor, I grabbed the flight strips from the printer. These strips represented the airplanes that were to take off in the next 30 minutes. I couldn't help but notice that two of the flights were headed to Minneapolis. Upon closer observation, anyone could see that one of the flights was the Chicago Blackhawks, while the other was the Minnesota North Stars.

I pointed out this seemingly mundane fact to the supervisor, and back came the reply, "Yes, Calvin, both teams are playing each other again tomorrow night."

Being a wise guy, I said to the diehard Blackhawks fan, "I guess they're going back to Minnesota to get their asses kicked again."

The supervisor smugly replied, "Well, Calvin, we'll see about that...maybe we can change that."

I didn't understand the meaning of the last comment, so I inquired further: "Oh yeah? And how are you going to do that?"

"Well, Calvin," the supervisor replied, "watch the master!"

So I watched the master and what I saw was totally beyond comprehension.

As the buses that carried both hockey teams drove on to the tarmac to the respective airplanes, a devilish smile magically appeared on the supervisor's face. Was it possible that this had been done before?

As both teams finally boarded their respective planes, the pilot of the Blackhawks called for his clearance. The supervisor, without hesitation, read the clearance to the pilot, gave them the quickest route to the departure runway, cleared them for takeoff and finally wished them a happy bon voyage, saying "Go Hawks." Not once did the supervisor hand off the flight to another controller in the Tower. He did it all by himself and didn't involve anyone else. It was the best service you'll ever see a flight get anywhere, particularly as it was just after 10:30 p.m.

When the Northwest pilot of the North Stars called for his clearance, that same supervisor, whom I'll call Tom, seemed to go into dreamland.

I said, "Hey, Tom, did you hear that clearance request?"

"Oh yeah," replied Tom, "clearance on request," which in aviation terms meant "I will have to go to the computer to find the clearance." Normally, the fairly routine Tower response would be "cleared as filed," meaning the aircraft could depart as soon as it was ready, since the paperwork filed by the company was in order.

I expected Tom to simply go get the strip and say the magic words "cleared as filed," but he instead typed the letters "RS," with the North Stars Flight number, into the computer. An "RS" is a remove strip (thereby removing the flight plan) action. By typing in the RS amendment for the North Stars flight, he had created a delay for the flight. Without a current flight plan, the flight could not take off until the company put in a new flight plan.

Apologetically, Tom told the pilot, "Sorry, Captain, we don't show any flight plan for Minneapolis for you... you'll have to refile. Go ahead and park in the nine right pad until we get your clearance."

So now the airplane, filled with anxious, strapping hockey players, had to sit in the equivalent of an aviation parking lot and wait till their company sent another flight strip through the government system and then into our printer in the Tower.

About ten minutes later, the printer spewed out a new flight plan. Looked like the North Stars would be able to go, right? Wrong.

To my surprise, about five more minutes went by, and while Tom glanced at the flight plan, he did nothing to help out the North Stars flight.

I sheepishly inquired, "Hey, Tom, are you going to get the North Stars out sometime tonight?"

Without answering, Tom stared at me for a second, smiled and then deleted the North Stars flight plan again, thereby deleting any existence of the flight.

It was painfully obvious where this was all headed, and rather than be angry, I became scared. I wasn't just afraid because I was worried about the potential for big scandal, but also sensed my life would be made miserable if I protested or became a whistle blower. Besides, how could I prove it, anyway?

The radio in the Tower was quietly sending me a message from the band Jethro Tull. The song "Skating Away on the Thin Ice of a New Day" said it all:

"For those who choose to stay, will live just one more day...

To do the things they should have done...

And as you cross the wilderness, spinning in your emptiness,

You feel you have to pray…

Looking for a sign that the Universal Mind has written you into the Passion Play…

Skating away…

Skating away…

Skating away on the thin ice of a new day…"

I knew I was on thin ice.

After about ten more minutes of silence, the North Star pilot inquired, "Hey, Tower, anything on that flight plan yet?"

Tom came back with a patronizing response for my benefit, "Sorry, sir, we still don't have anything on your flight… are you sure you refiled?"

The less patient captain replied, "Yes, and it's never taken this long to get a simple flight plan… Are you having some kind of problem with your computers or something?"

"We'll check on that," said Tom and back into his chair he went, ignorant and without any desire to help out.

So, if you're keeping score, the Chicago Blackhawks had not only departed, but were just about to land in Minneapolis, while the North Stars were still sitting on the ground in Chicago, getting angrier and more impatient by the moment, crouched in their seats, unable to get quality rest or sleep. One could only wonder how long this was all going to last. It can be gut wrenching to sit in an airplane going no-where, with no idea what is going to happen next. In today's world, sports teams travel in luxurious charter jets, and even large jets, such as the Boeing 757. Back in the day, however, most teams flew charters in the Boeing 727, which allowed little, if any, room for a even a small person to be comfortable. Legroom was never the best quality of the Boeing 727.

So now, for the third time, the North Star flight plan came out, and once again Tom strolled casually over to the printer and hit those two magic R-S (remove strip) buttons, without saying so much as a word to anyone. As he hit those keys, one of the other controllers in the Tower was smiling ear to ear. He may have known what was going on but chose to pretend not to.

After another ten minutes of silence, the captain shouted out, "Tower, anything yet on that clearance?"

From Tom came, "Sorry, Captain, try refiling one more time, and I'll follow up with Chicago Center if it doesn't come out."

After the clock ticked another ten minutes, the fourth North Star flight plan came out of the printer, but instead of deleting it this time, the supervisor simply placed it in front of himself on the counter and then slumped back into his chair, smiling at me before closing his eyes for a mock nap.

It was about this time of night that the City of Chicago called and asked to close some of the runways for maintenance, and by a stroke of luck, one of the closure requests was the runway that the North Stars would eventually be taking off from.

Tom answered the City thankfully: "No problem, City, you can have runway nine right and we'll simply send that one airplane waiting [the North Stars] to one of the other open runways."

How nice—now the North Stars would have to taxi to another runway, which is at the other end of the airport. During the time Tom is on the phone, his frequency, which was now over the loudspeaker (no need to use headsets late at night, since there is no other traffic), was blaring the desperate request from the North Star pilot for a clearance. "Tower, how's that clearance coming? Do we need to shut down?"

The pilot's concern was now fuel, because of the delay, and the fact that the engines had been running. If his engines kept running, it might have become necessary to go back to the gate and get more fuel. If a pilot knows his delay might be at least fifteen minutes, it is usually no problem to totally shut down either one or all three of his engines. But on this night, the Tower was giving no clues as to how long the "delay" might be. Pilots can be embarrassed to go back to the gate for fuel, especially when the flight to Minneapolis is only a little over an hour long.

So, to check the score again, the Chicago Blackhawks had probably already landed in Minneapolis, checked into their hotel, and were probably fast asleep, getting ready for the big game the next day against the team that was still sitting at the airport in Chicago. Meanwhile, the North Stars were sitting on a cramped B727, probably unable to get any kind of comfortable sleep and wondering if their airplane would ever take off. Some of the players might even be experiencing anxiety, wondering if there was some kind of mechanical problem.

In any event, the flight was almost an hour late, and so the pilot advised he had to shut down his engines completely or he'd need to get more fuel. The supervisor sensed he could buy more delay, and replied, "Yeah, go ahead and shut 'em down and I'll tell you when to start them up."

At this point, I had simply propped my legs onto the console, pretending I was asleep. The North Star pilot was totally disheartened. He knew he had several men behind him who could not wait to find a nice, warm bed in Minneapolis.

I figured if I was sleeping, I could hear no evil, therefore know no evil.

After a few more minutes of doing nothing, Tom picked up the flight strip and it appeared he was finally going to read it to the pilot so the flight could depart. But no. Instead, Tom picked up the phone to Chicago Center. As he talked to Chicago Center, it became apparent that he was trying to change the route of the flight under the guise of some weather still about 150 miles to the west. Unbelievably, Tom did receive an alternate weather routing from the Center. Was the Center in on this conspiracy also? Who could imagine someone being rerouted around weather that was clearly too far away to be a factor? At this point, having received the new clearance, Tom fell back in his chair for another five minutes to "relax." Certainly anyone watching this whole exercise would be exhausted.

As I watched Tom stand up from his chair, I thought surely this trickery was coming to an end. As a college and high school basketball official, my biggest nightmare was to be accused of fixing sporting events. I loved officiating and certainly if I were associated with this charade, it would cost me dearly. I'm sure my fellow controllers thought I was asleep, but actually I was petrified and couldn't wait for the North Stars to get airborne.

Tom finally gave into himself and contacted the pilot with news of a reroute and "Are you ready to copy?" Now, normally from Chicago to Minneapolis, most flights fly directly northwest and can make it in just over an hour. The new routing read to the pilot was unbelievable. He had to head southwest and away from his destination before being turned west and then back northeast to Minneapolis, all because of some bad weather out by Rockford, Illinois, to the west. New flight time to Minneapolis was about two hours. I wanted to crawl into the nearest hole and pretend it was all a nightmare.

Here was a team that had made it to the airport *last* night after 10:30 with the hopes of a quick flight back home. To add insult to injury, after being told he could start up his engines, the pilot was next informed that he had to taxi to the other end of the airport because the runway he was closest to had been closed for maintenance by the City of Chicago.

Upon reaching their new runway, it would appear all was a go for takeoff. But wait. There were aircraft landing on the same runway the North Stars were to take off on. Not really anything to worry about, though, because there was sufficient distance between successive arrivals to get out the North Stars. Or was there? Well, apparently Tom did not think so. He told the pilot he'd get him going as soon as he got a few arrivals on the ground. The distance between the first two arrivals was about 20 miles—all that were needed were about five!

Things were so quiet at the airport that the supervisor had control of *all* the frequencies in the Tower. He had combined all the positions, which was quite common at that time of night. That meant that Tom now had total control over the aircraft's fate on ground and local control. The other controllers in the Tower, who had been relieved by the supervisor, were downstairs on a long "break." Tom continued believing I had fallen asleep. The whole time I had worked my way under the consoles, pretending to be snoring.

"Hey, Calvin—time to get up," Tom said as he shook me to wake up. It was now time for Tom to get his break – his work was done.

As I looked out onto the airport, I was totally numbed at the sight of the North Stars Boeing 727 waiting helplessly at the approach end of the runway with an aircraft still at least ten miles away. When were we going to depart this guy, I thought? As Tom tried to give me the relief briefing, I asked him if he wanted to roll the North Stars.

Without hesitation, he stuttered, "Uh... no, not yet, I got someone landing out there."

"You mean that guy about ten miles out?" I asked in a very stern tone. Now he knew that not only did I know what he was doing, but I was also making it known that I was angry.

Not flinching for a second, Tom came back at me, "Calvin, just hold on and don't do anything till I tell you what's going on, understand?"

It was then I realized he was going to allow the North Stars to miss a good departure gap, and because of that, the next two arrivals were so close that the doomed flight would have to wait another five minutes for the rest of the arrivals (only two) within 200 miles to land. I couldn't even imagine what, if anything, the pilot was telling his passengers. What could he tell them? Weather? Mechanical problem? ATC delay? Having many times sat in a B727, I know it had to be pretty uncomfortable that whole time.

So as soon as Tom let me talk, I told the pilot to be ready to go after the next arrival. With a fake chuckle, the pilot said, "What, you don't think we're ready?" So with Roberts, Illinois, as the first waypoint for the North Star flight to fly over on his flight plan, I cleared the aircraft for takeoff and told them to turn southwest. As soon as the flight was airborne, I told him to "Contact Chicago Departure."

In untypical style, the errant flight flew southwest for at least 100 miles. At about 20 miles or so from the airport, Chicago Center took over and directed that airplane at least another 100 miles around that "lone" storm cloud in the

Midwest. Any ATC working that flight might have seen the absurdity of its path to Minneapolis, but nothing was said by anyone that night, or for the next several days.

The next night, the Blackhawks went up to Minneapolis and kicked ass.

One might argue that even with such a long and tiring flight, the North Stars still could have overcome the fatigue and put the Blackhawks away. But put away they couldn't. In fact, all the North Stars could muster at their home ice was *one* goal, and ended up losing four-one, after beating the Hawks six-four the night before. Go figure.

On a few other occasions, I watched different sports teams get unnecessarily delayed and, in some cases, even the home team was delayed! So it was possible that it didn't even really matter which way the fix was in. There were other times where one could speculate that the visiting sports teams were probably being delayed for their next game to play someone besides a Chicago team. So betting very easily could have been about teams other than Chicago.

A few controllers, over the years during the Chicago Bulls championship runs, often exhibited their disdain for the New York Knicks, one of the Bulls' biggest nemeses throughout the years. It wasn't unusual to see the Knicks experiencing delays on the ground under the disguise of bad weather between Chicago and New York. Most of the time it probably had nothing to do with sports betting—some controllers simply hated the Knicks.

I stayed clear in terms of involvement in such proceedings, but every time I saw a sports team taxiing out, I always wondered whose money might be influencing the movement of that airplane.

I have to admit when it came to the home team, I always gave my best to get them to their next destination, but never did I intentionally try to delay the visiting teams heading in or out of Chicago.

In the end, like many endeavors of society, the almighty dollar reared its ugly head. Whether in politics, sports, or even in a simple control tower, the bottom line ruled. Fortunately, the person responsible for the "fix" is long gone from O'Hare, and even Illinois. Coincidentally, he moved to Nevada. I really felt uncomfortable and sad about the whole situation throughout the years, so I guess being naïve is not such a bad thing after all. God help us.

Chapter 16

Captain Kangaroo Rules

DECISION HEIGHT: *The height at which a decision must be made by a pilot during any instrument approach to either continue the approach, execute a missed approach, or just shut up.*

The early 1990s saw the O'Hare workforce maturing to the point that cockiness was everywhere. After years of training, the pimply-faced kids who had first come through the doors of O'Hare in the 1980s, shaking in their pants, were now so confident that most couldn't even remember their first days at the Big "O." What made O'Hare work was the close relationship between the supervisors and the controllers. All the supervisors at O'Hare were home grown, so relating to the controllers just below them was never a problem. Controllers usually respected criticism from their supervisors *and* supervisors respected criticism from controllers. With seven supervisors and almost 65 controllers, everyone had an opinion.

At the top of the O'Hare Tower hierarchy were the three Area Managers, known affectionately as the "three-headed monster." Their job was to supervise the supervisors, but usually, with the Tower so crowded, they ended up being more of a distraction. Then, when someone new from outside O'Hare was promoted to area manager with little or no knowledge of the overall operation, just because some idiot at the Regional Office decided to promote them... well, then all hell would break loose.

My fondest example of the FAA promoting incompetence to a place they didn't belong was an area manager I'll call Merle. Merle had been in some type of evaluations at the Region, probably needed more money and, best of all, looked like Captain Kangaroo. O'Hare Tower was an attractive lure for a lot of the desk jockeys at the Regional Office just up the street, since the pay raise alone was substantial. The good money always overcame common sense for some of these people, so most of us figured this must be some kind of FAA practical joke.

Becoming an Area Manager in the Tower meant that technically, he could override any supervisor's decisions if he so desired. Most area managers at the time rarely got involved in the actual minute-to-minute supervising in the Tower, since the supervisors were always more than competent. The other reason was that although many of the area managers were home grown, some hadn't been in the Tower for years. Most Tower Area Managers were simply cruising into their retirements, and with retirement based on the highest three years' salaries, what better place to go than the highest paid Tower in the world?

Merle's first mistake was telling us about his experience in evaluations: assessing controllers at O'Hare. We always had wondered where these trivial and ridiculous evaluations came from, and now we had a face to dump on.

One of his crowning achievements, he thought, was having the ground controllers, and particularly the outbound ground, identify themselves to every pilot as "O'Hare Ground Control." The reality at O'Hare was, and still is to this day, that when an outbound ground control is talking to as many as 20 to 30 flights at one time, there is no time to become re-acquainted on the radios when the pilot has already talked to two previous O'Hare controllers. If a pilot didn't know he was at O'Hare by the time he got to outbound ground, he probably shouldn't be a pilot anyway. Get off that flight.

His priorities were quite comical at times, though. One of Merle's biggest worries was that controllers would steal the black government click pens. These unreliable, worthless writing instruments were never any of our favorites—most controllers used their own pen, anyway. To stem what could be an epidemic of thievery unrivaled in the Federal Government, Merle would rip apart the little pocket grabbers that were welded to the pens. Now it would be impossible for controllers to clip them to their pockets if they should decide to walk off with one. Life's a bitch when you're making almost six figures as a Tower Area Manager.

Time after time, Merle would attempt to make operational decisions on matters in the Tower, and when he did, entertainment in the Tower usually rose to all-time highs.

On a hot morning in July of 1989, excitement throughout the Tower was evident. The Russians were sending to Chicago the *largest* airplane in the world, the Antonov (An-124). This four-engine cargo jet was stopping into Chicago before heading up to the Oshkosh Air Show. It was the first time this Russian aircraft was to land in Chicago. It was part of the post-Cold War thaw, to show the Americans how technologically advanced Russia might be. Merle wanted to make sure that all the right people were controlling and talking to the Antonov. International relations were important to Merle. In short, Merle tried to make sure I wasn't going to be involved. Apparently, he had heard about my "flake" reputation.

At the time, I was working inbound ground, so normally when the Antonov landed, he would be told to contact ground and I would get to greet the Russians personally. *No way.* Instead, Merle opened up a *second* inbound ground control for the express purpose of talking to the Antonov only. Tim was given the job and I just laughed at being snubbed. Merle, however, couldn't have predicted what would happen next.

As the Antonov landed, it was hard not to be impressed by this flying oversized whale. It was as quiet as any big plane we had ever seen and seemed totally effortless. It defied gravity that anything that big and slow could even fly. As the Antonov rolled out toward the cargo area, Merle stood within a foot of Tim's headset to make sure everything Tim had to say would be by the book. International customs demanded it. At least, that was what Merle thought.

All of a sudden, a most unusual accent came into my ear. It was Russian. In spite of the fact that the local controller had switched the Antonov to Tim's frequency, the Russian must have instead gone by his book. He accidentally wanted to talk to Calvin all along.

As the Russian introduced himself to me, I replied, "Antonov, welcome to the good old U-S-A. How are you doing?"

In total shock, Merle leaped from Tim and was right next to my ear, saying, "Calvin, you better be careful, or you'll know what will happen."

I stared at Merle, laughed and then told the Russian, "Hey, Antonov, taxi to the cargo area, and Merle said to say hi."

The Russian chuckled for a second and then said, "OK, Merle, we go to the parking."

At that point, I could feel someone's index finger in my lower back, pressing hard. It was Merle and, boy, was he white-faced. All the oxygen was leaving his body. He quickly sat down to catch his breath.

"The Russian said you're the man, Merle," I proclaimed. Merle was the man. Having nearly had a heart attack, you would have thought Merle would leave me alone. *But no.*

It wasn't but a week later that Merle would try to impart another lesson.

On the start of a day shift one morning, just before seven o'clock, I was clearing aircraft for takeoff to the west. I was making sure to aim them over the point on the radar designated for noise abatement. In other words, I was taking aircraft over a pre-designated area that was not populated. It was my job to make sure that people in towns just west of the airport could sleep in till seven o'clock. After seven, I could wake up anyone I wanted. Those were the rules.

Because of some strong winds from the south, I had to adjust the assigned heading to the pilots heading west. With the winds blowing from the south at almost 30 miles an hour, if I had applied the normal noise heading of 290°, the wind would have blown the aircraft so much farther north they would be in the face of the aircraft landing on runway fourteen right. That would be a nightmare for both the pilots and me.

To solidify the unique situation, I coordinated, via the push-button landline, with the radar controller in the

TRACON so he would not worry that my departures would cross paths with his arrivals. I simply said, "Hey, Arrivals, don't worry—the departures off runway two-seven will be on a two seventy and not a two ninety."

The normal mocking answer then came, "Wow, Calvin, you're a genius."

The landline push button was the best way to talk and coordinate with another controller. By simply pressing a button, you would have instant communication with any other controller in the Tower or in the TRACON.

Just as I was getting into my rhythm, I got a tap on my shoulder from Captain Kangaroo who, in a lecturing tone, said, "Calvin, how come you're not using the two nine zero heading prescribed in the manual?"

Wow, the guy had actually read the O'Hare Manual. Unfortunately, what he wasn't considering was the strong crosswinds from the south that had to be adjusted for.

As I started to answer his question, he held his right hand up into my face and, very indignantly, said, "Stop there, Calvin, I don't want to hear it—do what you're supposed to and put those departures on a two ninety heading!"

I came back loud enough so the whole Tower could hear it, "Understand, Captain, you want a two nine zero heading!"

"Yes, Calvin, I want you to assign two ninety headings like you're supposed to!"

I had let the word "Captain" slip out, but I didn't care because I could see the supervisor behind Merle rolling his eyes up into his head. I followed with a mocking pirate, "Aye aye, Captain!"

I immediately hit the landline button to the TRACON to inform the arrival controller I was about to scare the shit out of him with my two ninety headings, and it was by direct command from Merle. As I started to hear the arrival controller yelling, I immediately pulled my finger off the landline button. I knew it would take some time before the TRACON controller could yell at the TRACON supervisor, who would yell at the TRACON manager, who in turn would use the ring line to Merle in the Tower.

On the Tower radio, Ted Nugent was belting out "Stranglehold" and inspiring my next move. Ted said, *"Got you in a stranglehold, baby… you best get out of the way."* It was time to put Merle in the "stranglehold." So for fun, I let a departure go on a two ninety heading. Not to worry, though, I only did it because there were no arrivals at the time that he could get close to.

As the wind blew the aircraft farther north than was acceptable, a loud voice from the TRACON came through a speaker at the supervisor's desk, screaming, "Stop the departures!" Clearly *Merle's* two ninety heading had got everyone's attention in the TRACON.

After about five minutes with no further word from the TRACON, I inquired of the supervisor if I could release the departures. He didn't say a word, but I could tell something was up, since Merle was back in the corner, desecrating government pens. I surmised that the supervisor, Bill, was being silent because he wanted no responsibility for what had just happened. After another five minutes, still nothing. As I apologized over the frequency to the pilots waiting to depart, I heard a loud thud from the door that opened up into the Tower just a floor below.

It was the Mish. Bob "the Mish" Mischke was the TRACON manager and had served his entire 40-year career at O'Hare, and not someone you wanted to get into an argument with over operations. He had ascended the elevator up to the Tower faster than Jesus at the resurrection. Ted must have heard the Mish because he belted out,

> *"The road I cruise is a bitch now, baby...*
> *But no you can't turn me round...*
> *And if a house gets in my way, baby...*
> *Ya know I'll burn it down!"*

The Mish was about to burn Merle's house down.

Even though the Tower and TRACON were separate entities, the Mish felt compelled to educate Merle. In uncharacteristically soft tones, a fully red-faced Mish was lecturing Merle. The Mish was doing a great job of holding back his anger and his blood pressure.

After a two-minute lecture none of us could hear, the Mish walked up to me and said, "Now go back to the two seventy headings, Calvin." Just as quickly, the Mish disappeared.

For the next hour, Merle said nary a word, but never did he apologize. I believe that was the beginning of the end, because to not admit when you're wrong when you clearly were in front of ten other controllers was paramount to losing any last ounce of respect you might have had.

By some strange twist of fate, in the next few months, Merle retired early.

Merle wasn't done yet, though. In retirement, he went on to be a "professional" court witness against the government in various aircraft accidents. I guess he never knew which team he was playing for.

Chapter 17

It's A NEAR MISS

FLIGHT PATH: *A line, course, or track along which an aircraft is flying or intended to be flown.*

January 20th, 1992—a day that "shall live in infamy." Plagiarizing Franklin Delano Roosevelt seems only logical, since I graduated from Roosevelt University in Chicago and it's the only description that comes to mind when I think of that day. Having seen many accidents and near misses by other controllers in the Tower, I seemed to have that false sense of security that bad things only happen to everyone else around me. Nothing could be farther from the truth. I never thought I would become the victim of a surprise attack.

The unusual thing about coming to work every day was the possibility that virtually anything could happen. Being somewhat superstitious, I never claimed as a controller that I had a perfect record of safety. I never wanted to brag that I had never had a "near miss." To do so would almost certainly invite a blemish on such a clean record. In fact, whenever I made speeches to small gatherings, such as Kiwanis, Rotary

Clubs, schools, etc., I would start out by saying that "my record of 22 dead, 32 injured, and only five missing" was one of
the best at the O'Hare Tower. I had to back off with this initial
approach when many in the audience wondered aloud what
the worst record was. So much for dry, dark, air traffic controller humor.

While I had witnessed actual airplane crashes in the
past, I had always been extremely careful not to put myself
in a situation that would cause one. Sooner or later, and especially when working hundreds of thousands of airplanes per
year, the human statistic eventually creeps in. I was no different. On a beautiful, sunny day in mid-January, my career as a
controller took a very serious turn "south."

It was around 12:25 p.m. that I caused everyone in the
control Tower to go totally silent while my drama played out.
While working the north side of the airport and responsible
for four departure runways, it was my job to depart aircraft
to their destinations. Very seldom does a single local controller (the controller who clears aircraft for takeoff and landing)
work that many runways at one time. In 2005, the rule was
changed, and now two controllers must work the same four
runways.

The reason we stopped the old procedure was simple—
too many airplanes for just one person. Otherwise, most of the
time, each local controller lands and departs just one runway.
But in 1992, I had *all* the departure runways, while on the
south side of the airport, another controller was landing the
only two arrival runways. In case an aircraft aborted a landing
on the south side of the airport, it was then my job to handle
that aircraft as a "departure," by telling the other controller which way (or heading) to send him. Usually the missed
approach from the south side was blended with the regular

departures on the north side. Basically, if a flight is unable to land, it is simply treated as a departure off O'Hare. So while I didn't necessarily talk to the aircraft from the south side, I basically left a departure path for him to fill. I oversimplify to clarify.

The only time there is any interaction or coordination between these two local controllers is when the south side landing controller has an airplane that, for whatever reason, is unable to land, a term known as the "go around." The "go around" phrase at O'Hare Tower, while normally a routine procedure, occasionally caught controllers off guard. Because of their unexpected, sudden occurrence, controllers must act quickly to mix the "go-around" aircraft first with the other departures, and then eventually back with the landing string of airplanes, where the aircraft will be given another chance to land. The initial coordination for a "go around" is usually a loud, "Hey, I might be going around!" or even "Hey, I need a heading for this go around ASAP!" The reason for the loud communication is that the two controllers are usually about thirty feet from each other, across the Tower.

An aircraft can lose its clearance or ability to land for many reasons. A controller usually issues a "go around" command for such situations as when a previous landing aircraft does not clear the runway, or when there is reported debris on the runways, such as uplifted concrete, rubber from blown tires, or even wild animals, such as coyotes. Any foreign substance ingested into a jet engine could cause harm on impact. Damage to jet engines can cost airline companies in the millions. No one wants to upset the bottom line.

It's also possible for pilots to initiate their own "go-arounds." Some pilots simply can't descend fast enough in time to land due to bad weather, strong winds, low visibility, etc. Some pilots are not used to flying in certain kinds of weather. While there are contingencies for missed approaches, published in the various pilot's manuals, they are seldom followed at O'Hare, due to the complexity and sheer volume of airplane traffic. Since controllers are almost always in radio contact with aircraft, it is usually possible to send the "go-around" in a direction that will make reentry to the airport easier than the published procedure.

In the midst of departing aircraft in rapid succession from one runway to the next, I was barely able to take a breath without saying something to someone. I rolled United 649 to the northwest on a heading of 330° off runway thirty-two left, and then immediately over to runway nine left, to roll a United 67 to a heading southwest on a heading of 140°.

At this point, the controller on the south side yelled over, "I'm going around," and before I could open my mouth, the "go around" aircraft appeared, coming from the southwest. It was aimed like an arrow that was fast approaching the United 67 heading southeast and just lifting off the runway.

Without further hesitation, I told the south side controller to put the "go around on the 140 heading," and I would turn the other aircraft United 67 back to the east (on a 090 heading) from his assigned 140 heading. It was a great plan, right up until I had a brain fart. When I keyed the mike, instead of talking to United 67, I transposed the call sign United 649 and told him to turn left, heading 090. Without knowing it, I was talking to the aircraft northwest of the field and in effect asking him to turn west, turn south and then again turning more to the left, until he was flying east. The biggest problem in this big turn was the aircraft course would take it right through the *flight paths* of two lines of aircraft landing on the two south side runways. I was, in effect, aiming an aircraft into two different straight-line strings of airplanes coming into the airport.

The pilot of UAL 649 must have known how bad my instructions were because he said, "Tower, United Six Forty Nine *understands* you want us to turn left heading 0-9-0?"

Not picking up on this important hint and feeling the need to take charge, I gently scolded United 649 and told him, "Yes, United Six Forty Nine, please turn left *now*, there is another aircraft off your immediate right, aimed right at you."

Without any argument at this point, UAL 649 made a hard left, which I couldn't see because I was looking visually at UAL 67 for the same turn. I had given the wrong instructions to the wrong aircraft.

The next words on the radio I heard were "What the hell?" and "What's this guy doing?" And then a shrill voice came from the other side of the Tower: "Hey, Calvin, what the fuck is your United doing?" the south side controller inquired.

Looking out the window to the west and then quickly to my radar screen, I could see the United pass right in front of a Northwest jet on a two-mile final for the west runway nine right. My heart sank and I could feel all the air leaving my lungs.

As I started to key my mike, I could tell the United was next headed for the airplanes lined up for runway four Right. Immediately I commanded, "United Six Forty Nine, turn *immediately* to the north heading three six zero," away from the landing airplanes, "and do it *right now!*"

It was all too late, however, and I had just missed taking out three different airplanes and around five hundred people.

Now I was shaking uncontrollably, but still trying to control the situation. As I started to talk, the supervisor already had another controller plugged in. The also visibly shaken supervisor, Darryl, leaned over my left shoulder and softly said, "Calvin, give Joe [my relief] your picture so he can take the position."

At this point I could hardly talk, and Joe knew it. Sensing my helplessness, Joe did the compassionate thing and said, "Don't worry, I got it… really, don't worry, Calvin, I'll talk now."

As I unplugged my headset, I looked straight into Darryl's eyes, but wasn't seeing a thing. After a few seconds of my complete silence and staring, Darryl said, "Calvin, are you OK, man?"

While I heard the words, I still could not speak. Part of me wanted to scream in pain and the other part wanted to cry like a baby. I think because of my upbringing, I did neither. Instead, I walked away down the stairs and to the elevator to get as far away as I could.

As I walked out of the elevator at the base of the Tower to flee the scene, there stood my area manager, Jim. It was clear that Darryl had informed Jim to run interference for my benefit. As I stood in front of Jim in the hallway, I could not say a word—nothing was registering. Jim's job as an area manager was to supervise the supervisors and answer to the number one man, Bill Halleck, who was the Tower Chief. While it wasn't necessarily Jim's job description to work and speak directly with controllers, I could tell this was going to be an exception. Jim's first words were eerily reminiscent from a few minutes earlier. In a low and concerned voice, Jim said, "Calvin, are you OK…you know it's gonna be OK, Calvin."

By this time, we were standing just outside Bill's office. I had no idea how I had got there, and then out from the office, with the most serious facial expression I had ever seen, was Bill. At first he said nothing, but put his right hand on my shoulder and gave me a little pat, as if to try and soothe my confusion and fear. I put my head down, trying to fight the tears from coming out.

Then, slowly, Bill began to speak, "Hey, Bobby, don't worry, man, these things can happen... We all make mistakes. Hey, Bobby, look at me."

It was very strange to have anyone call me Bobby, and in fact Bill was only one of a handful of people at the Tower who called me that. "Bobby" was a name I associated with my childhood, a place at this time I wished I could have crawled to. Only my closest friends and parents called me Bobby, so while Bill's voice sounded reassuring, it also caused me to break down and, silently, the flood of tears came.

Out of the corner of my eye, sitting at the receptionist desk, I saw Rocchina. For some reason, the sight of Roe made me feel like I was losing my manhood, as if I couldn't cry in front of a woman. I know Roe felt bad for me, but I really couldn't stand the idea of people feeling sorry for me.

I asked Jim if I could leave the Tower and maybe take a walk across the street in the terminal, simply to get away. Not only did Jim agree, but he followed me around for the next hour, from terminal to terminal. Jim spent most of the time talking about his own misadventures in air traffic, but then touched upon a subject I was most curious about—drinking. I knew I drank a lot, but I didn't know if Jim was aware of it. Apparently he wasn't, since his next move was to tell me about how he overcame his problem with drinking. His story struck me as being from his heart—it was a side of Jim I had never seen. In telling me about his own vulnerability, he was making my own situation seem not as horrible as I first thought.

Jim suggested strongly that I talk to a therapist of my choosing. When I told him I didn't think that was necessary, he shot back, "Calvin, I'm not asking you."

After filling out the appropriate paperwork, I took the next few days off, with Jim's blessing. When I got home, I attempted to tell my wife about the incident, but as I started to relive the experience, I could tell I was going to break down again.

Rather than go into detail, I simply told Debbie that I had had a small incident that needed to be looked into and everything would be all right. I knew at the time it was the wrong thing to do, but I honestly felt bad about having anyone else but me worry about this. I used this as my excuse not to confide in her.

To fulfill my promise of seeing a psychotherapist, I walked a few blocks away from my house to a place I had driven by many times on my way to and from work. When I walked into the Fillmore Center, I explained I was there to talk with someone about my job.

When the receptionist asked, "What do you do?" I softly said, "I'm an air traffic controller." As soon as I said the word "controller," I noticed a somewhat surprised look on her face. "Wow, that must be a lot of pressure," she proclaimed.

At that point, I didn't say anything, because if I had a dollar for every time someone said that, I would have retired already. I was always in denial about my job affecting my physical and mental performance.

As I sat in the waiting room and filled out the paperwork, I sensed I was being surrounded by mental weakness.

There were two other guys in the waiting room with me to see therapists, and neither one of them "appeared" sane.

It was right out of the song "No Rain" by Blind Melon.

"All I can say is that my life is pretty plain...

I like watchin' the puddles gather rain...

And all I can do is just pour some tea for two and speak my point of view...

But it's not sane...

It's not sane..."

One was a guy who sat there with a kind of nervous tic, jerking his head to the side about every three seconds. The other guy was having a conversation, with whom I couldn't tell because he was sitting all alone and there was no one within five feet. I started to believe I was in some kind of insane asylum. I froze in fear and was starting to think about just walking out. I figured I could always tell Jim I did go the Fillmore Center and leave it at that, but before I could walk away, this giant of a man came from behind the receptionist door and bellowed, "Mr. Richards, come with me."

The therapist's name was B.J. Parrish. He easily stood over six feet and was built like an offensive lineman. He was clearly older, with his thinning gray hair combed straight back, and he carried that smell of tobacco all around him. I was too proud to believe that this guy, or anyone else for that matter, could help me. When he asked me to sit down, I took my place on the nice soft sofa behind his credenza.

As he wheeled his chair around toward the sofa, he politely inquired, "So, what brings you here to see us?"

I next went into a very simple explanation: "I had a little accident at work and my boss thought it would be a good idea if I talked to someone."

After that short quip, B.J. came back with that all-too-familiar question, "So what do you do?"

I mockingly returned, "I'm an air traffic controller at the *entire* world's busiest airport."

And again, as if on cue, B.J. responded, "Wow, that must be a lot of pressure."

I quickly turned that around and said, "No, air traffic is easy, it's raising kids that's a lot of pressure."

After a slight chuckle, B.J. grew serious again. "I'm sure air traffic has a lot of pressures of its own."

Again, and in denial, I replied, "Sorry, B.J., I find my job a lot of fun and not stressing at all." Now I sensed inside myself I was bullshitting, but I wasn't going to admit it. I was too stupidly proud.

B.J. backed off from the verbal jousting for a second to explain that our sessions would only be beneficial if I "came clean" about things in my life. I simply shook my head, agreed to see him the next day, and then once a week for an undetermined amount of time.

A week later, I was still feeling depressed and at times not sure why, but I knew I would have to find a way to overcome my doubts. Up to the point of the "incident," I had always been happy and positive, but now I needed some help. I rationalized taking a magic pill that I had used for some back strain I had experienced earlier in the winter.

When I opened up my dresser, there was the answer to my sleepless nights and depression: a bottle of Vicodin. Vicodin spoke in the first person through the song "No Rain":

"I just want someone to say to me
I'll always be there when you wake…
You know I'd like to keep my cheeks dry today…
So stay with me and I'll have it made

And I don't understand why I sleep all day
And I start to complain that there's no rain...
Escape...
Escape..."

After I took the first two, I started to feel positive and happy again. In fact, I felt so good I deduced that I would be cured in no time with this enchanted remedy.

Everyone around me noticed the change from the week's previous funk. I had embarked on a new flight path. I decided to take my "medicine" when I wasn't working, because not only could it dull my back pain, but my mental pain as well. No one, including my wife, questioned it either—to her it was just Bobby being Bobby.

As far as my wife was concerned, she always had a hard time trying to keep up with my hyperactivity. There was so much I wanted to accomplish and experience in my life that there never seemed to be enough time in the day. Often, I would be starting one task before finishing another one I just started. I was always focused at the Tower but, outside of it, I was headed in many different directions. Most of the time, I was a very positive person spending hours laughing and having fun with everyone around me. I never wanted to let anyone be burdened with my sadness so I simply didn't let it out. I held it all in. Vicodin and working airplanes were the two things that kept my depression in its inner cage. Even though my wife knew I was prone to bouts of depression, she also knew that in time I would always rebound back to my "happy, manic persona." My view of reality was in constant flux.

But in time, I would eventually be faced with a new reality. What would I do when the magic wore off?

Chapter 18

Midnight Madness

SAY AGAIN: *Used to request a repeat of the last transmission. Usually specifies transmission or portion thereof sometimes not understood or received by older pilots.*

A s I gradually left behind the near miss of six months before, I began to understand what a waste of time it was to wallow in self-pity. Often, I would hear the Tower radio echo the song "The Real Me," by The Who. It reminded me of my favorite primary care doctor, known as Doctor D. In my mind, the words to the song would pierce my soul.

Can you see the real me, Doctor? Doctor?

Dr. D never understood I was escaping from the darkness of my life. Before that darkness could consume me, I'd head down to his office. I would be in and out of the doctor's office with another prescription for Vicodin. Dr. D felt good that he could make me feel well and happy again.

I basically had two "quasi" addictions. The first was work, because when I was in the Tower, nothing mattered. All

I could concentrate on was the airplanes and having "fun" with my co-workers. I could completely block out my personal life when I had my headset on. All I wanted to work was the heaviest traffic. The more traffic I moved, the more my mind couldn't focus on my personal plight. I didn't feel the need for any drugs or alcohol when I was working airplanes.

The second obsession occurred on my days off, or whenever I had a long break between work shifts. If I felt the need or wasn't happy, Vicodin and alcohol were the answers. I was so *anal* about not breaking the rules of not working traffic 24 hours after taking Vicodin that I became a "controlled" addict. I would systematically time my medication week in and week out to not break the "rules." Besides, my back was really acting up at times, and that was all that mattered. I could fix physical and mental pain at the same time.

One of the few things that kept my hopes up for the future was my two boys. Very often, their mere presence would keep me sober, happy, and hopeful. Only six and nine years old at the time, they were curious about everything. I could hardly keep up with them. They always made me laugh, particularly when they wanted to know more about air traffic control.

One time, on a red-eye flight out to California, I gave my older son, Adam, a bird's eye view of an airplane in flight. Before 9/11, controllers were allowed to ride the jump seat on a space-available basis in the cockpit, under the FAA program known as "Familiarization Travel." The program was designed so that controllers could observe pilots in action firsthand. Most often, the jump seat had a better view than the Captain and first officer's seats, since it was more elevated and slightly behind the two pilots. It was an extremely beneficial program that educated controllers into having a better understanding for dealing with pilots on a day-to-day basis. Being allowed a maximum of eight free flights a year, many controllers did a lot of traveling.

The program at times was so liberal I once had a DC-10 captain invite my nine-year-old son, Adam, to come up to the cockpit during the flight. During level flight at 33,000 feet, the first officer excused himself to go to the bathroom. Immediately, the Captain put on his oxygen mask, which was standard FAA procedure for whenever a crewmember left a two-person cockpit. As the first officer went out, Adam came in. The Captain told Adam to sit next to him, because now Adam was "helping to fly the plane." Adam could only stare at the Captain, since his voice sounded just like Darth Vader with his mask on, inhaling oxygen. For a few seconds, Adam really thought it might be Darth himself, but after a few minutes of my reassurance, he felt at ease.

As the Captain and I got entrenched in some innate conversation about procedures, a call over the cockpit loudspeaker came from L.A. Center: "United One Ninety Heavy say altitude." The puzzled Captain answered, "Level at Flight Level three three zero errrr... I mean flight level three two zero...standby, L.A. Center."

While the Captain and I were talking, Adam had turned the little dial button that regulated the altitude on the autopilot to Flight Level 290 (twenty-nine thousand feet). The plane was descending, and all the Captain could say was "Holy shit."

When he finally figured it out, the airplane was descending through thirty thousand feet. L.A. Center was getting a little more excited. "Hey, United One Ninety Heavy, *please* take it back up to flight level three three zero best rate of climb."

As the first officer made his way back into the cockpit, the Captain cleverly relayed to L.A. Center, "L.A. Center, United One Ninety Heavy, I think we have some kind of malfunction in the autopilot. We're headed back up now. Sorry about that."

L.A. Center paused for a moment and then calmly said, "That's OK, United One Ninety Heavy, there's no one within 50 miles. We got lucky. Give us a call when you get on the ground."

I knew the "phone call" was not a good thing, so I quietly escorted Adam out of the cockpit. Not knowing what had just happened, Adam exclaimed, "Wow, Dad, that was neat— can we do that again later?"

This was quality time with my boy. Because I wanted to spend as much time as possible with my boys, I decided to find a safer way to integrate them into my job schedule.

A controllers' workweek at O'Hare is one to behold. Initially, every controller bid to have two days off, and naturally the highest in seniority were able to get the weekends. Everyone worked the same five-day, compressed "hell" week known as shiftwork. I say "hell" because workdays one and two were night shifts, meaning Day One was a 3:00 p.m.–11:00 p.m. following into Day Two with a 2:00 p.m.–10:00 p.m. Day Three was either another 2:00 p.m.–10:00 p.m., or a day shift, 7:00 a.m.–3:00 p.m. Day Three meant the quick turnaround if you had a day shift. This first transition always guaranteed the fact that no one would get more than seven hours of sleep. You got off work near 10:00 p.m., drove home, tried to get to bed, and then started it all over when you woke up at 5:00 or 6:00 a.m., depending on where you lived. Try doing this to your body for 20 years.

Day Four was always a 7:00 a.m.–3:00 p.m. If you had a night shift the previous day, then this was your first transition. It was the Day Four to Day Five transition that presented the second quick turn. Just as you thought your body was adjusting to the weekly work schedule came the next shock.

After getting off shift at 3:00 p.m. on Day Four, Day Five would start just eight hours later, on the midnight shift from 11:00 p.m.–7:00 a.m. Again, you'd be lucky to sleep seven hours maximum. Quite honestly, not many people could sleep at all, waiting for the midnight shift, simply because it wasn't natural to sleep during the day and only one time a week.

The biggest problem of all, though, was the fact that it would often take an hour or two after a shift to simply wind down. Instead of falling asleep as soon as they got home, most lay in bed, staring at the ceiling, knowing it was just a short time till the next shift started. With an availability of 13 sick days a year, many controllers found themselves calling in sick on the quick turnarounds, such as the night shift to a day shift, and even the day shift to the midnight. You *never* wanted to come to work without any sleep, although I'm sure a few people tried. We had one controller so confused by his schedule that he would call in sick on his days off.

When I went to weekly therapy and explained to B.J. about our work shifts, his eyebrows rose about an inch and a half. I know a lot of people I had talked to outside of air traffic found it unbelievable that any human being could function with such odd sleeping habits. But since we were young and dumb, none of us really cared. The only work shift rule that made any sense was the law that we couldn't work more than two hours' overtime, or ten hours total in one day. Also, it was required that there had to be eight hours between shifts. At least two, and sometimes three, days a week, it was right at eight hours. As the years went by, I could see the older controllers becoming less patient with pilots, from the years of wear and tear on their bodies.

The midnight shifts were the easiest because the traffic was limited to a few passenger and cargo flights. Only four controllers were required to run the midnight shift, compared to 15 and 17 for the day and afternoon shifts respectively. The midnight shifts were so quiet many of the controllers would bring their kids in to hang out in the Tower. Here was my opportunity to spend more time with my guys. Adam and Andy would bring their sleeping bags, pitch them under the consoles, and then stare out the windows in amazement at all the bright lights that were the airplanes. When they felt like getting some exercise, they would run around the inside of the circular Tower, which resembled an indoor track. For the first few years, my boys couldn't get enough of the Tower. Then one day they both got the scare of their lives.

The scare came from a veteran controller by the name of Bill Norwood, Jr. "Woody," as he came to be called, was only the second African-American to enter the Tower in the last ten years leading up to 1992. His father was the first black captain at United Airlines, and one of the most respected pilots in the O'Hare arena. At six foot two, Woody was extremely stocky, strong, and, when he was angry, could scare the hell out of anyone with just a simple scowl. Conversely, he had a great sense of humor and loved to play practical jokes endlessly. His smile was so contagious people ended up gravitating to him without knowing why. He was so muscular that when he played with our Tower softball team, he averaged at least one homer in every three at-bats. He was so feared by opposing teams that most often he would be walked "intentionally." That may not sound unusual, except there were occasions when our opponents walked him with the bases loaded. They simply figured it was better to give up one run than a grand-slam home run.

During one midnight shift I was working with Woody, he started the shift on a break while I went straight up to the Tower. My two boys also came to the Tower, but stopped off in the break room to buy some snacks out of the machines and watch a little television before heading up. Unbeknownst to Adam and Andy, Woody had covered himself under a blanket, resting on a break room couch. My two boys had never seen Woody before. Thinking the blanket on the couch was simply bunched up and not a 220-pound man, my boys jumped on top of the unsuspecting Woody. It was as if they had attacked a wild bear. Both boys screamed in terror and Woody, sensing how much fun he was about to have, gave out a big roar. My boys had never run so fast to the elevator in their lives.

By the time my boys made it up to the Tower for reassurance, they were shaking beyond control and at first were not even able to talk. Finally, Adam took a few deep breaths and warned, "Dad, the big *black* man downstairs scared us, and he's still after us!"

I found Adam's characterization of Woody a bit unusual. Since Adam and Andy had grown up in a predominantly white neighborhood, I began to realize that they were more afraid of the fact that Woody was black than the fact he was big. Having never really been around black people, it was clear they were afraid because of their unfamiliarity.

For the next hour, my boys didn't stray more than five feet from me. I tried to reassure them that Woody was only joking around and they shouldn't be scared of him. When Woody came up to the Tower to relieve me, my boys scurried to take position as close as humanly possible to each one of my legs. As Woody entered the Tower and caught sight of my boys, he let out a boisterous laugh, as if he was Santa Claus.

"Hey, Calvin, your boys scared the shit out of me," Woody jokingly exclaimed.

I then looked to Adam and Andy and said, "Guys, is this the big, black man from downstairs?"

A confused Adam answered Woody, "I'm sorry, sir, we thought you were a blanket."

Woody just smiled and gave my boys a high five. From then on, they were no longer afraid of Woody. They hung around with him for the rest of the shift. They had befriended the "Wood" man and learned something special about race relations. *Priceless.*

The midnight shifts also gave some of the controllers time to give some interesting and educational lessons to controllers at other airports. Many of the controllers at O'Hare knew about a controller at Midway Airport, just ten miles to the southeast, who often worked the midnight shifts. The controller, who I'll call Ward, had been a controller at O'Hare for a number of years and was prone to being quick tempered. Having transferred to Midway Airport, a commercial aviation airport just like O'Hare but with considerably fewer airplanes, it was felt that Ward would not be as stressed out at a less busy airport. Nothing could have been farther from the truth.

One controller at O'Hare, who I'll call Marvin, decided while working his midnight shift at O'Hare that he would have a bit of fun with Ward at Midway, and usually around two in the morning when traffic was non-existent. Using a hand-held emergency portable radio and dialing up the frequency to Midway Tower, Marvin would transmit in the disguised voice of an old man, saying, "Midway Tower, Midway Tower, this is Cessna Three-niner- niner on the ground at Willy Howell looking for a radio check. How do ya hear?"

Normally, the response was silence for the first ten seconds, because with nothing else to do, Ward was probably taking his feet off the counter to answer at two in the morning. The reference to Howell Airport was used because its location was just a few miles to the south of Midway, and while it was common for pilots to call from there, it certainly was not common for them to call at two in the morning, looking for sound checks on their radios. Think about it—what is Grandpa doing at two in the morning with his single engine prop airplane?

Ward's response was usually very slow, as if he had just awoken: "Cessna ...uh....Three, Three, Niner...uh...*say again.*"

Marvin realized he probably had done the FAA a favor and was helping Ward's alertness.

Knowing Ward had read back the wrong call sign, the phantom old man said, "Midway Tower, Midway Tower, this is Cessna Three-*niner*-niner at Willy Howell for a radio check. How do ya hear?"

A less confused and angry Ward responded, "Cessna Three-*niner-niner* loud and clear—now don't call me *no* more, get your radio checks on another frequency, this is a busy frequency."

Ward was correct, because very rarely did any pilot call controllers on the Tower frequency, but this was an old, befuddled man.

As if he hadn't heard a word, the old-man-alias Marvin retorted, "Midway Tower, Midway Tower, your radios are weak, *say again.*"

The steam now started to hiss from Ward's head. "Cessna Three-niner-niner, *I told you,* do not call me *no more* on this frequency, you got it?"

A more bewildered old man came back, "Midway Tower, Midway Tower, we're having a hard time…I think…understanding you, is something wrong with your radios? *Say again?*"

Then came the Ward outburst: "Cessna Three-niner-niner, *Goddammit,* stop calling me on this frequency! I can hear you just fine!"

Without blinking, the old man shot back in a very cordial and condescending tone, "Midway Tower, Midway Tower, your radio is awful. I will call your regional office and let them know so you can get it fixed, OK?"

This was the last thing Ward wanted to hear, because if the Region listened to the tapes, they would be able to hear Ward screaming at a poor old man and using the word "Goddammit." Ward's now enraged voice was converted to Mister Rogers' soothing voice: "Now, don't do that, Cessna Three-niner-niner, we're good, man… that radio is excellent. You don't need to call anyone, OK?"

Marvin decided that Ward had learned his lesson and then let him off the hook. "Midway Tower, Midway Tower, OK. We hear you loud and clear. Now have a wonderful day."

Marvin would repeat the same lesson for Ward periodically over the next two years. As time went by, Ward, in his transmissions with the old man, would be kind and considerate, which were qualities he had rarely possessed when he was at O'Hare. Ward never figured out who the old man was, but he learned a valuable lesson on how to treat a fellow human being, which was something the FAA could never teach him. Marvin was a genius.

Chapter 19

You're Jammin' Me

LAHSO: *An acronym for "Land and Hold Short Operation." These operations include landing and holding short of an intersecting runway, a taxiway, a predetermined point or an approach/departure flight-path.*

As the workforce in the Tower and TRACON matured into the 1990s, the fruits of their experience began to show. The cohesiveness between the Tower and TRACON was apparent in everyday work and play. The O'Hare Tower softball team was unbeatable wherever they played. With a combination of both Tower and TRACON controllers, there was not a weak link throughout the whole lineup. The third through eighth hitters all had the potential to be long ball threats.

When I was hitting in the first or second spot in the batting order, I knew that if I got on base, there was a good chance I was not going to have to run hard because the guys behind me were all "home run" threats. Most often, I was trotting across home plate. At the bars after games, they were always reveling in the fact that they were like a group whose camaraderie was based on the daily wars with airplanes. Every controller believed that coming to work each day was a challenge to be better than the day before.

I was so excited to be working in the Tower I'd often stand up on the consoles to work airplanes. If I felt confident, I would even adapt the "Karate Kid" stance, standing on one leg bent with the other bent up in the air. Supervisors really enjoyed that move. To amuse my friend and supervisor, Dave Dobrinich, I would improvise bad "dance" steps while walking around the Tower to search out my airplanes. We made audiotapes to play on the Tower boom box, such as the bad '80s, encompassing the worst pop music of that era. Just listening to that music made us all laugh.

Dave, like many of the other supervisors, was aware of what kept controllers motivated and interested. He picked his spots when it came time to make decisions in the Tower. Most of the time, controllers were given free rein when Dave was in the Tower, but if he saw something get out of hand, he would jump right in and rarely would anyone question him. Dave was like a hibernating bear most of the time, but look out if you did something to wake him up.

On one occasion, Dave was informed by the TRACON that a single-engine Cessna was approaching O'Hare from the southeast and appeared to be lost. Dave informed the controller working the area not to launch any departures into that airspace, since the Cessna was not talking to anyone. The controller, who already had a Delta DC-9 sitting on the runway waiting for takeoff clearance, paused a few seconds, then, after seeing the Cessna target still six miles southeast, decided (on his own) there was plenty of room to depart Delta. Big mistake.

When the controller cleared Delta for takeoff, the captain hesitated a few seconds before finally rolling. As the Cessna made its way northbound and just to the east of O'Hare, the Delta DC-9 was now starting to look like an ICBM missile about to hit its target. At just one mile east from the airport, the conflict alert system engaged and made the noise that every controller fears.

Dave, who was on the other side of the Tower, quickly turned around and shouted, "Now what the fuck?" As he made his way over to the controller, he loudly inquired, "*Mike*, why did you launch that Delta?"

The controller, now too busy trying to stop a collision, meekly pointed out, "Well, I thought he could beat him."

Dave came back sternly, "Stop *fuckin'* thinking and do what you're told!"

To this day, that controller has never crossed Dave again.

Other times, I would sneak up behind other controllers and just stare. This maneuver used to drive Craig Burzych crazy. First, he'd pretend I wasn't there and then, in a matter of seconds, he would simply crack up in laughter. Craig liked to throw other controllers off by pretending to transmit to airlines that were long extinct. One time, with visitors from the regional office in the Tower observing, Craig and I went back and forth on our radios (not transmitting, of course). Craig would say in one transmission, "Hey, Eastern Three Fifty-two, how do you read, and Pan Am Seventy-six, what are you doing?" Trying to outdo Craig at the same time, I came with, "Braniff Fifty-nine, turn left, and Britt Air Twenty-nine, have a wonderful day." Most visitors just stared in amazement and must have figured they had entered the twilight zone. That was the effect we had on most visitors.

Most of the time my distractions were ignored, but often it was just comic relief from what was becoming an "assembly line of airplanes." Before air traffic could become simple factory work, controllers needed to find new ways to keep things fresh and interesting. Dave would say, "I just love coming to work for the entertainment." Dave could speak volumes.

Another time I played the role of a naturalist and rescued a group of baby ducks and their mother that I encountered one day on my way into the Tower from the parking lot. With the help of some TRACON controllers, we herded about ten baby ducks and their mother into a box and away from the busy street traffic next to the Tower. No one knew how the ducks had made their way to the Tower, but it was decided that I would take them home after work. I was so proud of myself and the TRACON controllers that I brought the box of ducks into the radar room to show the TRACON manager, the Mish. He was only mildly amused. When I realized I was late heading upstairs to start work in the Tower, I decided to leave the box in the TRACON.

Within a half-hour of being in the Tower, I heard the Mish's voice crackling through the Tower supervisor speaker: "*Calvin*, get those ducks outta here!"

Apparently, one of the TRACON controllers, while adjusting his eyes walking into the dark radar room from the lighted hallway, had accidentally knocked over the box with the baby ducks. In seconds, the Tower supervisor had me relieved and I was downstairs in the radar room, searching for the little guys. At first I couldn't see a thing. Then from the other side of the radar room, I heard a woman scream. It was Olivet Smith.

Olivet was the first and only African-American woman controller at the O'Hare TRACON and, later, the Tower. She was always a lot of fun, particularly in her younger days, and used to refer to me affectionately as her "blonde-haired, blue-eyed baby." But small animals in a dark room were not a favorite of Olivet's.

Working east departures, Olivet was so startled she just kept on screaming, "Something is nibbling at my dress, something is attacking me!"

I tried to assure her, "Olivet, they're just baby ducks."

Naturally, everyone else was laughing but the Mish. He, of course, would be responsible for any problems caused by Daffy and the guys. By the time I scooped up all the ducks, I had been given the rest of the day off, with pay. So was Olivet. It was fun having the TRACON living in the same house.

Even though up to 1996, the Tower and TRACON were collocated in the same building at O'Hare Airport, many of the TRACON controllers came from the Tower. Because of that fact, controllers in the Tower and TRACON knew each other's comfort level when it came to the number of airplanes each could handle at any one time. Very often when I was clearing aircraft for take-off, I would push the communication buttons to see who was working the departures. If I knew the person at the other end, I would usually appeal to their egos and say, "Hey, Richie, are you ready to get your ass kicked?"

The answer was usually, "Yeah, let's see what you got, Calvin, you weak stick." The "weak stick" reference was a joking comment designed to taunt other controllers, basically telling them they couldn't possibly send too many airplanes because they were too "weak."

Rich (Richie) Nemcek was a controller for many years in the Tower before transferring downstairs to the TRACON. At

six foot six and having played basketball at Indiana State with
Larry Bird, Rich was not about to back off from a little guy
such as myself, who had played guard at Roosevelt University,
a small, unheard-of Division II school. Outside of work, Rich
and I played in yearly basketball tournaments in Chicago. We
approached play just as we did work—like war. The energy at
work was what carried us outside of it as well. We were often
overachievers in three-on-three competitions, with five sec-
ond-place finishes in the 1990s against teams that were still in
their prime, playing Division I college basketball.

Depending on what kind of departures I had, there
were at least three and sometimes four TRACON controllers
controlling east, north, south, and west departures. Sometimes
the west and south would be combined, as well as the north
with the east. When O'Hare was busy, chances were all the positions were staffed. While Rich was working east departures, I
pushed the north button to see who was working there, since
I was departing east and north at the time.

The familiar voice at the other end was none other
than Bob "Hoosier Boy" Mathias. Bob was an Indianapolis,
Indiana, native: thus his nickname. For a while, Bob actually commuted the three-hour trip to Chicago weekly. Having
worked for years in the TRACON, since 1985, Bob was always
comfortable, yet never got too excited about anything. When
I went down to the TRACON to observe him work departures,
he was as smooth as ice. His transmissions were always perfectly measured, so he only had to say them once.

So I pushed down the north button and said to Bob,
"You ready to work some planes?"

Hoosier Boy, in his normal monotone, said matter-of-
factly, "You can't hurt me."

For the next hour I would roll airplanes as fast as humanly possible, only to hear Bob in my ear, saying "Is that all you got?"

Richie was just as diplomatic, saying, "Not bad, Calvin. I've noticed you've improved a little over the last few years."

Having almost *mastered* the art of separating airplanes, controllers sought out more innovative ways to move more aircraft. The obvious solution was to change the rules to allow more aircraft to land. Back in 1985, when I first arrived at O'Hare, there was a procedure known as "Landing and Hold Short Operations" (LAHSO), which was used to have aircraft landing one runway while simultaneously departing an intersecting runway downfield from the landing runway. What this meant was that aircraft landing had to stop near the end of the runway and prior to where the "departure" runway intersected.

At the time, LAHSO was used on runway 14 right to hold short of runway 27 left (see Appendix 3, airport map). The aircraft landing on runway 14 right had 10,000 feet available before they had to turn off prior to reaching runway 27 left. Aircraft departing runway 27 left could be rolling without any regard to the airplanes landing runway 14 right. Any aircraft, when cleared to land on 14 right, were also instructed to "hold short of runway twenty-seven left for departing traffic." If the aircraft said he couldn't hold short, we simply didn't depart runway 27 left until runway 14 right was clear.

Initially, this procedure was only used at a handful of airports, and not at all outside the United States. In fact, when a group of controllers from Canada and Europe came over to watch us do "LAHSO," they just about flipped out. Even though the procedure was only used when runways were dry, many foreign controllers felt the operation was too dangerous, and that O'Hare controllers were, as they put it, "plain nuts." They feared that aircraft landing 14 right would somehow find their way into the departure of runway 27 left.

In 20 years, we did not have a single collision on the runways. Asking aircraft to land with 10,000 feet available was not a big deal, since most aircraft were landing at other airports with runways half that length. *Any* close calls initially with LAHSO involved foreign carriers, so the FAA did the right thing and kept *all* foreign carriers out of the LAHSO program.

Because of the language barrier, many foreign carriers had a hard time keeping up with basic English, much less trying to learn complicated "American" landing procedures. Very often, if a controller was departing two or three different runways and a foreign carrier was involved, vigilance was at an all-time high. It was not uncommon for a foreign carrier to accept a takeoff clearance given to another flight simply because the numbers were similar.

On July 12th, 1988, I had an Air France Boeing 747 at the full length of runway three-two right, holding in position with a flight of two C130s Hercules (four-prop Air Force cargo planes) holding short of the same runway halfway up field from Air France. In deference to the United States Air Force, I was going to hold Air France while clearing the Air Force flight of two for takeoff. As I cleared the Hercules flight for takeoff, I noticed the Air France starting to move ahead as the first Hercules was taking the runway about 6000 feet up the runway. With the first Hercules revving up the props for takeoff, I noticed Air France had the brakes unlocked and was now rolling straight at the two Air Force bowling pins up the runway. I quickly made a decision.

Instead of talking to Air France, since it was probably too late and he probably wouldn't be able to hear me anyway with the engines roaring at takeoff power, I screamed at my Air Force buddies, "Voter Eighteen, flight of two, clear the runway *immediately*—traffic departing behind you!"

As the lead Hercules acknowledged, "We're doing it," both C-130s turned into the grass as fast as possible, and just in time. The Air France Boeing 747 "swooshed" right by, narrowly missing both aircraft. Both Hercules ended up stuck in the mud as Air France lifted, oblivious to missing his "spare try." Bowling airplanes, as we will see later with such airlines as Mexicana, would become popular. For now though came the first bowler at O'Hare—welcome Air France.

Since the Air France number was 87 and the Air Force was 18, it was easy to see what might have caused the Air France to roll. It was still no excuse, since the numbers were clearly different. The bigger question was how could three crewmembers in the cockpit not see two big Air Force cargo planes up the runway? The FAA answered that question by suspending the flight crew for one year from flying in the United States. It was a stiff penalty, but one no one questioned it, since that incident had probably taken a year off the life of anyone who witnessed it in the Tower. It was one of the main reasons that foreign carriers were left out of LAHSO.

In April 1999, the FAA updated LAHSO at O'Hare to include various other runway combinations. The biggest change was abandoning the runway 14 right-two seven left combination, due to the fact that ALPA (Airlines Pilot Association) felt that the procedure didn't take into account what could happen if the airplane landing runway 14 right were to abort landing and had to go around. Would that go-around be aimed at the runway two seven left departure?

ALPA felt there wasn't enough time to react in this situation. Over the years, this plan was modified several times, until the latest rule, circa 2007, that aircraft rolling 27 left had to be past the intersection of runway 14 right before the landing aircraft was at a location halfway down 14 right, a location known as taxiway turnoff T5.

O'Hare controllers constantly adapted to new "local" rules by enacting procedural changes known as "waivers." Waivers were basically procedures used at O'Hare throughout the years to bypass rules established in the National FAA Air Traffic Control Manual known as the 7110.65. This manual, often referred to as the "ten sixty-five," was under constant siege from the O'Hare controllers, since many of its rules and guidelines were outdated when compared to an airport as complex as O'Hare. While many of the waivers were beneficial and went a long way to moving airplanes, occasionally there would be one that everyone would question.

One of the most uncomfortable waivers in my opinion was the LAHSO of runway 22 right and runway two-seven right.

In this scenario, particular aircraft landing runway 22 right had to hold short of runway 27 right for landing aircraft (see Appendix 3, airport map). Only at O'Hare could you have two runways intersecting each other and landing at the same time. The aircraft on runway 22 right was the one required to hold short. The distance available on runway 22 right to runway two seven right is an interesting 6050 feet. I say "interesting" because most aircraft find that distance just barely usable at other airports. In my last three years at O'Hare, this procedure had become one of the most popular because of its ability to put more airplanes on the ground per hour than just about any other runway configuration.

The problem is that controllers have to work extremely hard to make sure the pilots turn off and clear runway 22 right immediately before the next aircraft can land. Very often, when arrivals on runway 22 right miss the turn-offs, they are usually sitting right up to the intersecting landing runway, with nowhere to go except to wait for the runway two seven right arrival to be out of the way. By this time, the next arrival on runway 22 right is looking straight ahead at the previous aircraft sitting on his/her landing runway.

With no place to land except on top of the preceding arrival, the runway 22 right arrival has no choice but to abort his approach and go-around. There's no fun if you're a passenger on a go-around. Chances are you'll be adding anywhere from ten to 20 minutes to your arrival time. It takes at least that long to get aircraft back into the long stream of arrivals at O'Hare.

Very often, the aircraft on runway 22 right were at the minimum three miles intrail spacing, meaning there was little time to react when landing aircraft missed the turnoffs. When controllers felt overwhelmed by this operation, they would yell out to the supervisor, "Hey, the TRACON is jamming me!" Often the Tower radio would even echo the predicament, from the group Tom Petty and the Heartbreakers and the song "Jammin' Me." As I was being "jammed" I could hear Tom Petty singing,

"You got me in a corner...
QUIT JAMMIN' ME."

Most supervisors reacted quickly and tended not to be very tactful when calling down to the TRACON, saying, "Knock the shit off, the twenty-two right final sucks, open 'em up to at least four miles!" Controllers who normally didn't curse were often so angry they let out the f-bombs in frustration. I know I did.

In my last two years as a controller, I saw no less than three errors involving this operation. One is too many. Many controllers in the Tower today refer to this operation as the "widow maker." It is an accident waiting to happen. There simply is not a lot of room to maneuver aircraft. Many other controllers besides me expressed our concerns about this operation, but to this day nothing has changed. Many in upper management still believe the gains outweigh the risks. I totally disagree and hope never to have to say "I told you so."

So if you're flying into O'Hare, listening to Channel Nine at United, and landing runway 22 right, make sure you look out the left side of the airplane to see where the other landing aircraft is. Hopefully, the sight won't be as scary as it sometimes looks. I know a few pilots who've told me they needed to get their trousers cleaned when they were involved in this operation for the first time. Then they actually said it didn't get any better the next time. Good luck with the cleaning bills.

Chapter 20

Hey, Mr. President

LIGHTS OUT STANDBY: *involves the staging of emergency vehicles, such as fire trucks, ambulances, etc., near the runway of any arriving or departing VIP (Very Important Person, such as the President, Vice-President, Heads of State, etc.). All standby vehicles have their lights out during any staging.*

O ne of the great things about being at the world's busiest airport as an air traffic controller was having the opportunity to take on some nice "side jobs." Periodically, volunteers from among the controller ranks would be chosen for special details, such as quality assurance, plans and procedures, and various other part-time desk jobs. The good thing about these details, which lasted anywhere from 90 days to two years, was that you could still spend many hours per month working airplanes in the Tower. Equally great was the fact that you could be away from the Tower on some cool "gigs." Well, I was fortunate to get one of these sought-after details, known as Plans and Procedures.

While much of the time in this two-year detail was spent at a desk doing FAA paperwork, every once in a while, a fun assignment would come up. When the President of the United States came to visit Chicago, I became the FAA representative, or liaison, to the Secret Service. Now this was fun! Part of this part-time job entailed my presence at the Secret Service advance meetings to coordinate the presidential itinerary. Representing the FAA and the control tower, it was my job to make sure everyone in the Air Traffic sectors knew and understood the President's flight schedule so we could work around his every movement, from landing at O'Hare and providing air control support for Marine One (the presidential helicopter), before he departed back to Washington.

As is my nature, I quickly endeared myself to many of the Secret Service agents who, after a while working with me, gradually began to accept me as one of their own. Even though it wasn't my job description to follow the agents everywhere they went, I soon became curious about what I considered to be their very interesting job. It got to the point that my relationship with the Secret Service was so good that whenever the First Lady, Hillary, or President Clinton came to town, I was allowed to get within an arm's length of them, as if I was an agent myself. I even went out and bought a trademark Secret Service trench coat. After a few visits from the President, many of the other agents actually believed I *was* an agent. Since I had the proper government identification and a security clearance, I was now a "G-Man."

One of my favorite agents was an agent I will call Greg, who, after a few short meetings with joking and laughter, let me tag along everywhere. People always sensed my genuine enthusiasm for life and interest in their jobs and consequently let me go places in their lives that no one else would. Greg enjoyed my openness, especially with the other people I worked with and some of his own superiors.

I didn't always work alone, and one of my FAA counterparts was another specialist named Mike. Mike represented our sister facility, Chicago TRACON. Mike was at times an overly serious, law-enforcement wannabe who joked around about as much as pigs could fly. I've never taken myself very seriously anyway and, thank God, neither did most of the people I worked with. It was my mocking of Mike that the Secret Service and the other government agencies thoroughly enjoyed and found quite entertaining.

Before any arrival of the President in Chicago, I had to attend the advance presidential meetings, which included the heads of various law enforcement agencies, including Customs, the FBI, and immigration. At these meetings, TRACON Mike, very often and without warning, would point out what he thought were shortcomings in the Secret Service or FBI operations. At first, the Secret Service must have thought Mike was some kind of FAA big shot with a law enforcement background. Dressed as he was in a tie with corduroys, I don't think anyone at the meeting knew what to make of this "FAA authority." Critiquing government agencies was *not* part of Mike's job description. Since the most experience Mike had in law enforcement was years ago as a security guard at a local department store, his attitude led to some great practical jokes.

One time, Mike launched into one of his lectures on how the Customs people could enhance their security. Due to the fact that Mike had *zero* experience in Customs, many at the meeting just rolled their eyes in total amazement. I, however, remembering the old TV show *Get Smart*, with its often-comedic pokes at law enforcement, decided to take a page out of the book of Agent "Maxwell Smart."

On the old TV show, Agent Smart would often take phone calls with his "shoe" phone. He would actually take off the shoe he was wearing and answer it when it rang or vibrated, just as people with cell phones do.

Right in the midst of Mike's lecture at one meeting, I jumped up suddenly and clamored, "Hey, Mike, hold on!" Reaching down to my foot, I took off one of my shoes, walked around the table to where Mike was sitting, put the shoe to his ear and exclaimed, "I think it's a very important phone call from the White House, Mike. Your country needs you."

The conference room exploded with laughter. Mike just glared straight ahead, but upon sensing all the frivolity around him, let out a loud chuckle of his own. He *finally* understood how important it was to joke around once in a while.

It was quite unique to be in a room with many older, dignified heads of other government agencies, such as the FBI, Treasury, and Secret Service, and see them let their guards down and have a good laugh. So often the situations that these people faced involved a sense of drama and seriousness, which, like all things, must grow old by routine.

I reveled in the moments of interacting with people who at times thought they were way too important for anybody or anyone else. I always felt it was my duty to either trim them down to size or thoroughly satirize them to the point that even they would see their own foolish pride and come back down and rejoin the human race.

During my initial tenure as liaison to the Secret Service, I rarely had any personal contact with then president, Bill Clinton, First Lady Hillary, or other important dignitaries. I often simply followed them around like a happy toy poodle, without a care in the world. That would all change in January of 1994. That year, the President came to Chicago on one of his many fundraising visits. This particular visit was very important to the President who, after landing, was to proceed immediately via Marine One (the Presidential helicopter) to a local fundraiser almost 20 miles south of O'Hare to raise money for one of his constituents. Land transportation via motorcade was not a good alternative, as it would have tied up many of the suburban expressways and their exits, especially during rush hour. President Clinton's staff was aware that upsetting rush hour drivers might translate into disgruntled voters. So the plan was to fly Marine One from O'Hare soon after the President landed. Sounds routine—but wait a minute.

Typically, as Air Force One touched down at O'Hare, the Secret Service and I would follow the Boeing 747 as it rolled down the runway, in two Chevy Suburbans. It was one of those duties that weren't in my job description, but once again it was Greg the agent who got me in everywhere the President went. The Suburbans themselves were equipped with weapons and an assortment of equipment designed to take out anyone who might advance suddenly on the presidential aircraft.

The weather that day was dark and overcast. Air Force One was running late, and typically when that happened, it could cause the commercial airlines to be late as well. FAA standards dictated the separation standards between Air Force One and the rest of the airlines. Frequently, the President would land on the *north* side of the airport. For 15 to 20 minutes preceding landing and following takeoff of Air Force One, no other flights were allowed to land or take off. It was important that the Secret Service and I kept to the schedule. Any deviations or delays in that schedule usually cost the airlines a lot of money in fuel and upset passengers who were always in a hurry, anyway.

Upon landing, the main door of Air Force One opened and for a brief moment the President stuck his head out to observe the waiting press. The press often preceded the President in their own chartered airplane, landing usually within a half-hour of the President. Like wolves, they waited anxiously for the President to come down the stairs to make a few short quips. So here I was, dressed in my Elliot Ness, J.C. Penney store-bought trench coat, looking the part of Secret Service Agent. I even conned one of the Secret Service agents into giving me a pair of his special Ray-Ban sunglasses. All he wanted in return was an O'Hare air traffic controller T-shirt. A small price to pay to be cool.

Feeling like a cross between Tom Cruise and Clint Eastwood, I stood at the bottom of the steps where the President would be leaving. This was somewhat more intense and intimidating than one might imagine, because no matter who the President is, he is still the most powerful person in the free world.

Once again, the President stuck his head out the door of Air Force One, but this time he quipped, "This does not look good!" This was an obvious reference to the fact that the trip on the Marine One copter might have to be cancelled due to inclement weather. For the next ten minutes, an eerie silence prevailed on the tarmac. The press was getting restless and clearly not used to the President taking so long to disembark from Air Force One. And then my country called.

One of the advance agents on Air Force One, knowing who I was, hustled down to the bottom of the stairs and asked if I would please come with him. While I had been on the airplane before, I had not been on it when the President was present. As I was whisked into the airplane, I could sense a kind of urgency from everyone within the President's circle.

Before I could say "where the hell are we going?" I was standing inside the Air Force One office, which was complete with a desk and even a little boom box on top. I couldn't help but notice the President's song list, including Dizzy Gillespie and "California Dreamin'" from the Beach Boys. Wow, the Prez is cool on the Beach Boys, I thought.

Also in the office were the flight crews from Marine One, Nighthawk 1 and Nighthawk 2 (the other Presidential helicopters), some of the President's staff, and two Secret Service agents, including Greg. The office itself was very small, probably in the range of 12 by 12 feet. The smell of pine from the presidential desk was unmistakable. I was then asked to sit directly in front of the President's credenza. Then, without warning, the President himself walked briskly through the door. Like in my old Air Force days, everyone stood up immediately, as if a four-star general had just walked in amongst the troops.

Having been out drinking with some other controllers the previous night, I was still feeling a bit groggy, but alive. I felt totally out of place. Here I was, some lowly, broken-down air traffic controller, amongst people who make big decisions for our country every day. What could they possibly want with me?

As the President sat down, so did everyone else, in almost perfect unison. I was the last to sit down, but alas there was no chair for me. Here I was, standing there, feeling almost totally naked. I was totally mesmerized by the President. At about six foot two inches, this was one imposing man. As he sat, he leaned over to one of his aides, whispered something and then looked directly at me. For a few seconds, he simply stared at me. I thought I was going to wet my pants. What in God's name did this man need from me?

Then the President spoke. "Mr. Richards, I need your help." How incredibly strange. The leader of the free world, mom, and apple pie needs my help? Whooooo! This must be some kind of dream. He then continued, "As you know, Mr. Richards, my pilots are a little concerned about the weather down south. Can you chart us some kind of path they would be comfortable with?"

The President's request was very elementary. Because of the low ceiling of the clouds, it was necessary to find a path where the cloud decks might at least be high enough for the Presidential copters to operate. The President's flight crews could have done that themselves, but for some reason seemed hesitant. At that point, I sensed the cloud ceilings were too close a call for them. Maybe they wanted a second opinion— or, more important, someone else to blame.

Not wanting to let down my country, I quickly asked for a cell phone to call the Tower and get the weather at all the local airports along the route of flight. When I asked for a cell phone, about four different people pulled their mobile phones out and handed them to me. I simply grabbed one and put two in my pocket. It seems I was simply not able to go longer than a few minutes without having fun or playing a joke on somebody. Everyone chuckled at this childish but innocent act, including the President, who almost seemed entertained by my circus-like mannerisms. When he laughed, everyone laughed, like some bad "yes" men.

When I called the control Tower, they were equally amazed. I first told them the President needed my help. The laughter in the background was almost embarrassing, since the volume on the cell phone was loud enough for everyone in the room to hear. I pleaded with the Tower again. "Hey, guys, I'm not kidding, I need those weather observations from Meigs Field and Midway Airport." Then the jokes from the Tower came. "Hey, Calvin, we need your help, how about getting us a pizza—or better yet, the garbage here is getting a little high, what do ya say?" Everyone in the traveling Oval Office was leaning my way and fast growing impatient.

Finally the supervisor in the Tower, Stan, also known as "McGarrett", grabbed the phone. Stan, who closely resembled the character Steve McGarrett, played by Jack Lord in the old TV series *Hawaii Five-O*, wasn't about to have the airline industry delayed any further. His demeanor became the same as the fictional head of *Five-O*. "Hey, Calvin, everyone here," meaning the flights waiting to go, "is waiting for Marine One to leave. What the heck is going on?"

I replied, "Well, Stan, nothing can happen over here till you give me those local ATISs" (automated weather info for any specific airport). (I really wanted to say, "Book him, Dano," but even I knew that wasn't the time for that). The Tower was waiting for Marine One to take off before releasing any of the commercial flights. In the Tower, Stan was taking phone calls from irate airlines about their long delays on the north side departure runways of the airport. The next words from Stan were very revealing: "*Goddammit, Calvin,* you're killing me!"

I simply replied, "I love you too, Stan." Now the confusion level in the office was at a new high. No one in that room spoke, as if their very lives hinged on my every word and action.

As Stan rattled off the weather observations, I knew exactly what I would have to do. I knew the President's trip would be a go, but I still wanted to have fun with this overly captivated group of people. I proceeded, "OK, Stan, let's clear the area for Marine One, rack 'em and stack 'em." The rack-and-stack reference was an old ATC saying about moving airplanes. It was out of some bad, old aviation movie.

When I hung up the phone, I gave a simple thumbs-up to everyone around. In spontaneous unison, everyone let out a small cheer. I had lived up to my governmental duty. I was now a local hero.

The President, seemingly relieved, said, "Thanks, Mr. Richards. You guys in the FAA are always there for us."

Upon saying, "You are welcome," to the President I couldn't help but notice a box of M&Ms Plain, with the presidential seal, sitting on the President's desk. As Clinton started to head out, I quickly asked, "*Hey, Mr. President*, excuse me, but I think it would be really cool... I mean, is there any chance I could get a box of those presidential M&Ms for my kids?"

As everyone was trying to leave, they stopped in mid-stride. The President slowly and gently replied, "Why, sure, just go ahead and take that one."

Then, as the President started to walk away again, greed got the best of me. "Uh, Mr. President, I hate to ask you this, but..."

Quickly the President replied, "Sure, go ahead."

Without hesitation I continued courageously, "Well, Mr. President, I have more than one kid, and you know I could hardly get a box for one and not the other."

The less-amused Clinton now looked at me with a smirk and stated, "Well, how many do you need?"

I retorted, "About fourteen."

Again laughter filled the room. The President then leaned over to his credenza, reached into a drawer and pulled out a big box of presidential M&Ms. "Will this be enough?" the President queried.

And with an impish smile, I replied, "Yes, sir, all my kids thank you, Mr. President!"

This time, instead of heading out the door immediately, the President simply looked at me and said, "If you need anything else, please don't hesitate. I'll be back shortly."

I have to admit it, I was having a lot of fun bantering back and forth with this jovial President who, at times, seemingly didn't have a care in the world.

On my radio to the Tower, supervisor Stan was in quite a bad mood. "You know, Calvin, we have about thirty flights here sitting on the ground. Do we have your permission to get them going or are you still shopping on Air Force One?"

I simply said, "Go for it, Stan!"

The rest of the day became even more surreal. I spent the next few hours touring Air Force One with the President's advance agents, while the President departed in his four "shell game" group of helicopters. The President often travels with an entourage of three or four helicopters for many reasons. As the copters lift in unison for their destination, no one on the ground along the President's path would know which copter the President is actually in. Hence, the shell game. Add the firepower of all the copters to protect the President, and you have the ultimate security force.

Touring Air Force One was like observing a flying hotel. Just below the cockpit was a full-scale presidential bedroom, complete with a bed, mirrors (but not on the ceiling), and amenities fit for a king. Throughout the room was a sound system that echoed a continuous play list selected by the President himself. I quickly grabbed an extra play list to see what made the President tick. I have always experienced music as one of my true passions. Different songs have always evoked different feelings for me, both in the Tower and outside it. Thinking the President must feel the same way, I noticed the diverse collection that he himself had picked out. Most of the chosen songs were upbeat tunes from the 1960s, such as "Good Vibrations" by the Beach Boys, "Hot Fun in the Summertime" by Sly and the Family Stone, "Summertime Blues" by Eddie Cochran, and many others that were all simply a part of the President's "Songs of Summer" collection.

Also in the list of songs was a jazz collection to reflect his love of the saxophone, including "Benny" by David Sanborn, and "Sarah Jane" by Ramsey Lewis. There was also a country list with the majority of songs by Brooks and Dunn. I have to admit I was impressed with the endless variety. Not wanting to forget this wonderful experience, I borrowed a play list just as the advance agents came rushing towards me to say the President's return was now just a few minutes away. I was fairly confident the President knew the list by heart anyway and wouldn't miss it.

When it came time for the President to return from his short, two-hour fundraiser speech, it was just enough time for me to get back to "work" outside Air Force One. As the Secret Service made a "human boundary line" for spectators behind some ropes away from the Marine One landing site, I noticed the inevitable group of dignitaries known as the "shakers." This slang term was used by the Secret Service to describe the group of people whose job was to form a line next to the Air Force One Boeing 747 and simply say goodbye to the President with a simple handshake. Behind the shakers was the line set up by the Secret Service where the press, military personnel and their dependents from the base, and various other government officials were located. Many had come to simply get a glimpse of a man they had all heard so much about. For most, seeing the President, no matter who he is, becomes a life moment. Many of these people may never have the opportunity to see one up close again.

As the three Marine helicopters made their way towards the tarmac, I couldn't help but feel the adrenaline that all the Secret Service must be feeling. As everyone knows, life can turn on a dime and often does. It's when you expect things the least that surprises usually occur. This time was no different.

As Marine One started to land, I couldn't help but observe the different agents situated strategically all over the tarmac. Two agents were sitting on top of the airplane hangars. Those were the sharpshooters who hoped to never have to use their rifles. Near the ropes cordoning off the spectators stood six or seven agents, approximately 15 to 20 feet apart. All had the G-Man look, sporting old, oval-shaped Ray-Ban sunglasses and trench coats. They kept a constant watch on the crowd of about 200 people without ever flinching a muscle.

In my totally Waldo pose, I was situated alone, about 50 feet from where Marine One would land. The only people closer to the landing spot than me were two agents about 20 feet on either side of me. Each of them was concealing a long automatic rifle hidden by their long G-man trench coats. I was the only unarmed person within 100 feet of the President's landing site. As the support helicopters landed at other end of the tarmac, right behind them was Marine One. As Marine One landed, I could feel the brisk wind of the rotors pushing me backwards.

Then, without warning, I heard the sound of a female screaming out. As I turned around to see the commotion, I spotted a six-year-old boy running from the barricades, towards Marine One and myself. In quick pursuit were his parents, who were quickly detained by startled agents. At about the same time I scooped up the kid, the other agents were screaming, "Don't let that kid go under *any* circumstances!"

At the point, Marine One touched down and I suddenly noticed the sharpshooters on top of the hangars aimed at me. I couldn't help but remember a story one of the shooters had been telling me earlier about how in some countries, such as Vietnam, the Vietnamese children were actually used to commit terrorist acts. While I doubted this small American boy was part of a terrorist plot, I knew the agents were taught to shoot first and ask questions later. So I put the death grip around the small boy, sensing that if I let him go, the Vietnam vet on top of the hangar would make Swiss cheese of the child or me in a Secret Service nanosecond.

As agents held the boy's parents and I gripped on to the boy for my life, Marine One touched down. Unbeknownst to the President, there were a lot of shaky and nervous agents who never saw the young boy run from the crowd until the parents came following after him. As the President made his way to the bottom of the stairs, one of his advisers talked with him at the bottom of the stairs for almost three minutes. Upon the end of their conversation, the adviser handed the President a bright, shiny object I could not discern. The schedule next called for the President to go by the line of shakers, say goodbye for a few minutes, then board Air Force One and be gone.

Just as the President was about to approach the shakers, he diverted his path directly towards me. I couldn't believe it. Here I was, heart beating 200 times a second, trying to hold on to a kid who was squirming, scratching, and whining out of control. The bite marks on my arm reminded me of just how upset this kid was. The agents, seeing Clinton approaching, closed in on either side of me to make sure all would be OK with the President's impromptu visit to Calvin.

As the President walked towards me, I suddenly noticed his right hand extending towards mine. Somewhat surprised, I switched the boy to my left arm and shook hands with the President. With a very firm handshake, Clinton proclaimed, "Thanks again for everything you've done for us today to make our trip smooth and successful." Then Clinton pulled out the shiny object he had been handed earlier and said, "I would like you to accept this as a sign of our thanks." It was an Air Force One Presidential tie clip.

Thanking the President, and impressed by his unnecessary gratitude, I seized upon a moment I have been waiting for on many of his previous visits. I had always carried a small camera in my pocket and I wasn't about to let this opportunity go by. So I confidently asked Clinton, "Hey, Mr. President, can you do me small favor?" Without flinching, and remembering our previous M&M incident, Clinton deadpanned pleasantly, "And what would that be this time?"

Pulling out my camera, I asked if we could take a picture or two. The jaw of the agent standing to my left side just about fell off. It was as if another agent had stupidly asked the question. How unprofessional. Nearer to me, on my right side, was a second agent who was busy observing the crowd nearby. So without hesitation, I asked the nearer agent, "Excuse me, can you take this picture, please?"

As the agent shrugged his shoulder, he had to pull his hand out of the inside of his coat, which was holding his automatic rifle. "Excuse me, Calvin, you want me to do what?" the puzzled agent asked.

With complete body language, the President smiled at the agent, as if giving the OK for such an insane photo shoot.

Meanwhile, in the background, the shakers were getting nervous and anxious, having to wait for the President to shake hands with a lowly government worker. I could hear radio transmissions between the Air Force ramp coordinator, Bob Regan, and my supervisor, Stan, in the Tower.

Stan was growing increasingly impatient with Air Force One's lagging schedule. He kept saying, "What the hell is going on there, Calvin? We are getting behind up here with departures waiting to go. And where the hell are you, Calvin?"

Since I had turned down my radio to "visit" with the President, Bob became the new temporary Tower coordinator. His answer was simple: "Yeah, Stan, the holdup is the President talking to one of your employees."

Stan inquired, "Well, Bob, now who would that be?"

"Uh, just Calvin, Stan," Bob answered.

It was then that Bob had to turn his radio volume down. *"What the hell is Calvin doing? Goddammit, Bob, get his ass moving, the airlines are all over my ass!"* Stan was fuming. I had never heard anyone scream so loud into a radio.

As a puzzled agent grabbed my camera, Clinton put his arm around me and we took at least three different pictures from different angles. My whole visit took about five minutes, but for those responsible for the President's schedule, it must have seemed like a lifetime.

President Clinton was so far behind on his schedule that his advisers scurried him straight past the shakers and into Air Force One. Mayor Richard Daley of Chicago, with his entourage, just stared at me as if I had robbed them. As the somewhat-hurried Clinton went up the stairs, the shakers turned around and looked at me with expressions that said, "How dare you take away attention from us?"

Reveling in this Kodak moment, I simply gave back that wonderful smile that to the shakers must have been the same as that "punk kid" grinning at them. And then I snapped *their* picture. Just another important group brought down to size.

Chapter 21

Goodbye TRACON

FLAMEOUT: *An emergency condition caused by a loss of engine or human body failure.*

Breaking up is hard to do, but that's what happened in October of 1996. I'm not talking about my own marriage, but rather the union that was the O'Hare Tower and the O'Hare TRACON. Upper management had decided years before to create super-TRACONs all across the United States. Instead of major airports having the Tower and the TRACONs collocated, the new trend would be twofold.

First, the Towers would still be located at the airports— that was a no-brainer. Secondly, though, and most dramatic, the new TRACONs would be broken off from the Towers and located anywhere from a few miles to as much as 100 miles from the airports they served. The Southern California TRACON in San Diego, for instance, is the largest in the country, and services 62 airports, including San Diego, John Wayne, and LAX. Years before, each one of those airports might have had its own radar room, located under the Tower, or even in the

Tower itself. Today, however, the FAA goal is to save money, so the idea is to place many radar controllers in one big building to serve a vast area of airports.

At O'Hare, the shock of breaking up was evident. The O'Hare TRACON was moved 40 miles to the west of Chicago in Elgin. Initially, as a joke, many in the Tower referred to the new TRACON as the "Elgin Departure Control" instead of the more prestigious "Chicago" or "O'Hare" departure control. The last thing said to flights being handed off from the Tower to the TRACON was "American Four Twenty-eight, contact Elgin Departure." The first transmissions from pilots to the TRACON would then be *"Elgin departure,* this is..."

The pilots knew we were mocking our friends at the TRACON. While many at the TRACON could take a joke, the "Elgin Departure" reference wore thin after only a week, especially when controllers at the TRACON were told they would be taking a ten percent pay cut because the cost of living portion of their paychecks had changed, now that the new TRACON was located in Elgin and not Chicago. It was far more expensive to live in Chicago than the remote suburb of Elgin.

In the first few years, the operational aspect of moving airplanes remained relatively unchanged. In 1998, the O'Hare Tower incurred six operation errors, or "close calls." The following year, the number of errors dropped to just one. That year we were recognized as the "1999 National Level 12 Terminal Facility of the Year." In one stretch, from July of 1999 to June of 2001, the crew of seven controllers I worked with didn't have one error. We had worked nearly 1,800,000 airplanes in that span. It appeared the Tower had reached its goal by being full of experienced and seasoned veterans.

Teamwork between the Tower and TRACON remained strong, but every once in a while, a question would come up about the handoffs. In the past, any problems were resolved between combatants from each facility at the base of the Tower or in the break room. Now, with the TRACON 40 miles away, issues had to go through a controller's immediate supervisor. When the TRACON and Tower supervisors couldn't resolve the issue over the phone, it would be passed up to higher management, the area managers. When the area managers disagreed, it would be passed up to the chiefs of each facility. With the chiefs unable to work together the last three years, far too many issues were left unresolved and with bad feelings.

Before long, the trust factor between the Tower and TRACON had eroded so badly that some controllers were looking for potential operational errors by the other facility. While the general standard longitudinal separation for non–heavy airplanes landing and departing was three miles, some controllers were measuring the distance to actual tenths of a mile. For years, three miles was more or less eyeballed on the radar by the dashed lines embedded in them. If aircraft got down to two and a half miles, then action was taken to pull the arrival off the flight path or a departure turned, if he was getting too close to the previous departure.

When I pressed the communication buttons to see who was working my departures, I began to realize I knew fewer and fewer of the voices at the TRACON. In just the five years after the split, so many controllers were added and subtracted at each facility that it was impossible to know who was at the other end of handoffs. I found myself no longer *caring* about moving airplanes expeditiously. Instead, the priority became increasing the separation so as not to be accused of being anywhere near violating the three-mile separation standard. Most Tower controllers stopped trying to figure out what the TRACON comfort level was at the other side of their handoffs.

Conversely, when I talked to familiar TRACON controllers, they said they were approaching it the same way because they didn't trust anyone in the Tower.

Isolation and uncertainty breed contempt and, ultimately, paranoia. In November of 2006, I witnessed a Tower controller given an operational error for 2.86 miles of the three-mile required separation. If that same measuring stick had been used in the 1990s, O'Hare would have had tens of thousands of operational errors.

In response to the "trust issue," upper management decided the best solution was to allow controllers "familiarization trips" to the TRACON. You know, let's get reacquainted again. Controllers at O'Hare were typically given a *whole* one day a year to spend observing their counterparts at the TRACON. In the days when the TRACON was collocated with the Tower, this scenario was a given. Controllers in the Tower would spend hours of their breaks in the TRACON, because they enjoyed watching. Conversely, TRACON controllers would do the same in the Tower. How do you become familiar with what someone else does in one day? The management response was like a guy dating a girl one time and then proposing marriage. It might work great in India, but not here in the good old USA.

In the 1990s, air traffic moved with a "controlled" reckless abandon. Safety was never an issue. Everyone in the facility knew the limits of the others and, if they didn't, all that was necessary was a simple discussion. With the old standard being enforced so rigidly, it had become necessary for today's workforce to be ultra-conservative when moving airplanes across the sky. There isn't one controller alive (that I knew) who wanted to challenge the three-mile rule. With O'Hare at the center of the country, it is easy to see how any changes there would have a domino effect across the country. The other reality was that if you received three operational errors in your lifetime, you could get dismissed from a very fun, high-paying job. It simply wasn't worth it.

To get the necessary three miles of longitudinal separation, controllers are now using cushions of one and even two miles. That may not sound like much, but when you multiply that by the thousands of planes that land and depart each day, there is a definite domino effect. The fuel bill alone caused by this change in work habits has cost the airlines *millions* of dollars and will continue for some time to come.

When an airplane takes off from anywhere in the United States to Chicago, as soon as it is airborne, it has a sequence to land at O'Hare from as far away as 1000 miles. FAA Central Flow in Herndon, Virginia, monitors every flight in the sky and ultimately determines which flight should and should not be delayed.

That's why on even the most beautiful of aviation weather days, John and Jane Q. Public still sit delayed on the ground at other airports, waiting to get to O'Hare. In the airplanes, the announcement from the cockpit to the passengers is usually something on the order of, "Ladies and gentlemen, we are sorry to report we have an *air traffic* delay. We'll keep you advised."

Then when the thunderstorms, snowstorms, fog, and all the rest of Mother Nature comes knocking on the FAA door, plan on sleeping on the airport floor in the baggage area. The reason is because your flight is likely to be cancelled since it can't make it to Chicago, and all the local hotels will be filled with other delayed passengers just like you. In my last two years at O'Hare, I saw the city opening up portable bedding space in the baggage areas for "overnight passengers" more often than in the previous 18 years combined.

Because the system has become so stretched out, it has become too fragile. Most airports are already operating at full capacity in terms of their ability to handle arrivals and departures. The next step will have to be adding more runways and/or better procedures. In both cases, the FAA is lagging far behind. Most of the separation standards that exist in the FAA are outdated. Controllers across the country proved that in the 1990s, when moving airplanes was an art and standards for separating airplanes were flexible and not chokingly rigid as they are today.

Each year the traffic count at O'Hare would steadily increase, and as it did, so did the stress levels of each controller. Controllers are markedly adaptable, but I think only to a point. As the hurdles became larger, the effort to overcome them became more draining. It is very hard to describe to someone who is not an air traffic controller what takes place in just one hour of working over 100 airplanes on ground control.

Your body is literally pumped by its own adrenaline and, by the time the hour is up, you might feel as if you had several cups of super-caffeinated coffee. In the breaks taken after a "fun hour," your body attempts to calm itself down. You can find most controllers lying on one of many couches during their breaks, but before their bodies can return to normal, it's time to go back into the Tower to do it all over again. And if the weather becomes a problem—forget it. The workload increases threefold with multitudes of airplanes slowed down by the weather.

Even the supervisors felt the pressure, particularly when a medical emergency was involved. At least once a shift you could count on a passenger from one of the airlines to have some kind of medical problem. I have experienced hundreds in my career at O'Hare and very seldom have I had any problems not being able to give the emergency the best service.

However, when there was a problem, we were usually quick to correct it. A perfect example was a medical emergency that occurred when a pilot 50 miles out radioed that he had a hemophiliac boy that was encountering some kind of uncontrolled bleeding.

Working Local Control at the time I cleared the aircraft to land, kept him on my frequency and turned him off the runway at a point which the plane would be facing the alley where the arrival gate was located thus insuring immediate medical attention. As the aircraft entered the alley, American's gate control pushed back an aircraft in front of the emergency aircraft thereby blocking access to the gate area and the awaiting ambulance. At this point, I totally lost it.

Having two small boys of my own and pretending as if the hemophiliac boy in the airplane was my own, I screamed at the pilot, "Tell your company to move that other aircraft back in the gate or I will personally come down and strangle them." The pilot, already brutally aware of the perceived insensitivity of his company, replied, "Don't worry Tower we're on it."

I could already hear one of the supervisors, Eddie Gish, also yelling on a phone to American gate control in the background, "If that American doesn't push back into the gate to allow that emergency to get by then some shit is going to fly, you got it!?" He said it so the whole Tower could hear it. In just seconds of that phone call I noticed the blocking airplane moving swiftly back into his gate. As the emergency flight finally taxied into the gate, Eddie came up behind me and said, "Just another day of going down the shitter!" If that wasn't enough to keep us distracted, every so often our regional office up the street would send someone into the facility to harass us.

One day the region sent in a "bean counter" from FAA headquarters to interview a supervisor in the offices downstairs about possible abuse of sick leave in the Tower at O'Hare. As word spread throughout the Tower of this FAA Inquisition, just about every controller in no uncertain terms made his or her opinions known to the prosecutor. In fact, at one point when the "beaner" came up into the Tower to look around, the controllers in unison "tore the regional puke a new *one.*"

It was like watching a pack of wolves attacking a wounded animal. Many asked the administrator where he worked before his top job in Washington. When he answered with "Well....I wasn't a controller in a Tower but at Flight Service," the Tower went up for grabs.

This guy knew *nothing* about being a controller, only that sick leave cost the government money. This was one of the first times I realized that people outside of O'Hare had *not* a clue what we were going through nor did they really give a shit. To them it was all about the bottom line.

It didn't matter that we were making the system work almost flawlessly in spite of getting our bodies beat up day after day. It was because we were all still fairly young that we could take it but time would only tell. We never saw that low-life snitch again. The FAA every once in a while would *talk* about how hard shift work was but never was anything done about it. The people that made the policies at the Region usually worked five-day shifts and had all the holidays off. Many of the controllers on the other hand were working six-day workweeks in shift work and very rarely had a holiday off.

It was an automatic that on a work shift that included delays due to weather, controllers were making arrangements to unwind somewhere by the time the shift ended. Whether at a bar or in front of a television for a few hours, a release from the day or night's barrage was forthcoming. It wasn't born out of fun, but necessity and survival. If you worked the night shift after getting your ass kicked by "herds of airplanes," there was no way you could go home, hit the bed and be fast asleep. Your body was wound so tight from work it took hours to return it to its normal mode. I was always in complete denial about adjusting to it all and adopted an attitude of invincibility.

Once in a while I would take a few Vicodin, but that calming effect was temporary. Since my health was OK and I was still actively exercising and playing basketball, it was easy to think my body was "Superman." Often on the Tower radio, the group REM would remind us of our superpowers:

"I am... I am... I am superman... And I can do anything."

Unfortunately, even Superman and controllers have their limits.

On a vacation with my wife to Puerto Vallarta in June of 1997, I could tell my body was starting to turn on me. The adrenaline rush that I experienced at work would sometimes linger not just for hours, but even days. I was hyperactive beyond anything I had ever experienced. As I sensed I was losing control of my body, I turned to more alcohol.

It got so bad that I found myself alone on a seventh-floor Mexican balcony, standing at the edge, overlooking the concrete street below. I had no intention of jumping, but rather I was doing the same thing on vacation that I was doing at the Tower. I was working at the edge. I was pushing the envelope just to get that high of achievement. Hard to explain for sure, but when my wife, Debbie, spotted me from inside the room on the balcony, she let out a scream that *almost* sent me over the edge. As she tried to console me, I remained isolated from the world. I simply told her it was a joke—a very bad one. I know she didn't believe it, but I had no idea what to tell her, because I couldn't explain it either.

As we walked the streets of Puerto Vallarta, my adventures continued. Leaving a small neighborhood restaurant, my wife and I noticed a large number of small kids following us. It was clear to me that this was not a new experience to these children, following American tourists around for handouts. Their performances were very polished and sentimental. As they handed out small wrapped pieces of gum, it was hard not to feel touched by their seemingly cute and kind actions. I knew what I had to do next.

I had a large stack of one-dollar bills in my wallet, usually to tip and spend while on vacation. As I unleashed them from my wallet like confetti at a parade, I proclaimed in my drunken stupor, "Hey, kids, you know who Michael Jordan is?"

Amazingly, the kids answered in English, "Are you Michael Jordan, senor?"

Touched by that cute reply, I let it all out, "Yes, I am, kids," and then I started tossing numerous dollar bills everywhere. I was having so much fun, but I could tell my wife was getting scared.

What had once been a handful of kids became a mob. As my wife whisked me away, she was sobbing. I passed out shortly and didn't wake up till the next day, with the worst hangover in my life. My body was headed into a type of "flameout." I was spiraling downward but could never acknowledge it to *anyone*. I was concerned that history was repeating itself and I was becoming more detached than my dad had ever been.

Chapter 22

Yahoo Mexicana

OFF COURSE: *A term used to describe a situation where an aircraft has reported a position fix or is observed on radar on a point not on the ATC-approved route of flight.*

Mexicana pilots always had a special place in the hearts of controllers at O'Hare. It was their total unpredictability that kept us on our toes. It wasn't that Mexicana had bad or even unseasoned pilots. It was more a case of inexperience, flying into a foreign land on a very limited basis.

Mexicana pilots, for instance, had little experience with snow and low visibility. When confronted with these flying conditions, anything could happen, and usually did. On one particular midnight shift in early January 1998, the visibility at O'Hare was down to less than one-half mile due to a snowstorm. The winds were extremely brisk and everyone was having trouble with their landings. On Mexicana's initial contact seven miles out, my supervisor, Tim Fitzgerald, and I knew Mexicana was going too fast and high to land. Add on heavy snow blowing across the landing runway, and you had all the ingredients for a wild Mexican air show.

On this snowy night, both Tim and I were keenly aware of the possibility that immediate action would have to be taken if Mexicana could not land. Normal procedure if Mexicana had to abort its landing would be for the aircraft to proceed away from the airport to try an approach possibly to another runway better lined up into the wind. Upon initial contact with Mexicana, clearance to land was given. Mexicana's response was a straightforward Spanish inflection of "Royer" instead of "Roger," which was simply acknowledgement of a landing clearance. But with winds kicking up to 34 to 40 knots and the visibility getting even lower, even the most seasoned of pilots would have problems trying to make a solid landing.

The pilot, sensing the landing's complexity, quipped, "Hey, Toyer, it is a very bumpy ride out here. We try to make it!"

On the radar, we could see the flight path of the Mexicana flight along the solid dashed line, which was the extension of the landing runway. Normally the target of landing aircraft would move precisely across this line, but this was a large Boeing 727 encountering severe crosswinds. As the meandering plane approached closer to the airport, it appeared extremely left of course, which made our Tower a nice target. Unknowingly, we had become a number seven-pin spare pickup, with Mexicana as the bowling ball.

Before we could even react, we heard a loud rumble of thunder, the same as often described by people who have experienced being near a tornado. As we looked out the window, where we could only see about a quarter mile, a sudden burst of light appeared through the foggy mist. There was Mexicana, not even 100 feet from the Tower and at perfect eye level. As the lights of the windows passed by us, we could literally see the shocked look of people's faces from about row ten to the back of the airplane.

In the Tower, the boom box was blasting music from Van Halen, one of Tim's favorite bands. On his screaming guitar, Eddie Van Halen was belting out "You Really Got Me." It was as if Eddie himself had seen Mexicana:

Please, don't ever let me be...

I only wanna be by your side...

Well, Mexicana almost "got" us. It was a sight as unbelievable as any hallucination I ever had. I doubt the pilots even saw the Tower, it happened so fast. I screamed, *"Yahoo, Mexicana"* while Tim just shook his head and thanked God.

I'm sure my response made Tim a little uneasy if for only a few seconds. My behavior change had become so gradual and subtle that most people figured that was my *real* personality. Even my wife started to get used to the "new" Bobby. If she couldn't see the change then how could anyone else? The pressure of the job was making me more manic to the point of simply not caring. In my world I continued to believe pressure did not exist. I was throwing my emotions around like the dollar bills in Puerto Vallarta.

Onward Mexicana.

In the late 1980s and even into the 1990s, the Mexicana plane of choice was the Boeing 727. They must have been the older ones, because just about every departure I observed used every inch of runway length for takeoff. When the planes were taking off into a direct headwind, there was usually a little room to spare at the end of the runway, but when winds were light, takeoff was based solely on those three ancient airplane engines trying feverishly to carry the flight airborne. It is a simple matter of physics that the more wind into the nose of the airplane, the better its lift capability.

The other factor impacting takeoff was the fact that most of the flights were at maximum weight due to passengers and cargo operating at full capacity. Aircraft were often so slow in climbing that we would have to abandon noise abatement headings on the midnight shifts so Mexicana didn't fly into the radio antennas just a few miles west of the airport. Violating noise abatement meant the loud, noisy aircraft would be waking people up in the surrounding communities, such as Schaumburg and Elk Grove.

Noise complaints were common when this happened, but safety ended up overriding sleep. Many controllers learned this lesson the hard way. If they hadn't any previous experience with low-flying Mexicanas, they usually learned after their first encounter. It was a banner day when Mexicana retired the Boeing 727s and switched to the more modern and aerodynamic Airbus 320. Controllers could now breathe a sigh of relief.

Because of the language barrier and unfamiliarity with O'Hare, many Mexicana pilots could barely read back verbatim controllers' commands and very often did so in such a heavy Spanish accent that we were often left wondering what was said. Time was always of the essence when taxiing as many as 20 to 25 aircraft at a time to departure runways, so finding ways to limit our long directions was essential, if not critical.

Often on ground control, we might ask an aircraft from one airline to follow another aircraft from another airline to a particular departure runway. Saying the word "follow" made it easy for us, since we then didn't have to issue the same long, complicated taxiway instructions to each pilot. One time, while working outbound ground, I asked a United jet to follow Mexicana to runway nine left. Before the United could even answer, the Mexicana pilot shouted, "Hey, Tower! I do not think that is a good idea." Even many Mexicana pilots knew their limitations, trying to learn a complex foreign airport such as Chicago.

Mexicana scheduled many of their passenger flights on midnight shifts and mainly at around two in the morning. I was never quite sure why they flew a lot of their flights at this time, except possibly because at that time of night, the skies were empty, with no other passenger airlines to compete with. Because it was flying during a time when there was little or no other passenger traffic, all Mexicana had to do was share airspace with a few cargo planes, such as UPS, Fedex, Airborne Express, etc. That meant that if Mexicana made any mistakes in moving on the ground or in the air, anyone else flying might only be "mildly" affected.

On one particular night and with no one moving anywhere, we told a Mexicana that had just landed to "taxi to the gate." Now, while this may seem a very simple instruction, at O'Hare it was not. Our airport is laid out like a jigsaw puzzle. There are many twists and turns to get to a particular gate, and normally we give directions in the form of many taxiways, such as, "Hey, Mexicana, taxi to the international via juliet, bravo, and delta." To the domestic carriers, these instructions are routine, but to a Mexicana pilot or any foreign pilot, it might just as well be gibberish.

As Mexicana landed, and since it was the only airplane moving on the ground, I simply told Mexicana to "taxi to the gate." While this particular command may sound very elementary, it still involved two Mexicana pilots pulling out their ground maps of O'Hare to find the best route. Many foreign pilots in this situation would ask for directions, but we had come across the ones too proud to do so. We were awestruck as we continued to watch Mexicana maneuver. First clearing the runway known as 14 right, it would have been necessary to make some kind of left turn into the terminal, but instead Mexicana went straight on to taxiway "Tango," which paralleled the runway it had just landed on, and was headed towards another active runway. During the day and with other airplanes present, this maneuver would have caused panic in the Tower but, with no one around to cause conflicts with Mexicana, this was a true human experiment to see how far someone would proceed before sucking up their ego and asking for help to get them to where they were going.

Most controllers respected a pilot who would acknowledge his/her unfamiliarity with moving in and around O'Hare. It would allow us to keep a closer eye and be ready to stop any sudden or wrong turns. To "pretend" you were familiar when you weren't was certain trouble. It has always been known throughout the aviation community that O'Hare is the hardest and most complex airport when it comes to ground control, and not just for pilots. Most controller training failures occurred at the ground control position as well.

So there went Mexicana, plodding along aimlessly, and then, without warning, he crossed an active runway. Under normal traffic situations, most controllers would be screaming at these maneuvers or lose two years off their life, but it was two in the morning and we were just two bored air traffic controllers. A pilot can be seriously reprimanded for crossing an active runway without a clearance, but these pilots apparently had no clue or conscience while still trying to find their gate. Crossing an active runway at O'Hare is like crossing the lanes of the Indianapolis 500 without looking. Disaster could be right up the runway at any second.

On Mexicana's next left turn, he ended up in a run-up pad and far from the terminal.

Unfortunately, this is how some pilots learn—the hard way. Now, at a total stop, there was still no communication from the lost jet. Within two minutes, the wayward plane was on the move again. We could only ponder that the passengers must be thinking how far their landing runway was from the terminal. And sure enough, Mexicana made his move and *again* crossed the same active runway he had crossed only a few minutes earlier. And then another right turn, and now Mexicana was headed for the east end of the airport, and again far away from the terminal.

Still not requesting assistance, the flight stopped in a different holding pad, which was simply a giant parking lot for aircraft without gate assignments or unable to depart due to weather.

At this point, with the experiment having gone far enough, I politely said to Mexicana, "Hey, Mexicana, buenos días, amigo. ¿Cómo está?"

From the flight deck of Mexicana came the much-awaited but confused response, "Buenos días, amigo, I think *me* need progressive to gate."

After giving proper directions to the Mexicana, I concluded with a simple "buenos nachos," while purposely using the word "nachos" (as in the tortilla chip). Till the day I retired, I said "buenos nachos" to every Mexicana pilot. Many came back laughing, but mostly all felt relaxed, knowing Americans were just as capable at making simple mistakes.

In my most profound Mexicana-related incident, I was training a very angry new controller named John on the position known as ground metering. The only function of ground metering is to tell the pilot who has just pushed back his aircraft ready to taxi for takeoff to monitor ground frequency 121.75. The next step is to place a flight progress strip on the board of ground control, who could now deduce that said aircraft is expecting to eventually be called in the order presented by ground metering.

The idea here is that the ground controller, at his leisure, can talk to many aircraft waiting to taxi and not be subject to countless calls of "I'm ready to taxi."

Very often, John would be very short with foreign pilots, and even make comments (between broadcasted transmissions) to me while training about "why can't these idiots learn English?" It always upset me that some of us didn't have the understanding or the patience to realize how hard it might be for us, as Americans, to be put in the same situation in another country. Most of us would certainly be confused in a foreign land, but not this trainee. He knew it all.

So at this point I felt the need to impart a lasting education on his international relations skills. As an instructor, I had the ability to override any transmission at any time I pleased, but also I could press the microphone foot pedal, and then both our mikes would be transmitting our every word.

During one session, Mexicana called John, looking for clearance and taxi. Barely able to understand Mexicana's broken English, John became enraged.

I simply said, "John, it's not healthy to hold in those angry feelings, simply let them out when you unkey your mike—you'll feel much better."

So John, just like an angry truck driver, let it all out.

To one confused American pilot, he gave an appropriate clearance, then unkeyed the mike and said, "What a jag off!" To a puzzled female United pilot, he said, "Thank you, ma'am, have a great day," and then off mike he quipped, "Wow, what a dumb ass!"

It was then that one of my silly experimental ideas popped into my head. You know those strange voices that come into our head from time to time. I decided that whenever John was done speaking and unkeyed his mike, I would automatically rekey it by pressing the foot pedal so that all the pilots listening on our frequency could hear his valued entertainment and comments.

So when a bewildered Delta called, John responded, "That read back is correct, Delta." At this point, John unkeyed his mike just as I keyed us back in, and he said, unknowingly, over the airwaves, "Yeah, right, Delta is ready when you are, what kind of shit is that?"

As I tried to withhold my laughter, another voice came back over the airwaves and responded, "Wow, go get 'em."

Still not suspecting, John simply looked at me and said, "Who's that idiot?"

Then my favorite, Mexicana, called for a clearance, innocent and meek. After Mexicana gave a vague but correct response to John's command, John responded, "That's correct, Mexicana." And then just as John unkeyed, I rekeyed us in, only to hear John say to the world, "Adios, motherfucker!"

I didn't know if I should laugh or hide. John had just called Mexicana a "motherfucker" and didn't know it until the response came, "Uh, Tower, this is Mexicana. What you say about mother?"

John just looked at me totally red-faced and said, "I can't believe you did that."

I said, "I can't either, but I bet that will teach you to be careful about what you say on and off the frequency."

John never swore in the Tower again, as far as I know. He transferred a few months later. Adios, motherfucker.

Chapter 23

Mickey's Army

EXPEDITE: *Used by ATC when prompt compliance is required to avoid the development of an imminent situation or delays to the flying public.*

The best quality a supervisor could possess was unquestioned loyalty from the controllers who worked directly under him/her. If you got into any kind of problem situation, it was understood that supervisors would settle it themselves and not go to upper management to seek punitive action. This factor was the main reason most employees gave their all to certain supervisors. I was never in fear of retaliation from management when any supervisor chewed me out for not moving traffic properly or just plain misbehaving. Most of the time it could be very comical and still be a good learning experience.

Many of the controllers in the 1980s who became supervisors in the 1990s followed Jon Fieweger's example right up to present day, where some of them have taken parts of Jon's managerial style and made it their own. Mike Vandini, a present-day supervisor, was one of those influenced by Jon, whether he knew it or not. His given Tower name was Mickey, but even though he stood at a mere 5'6", he was no mouse. His first and only controller duty station was O'Hare—only a handful of other controllers could say that.

He combined his passionate Italian heritage with a passion for making sure airline passengers were top priority. His dedication to his subordinates was beyond reproach. Just as in the movie *The Godfather*, Mickey was fiercely loyal to those who were loyal to him. Mickey even had a friend, Timmy, who looked and talked exactly like the actor Joe Pesci. Anytime I was in the same drinking establishment as Mickey and Timmy, I always felt like I was on the set of the movie *Goodfellas*.

During one of the many years we played in the annual FAA softball tournament, Mickey was our manager. One year he had taken us all the way to the championship game. In the first inning of the big game, I led off the game with what appeared to be an inside-the-park home run from a line drive hit down the first base line. Mickey was coaching third base at the time and observed as I circled third base, even leaving an imprint of my "Nike" cleats across the edge of the bag. Upon my scoring, the opposing team appealed third base, saying I didn't touch it. The umpire upheld the appeal and ruled I was "out."

Just as I started to scream and argue vehemently, Mickey grabbed me from behind and surged towards the home plate umpire with such force he just about knocked the man in blue over. Well, needless to say, Mickey was tossed from the game, saving me from being thrown out. As he left, he sent garbage cans flying into the parking lot. Billy Martin would have been proud. Our motivation at that point was clear. Our team wasn't going to simply beat the other team, we *all* wanted to *decimate them*. And annihilate them we did. Very few people I knew could get that kind of response from their peers. This was the same Mickey at work and play.

In the Tower, there was no differentiating between the supervisor and the baseball manager. Mickey was the ultimate taskmaster, sporting his trademark Marine crew cut. While most supervisors might sit back and let the operation run itself, Mickey would get involved in everything and everybody in the Tower. If departure runways were not evenly balanced, he would let you know about it. If airplanes weren't moving on the taxiways, Mickey would jump up and down, barking orders such as *"Expedite"* behind the controller responsible for the gridlock. If he thought for just *one* second you weren't giving 100%, Mickey was in your face, letting you know about it. Worst of all, if you disrespected or talked back in a demeaning manner, you usually got to hear Mickey's most famous line: "Get 'em outta here!" Within seconds of that last exclamation, there was usually another controller ready to relieve the one who was "outta here!" (If that all sounds familiar, see "Fun With Fieweger," Chapter 13.)

Often the Tower radio would play George Thorogood's "Bad to the Bone" as a dedication to Mickey. George would sing about Mickey,

> *"On the day I was born, the nurses all gathered 'round*
> *And they gazed in wide wonder, at the joy they had found*
> *The head nurse spoke up, and she said leave this one*
alone
> *She could tell right away, that I was bad to the bone…*
> *Bad to the bone..".*

There was no guessing Mickey's intentions when he was in charge. He was "bad to the bone." Mickey always decided which way the airport taxiways would flow and not leave it up to the controllers, as other supervisors did. He would make sure that the right people were working the proper positions at the proper times. If he could tell someone was having a bad day, he would make sure that person was not exposed to too much of a bad thing, by having them spend timing working in the "comedy corner."

The comedy corner encompassed the two docile positions of clearance delivery and ground metering. Both positions involved either reading clearances or simply saying over and over again, "Monitor ground on one two one point seven five." It required much less thought processing than ground or local control and, ultimately, less wear and tear on the psyche. If a trainee working any of the positions was delaying or impacting the airlines, Mickey would order the trainer to immediately start talking or face the consequences. Mickey was the airlines' best friend. When he was in the Tower, delays were at a minimum. If I was flying somewhere, I knew I was going to get out in record time if Mickey was in the Tower. Professional courtesy ruled. If Mickey ever retires, he could probably start his own airline and be very successful.

I especially enjoyed watching Mickey's interactions with other air traffic facilities, such as the TRACON. He used terms such as "we need more metal" to describe the fact that other controllers at other airports and the TRACON could not give O'Hare enough arrivals.

When there weren't many departures on the ground waiting to go, he would call down to the TRACON and tell them to "tighten up" the arrivals. Then he would tell us to "pucker up." While spacing may have been five miles to depart aircraft across intersection runways, Mickey would bring the spacing to the minimum of three miles. It wasn't a dangerous move, but just common sense, since there weren't many departures waiting to go. This simple, real-time move saved all the airlines millions of dollars in fuel, since every flight got on the ground much faster than if he had done nothing and left spacing at five miles.

He even took on the FAA's new central flow bureaucracy in Herndon, Virginia, which regulated flight delays across the country, particularly when volume was at its maximum or weather was at its worst. Even though the Tower and TRACON would establish an hourly rate for the number of airplanes landing at O'Hare, very often Central Flow would give errantly long flight delays that left a lot of gaps between landing aircraft at O'Hare. We knew the delays were too long because all the controllers in the Tower could see the real-time inbound aircraft on our ASD (Airport Situation Display), which showed all the airborne aircraft on a world map inbound to O'Hare.

Too often, Joe Q. Public might be sitting on the ground needlessly in Phoenix or Ft. Lauderdale for as long as an hour, when maybe only 15 minutes was necessary. Mickey would implore Central Flow by getting on the direct line and, in a sharp tone, say, "Hey, what's the problem, we've got room, bring 'em on." Like General Patton, Mickey believed not just in holding the line, but advancing (landing) constantly until you ran out of room to park airplanes. Working in the Tower with Mickey was like an army advancing constantly.

To the workforce in the Tower, Mickey was one of them. He was one of the few supervisors who would actually put on a headset during peak traffic periods just for fun or to show a new controller "how to do it." You couldn't bullshit Mickey, either. He understood air traffic procedures backward and forward. Most people with a professional disagreement with Mickey usually ended up with apparent speech impediments, such as "ah, well, ah..."

One controller, Gary Bahler, used to do a hilarious impression of Mickey that was so funny most people would end up in tears. For years, though, Gary felt somewhat awkward about doing it in front of Mickey. Initially, not wanting to offend Mickey, Gary's act was based on Mickey's less than average height. Mickey was all of 5'6", and to demonstrate that quality, Gary would walk around the Tower on his knees, barking out random orders such as, "Tommy, Tommy, your head is up your ass, get 'em out of here!" Of course, he did this when Mickey wasn't in the Tower.

One day I decided to put Gary on the ropes. While Mickey was standing next to me in the Tower, I yelled over to Gary, just a few feet away, "Hey, Gary, how about doing that impression of Mickey?"

At first, Gary stared at me, looking like death warmed over. Then Gary relented. Getting on his knees, he did his whole routine, complete with vocals. To some people's surprise, Mickey laughed as hard as everyone else. Mickey knew life was good in the Tower and never took himself so seriously that people couldn't approach him, even on their knees.

But things weren't always easy for Mickey, either. Most of his friends were Italian, and all too often we would joke about his "mafia" friends and relations. Well, things came together one time in the spring of 2001 to make things in our Tower interesting. As was customary in the Tower, whenever one of our own or a close relative was flying, we would try our extra best to give that flight the most "caring" and expeditious service.

At times, controllers would taxi their friends, usually with greetings such as, "Hey, United Three Twenty One, say happy birthday to my uncle in seat three c, he's fifty today." In return, very often the flight crew would show their appreciation by sending a bottle of bubbly to the "special passenger" or, in some cases, move that person or persons to first class. I must have had at least 2000 relatives over the years, flying all over the world. I was related to everybody. It got to the point that people would call me on their days off when I was at work in the Tower. Most often it was to "take care of my mother" or "my wife and I will be on American, take good care of us."

One day, Mickey called me in the Tower from his house on his day off. He made a very simple request. A friend of his had just got married over the weekend and was on his way to Hawaii for the honeymoon. The friend's name was Mike Cicero. While normally in Chicago this name might be associated with the supposed Cicero crime family, Mike was simply a regular guy with a regular job who happened to be one of Mickey's friends. Without the knowledge of me and many of the other controllers, the *Chicago Tribune* was doing a story about delays at O'Hare and was perched in a smaller adjacent tower, monitoring the radio frequencies.

When the "Cicero" flight taxied out on my frequency, I gave the pilot ground instructions to the longest runway at O'Hare (runway 14 right), per his request. The only aircraft that used this runway were usually the flights traveling overseas or the big cargo planes. While most of the other westbounds depart from the adjacent intersecting runway (27 left), runway 14 right is our primary landing runway.

What that meant was that the controller landing runway 14 right had to find a hole between the landing aircraft much bigger than the normal three miles to get the "Cicero" departure out. Normally, as soon as a controller recognizes a hole larger than three miles, the departure aircraft at 14 right is allowed to depart immediately, while the flights at runway

27 left have to wait. At O'Hare, this has always been the kind of exception to the rule that whoever gets to the runway first is next.

While the "honeymoon" aircraft was taxiing to the runway, I found a few seconds to say to the pilot, "Hey, American Seventy-three Heavy, if you would be so kind, say happy honeymoon to Mr. and Mrs. Mike Cicero, seated in the back, from Big Mike." By total coincidence, "Big Mike" was simply an endearing nickname I'd made up at the moment, so the Ciceros would know who from the Tower was wishing them well. The pilot, as with most of these requests, replied enthusiastically, "You got it, ground [control]."

When the aircraft was finally clear of all ground conflicts to the runway, I switched him over to the next frequency and the controller who would be responsible for takeoffs and landings of both runways 14 right and 27 left. Since these two runways intersect each other at an almost 90° angle, only one controller is needed to provide service for this two-runway operation.

Before American 73 got to runway 14 right, there were at least 15 other west-bounds waiting in line for departure at the intersecting runway 27 left. As luck would have it, the runway 14 right arrival corridor had an eight-mile gap about ten miles from the airport and just enough to depart the American.

With no other gaps visible, the controller working American 73 transmitted, "Hey, American Seventy-three Heavy, be ready to go on the runway after the next arrival lands and turns off the runway." There was little time to waste once the American departure took the runway, since the next arrival was only four miles from the landing threshold. But even in this tight situation, Buzz the controller took enough time to reinforce the greetings, saying, "Hey, American Seventy-three, I hear you have a special visitor today."

At this point, the *Tribune,* in the adjacent Tower, had heard all the exchanges. All they saw was a westbound departing immediately upon reaching runway 14 right ahead of the west-bounds still waiting at runway 27 left. They also knew the Cicero family was onboard and "Big Mike" must have had something to do with it.

The next day, armed with transcripts, the *Tribune* confronted our Tower Manager, Pete Salmon, ready to expose the "mob influence" and pull off a Chicago exclusive. Pete was a career O'Hare controller, having worked in both the Tower and TRACON. He knew us like his own kids. It took him a while to explain what his kids had done.

I'm sure in the minds of the *Tribune* investigators, "Big Mike" was calling the shots. But "Big Mike" was not a mobster, simply an O'Hare supervisor, and the procedure used to depart the Ciceros was totally by the book (for once). Mike Cicero and his wife fared much better, though, getting an extra serving of cheesecake. I'll bet they felt special.

After a few days of investigation by the local FAA regional office and conversations with Pete, who understood what had happened, the *Tribune* finally saw the light and backed off. Where was aviation expert Jim Tilmon when you needed him?

Chapter 24

They Almost Killed Kenny

DISTANCE MEASURING EQUIPMENT (DME):

Equipment (airborne and ground) used to measure, in nautical miles, the slant range distance of an aircraft from the DME navigational aid or the "dumb ass" in the Tower.

With the 1990s coming to an end and others fearing the end of the world with the millennium around the corner, my life was turning into a "circus of chaos." It was probably time to leave the O'Hare big top after having spent almost 14 years being beaten mentally, but my ego would not even entertain that idea being put forth in words. My trips to B.J. were becoming more frequent. I used to go to therapy maybe once a month when I first started in 1992, but by 1999, I was in at a rate of once or twice a week.

The issues were simple. I felt that I didn't need any help with my problems, whether personal or work-related. I viewed vulnerability as a human frailty to be disdained. Occasionally, I would fall back on Vicodin and be all mellowed out again. Vicodin made me not care, and that was fine with me. *No one* knew I was taking it, except Doctor D, who never questioned it. All I had to say was "back pain" and "can't sleep" to get a prescription.

I had always been taught to be strong and not let people know when I was feeling bad. Something was missing. I couldn't trust anyone—not even my own wife. Part of her anxiety was caused by my own aloofness.

Especially ironic was the fact that as much as I wanted to solve my own tribulations, I was seeing B.J. more and more. I couldn't have been lying more to myself. It became a competition. B.J. would say I was overwhelmed regarding my "ability to express myself honestly." I would say no way and give a multitude of bullshit reasons why he was wrong and I was right. I guess all along I knew he was right, or why else would I have kept going? As I started to break down emotionally in B.J.'s office, I was also starting to feel the effects at the Tower.

Early one morning, I was working Local Control, with the weather as bad as it could get. With fog restricting visibility down to half a mile, I was working runway nine right. It was my job to land flights on the runway while simultaneously putting out one departure between successive arrivals. To "see" the aircraft, I had to look to the radar when the aircraft was in the air, and then the ground radar known as the ASDE (Airport Surface Detection Equipment) when the aircraft touched down.

Most of the time, when I was working, nothing else mattered. I was usually totally focused on the job at hand. This time was different, though, since I hadn't been able to solve my mounting personal problems. My mind was wandering back and forth. I told myself to knock it off and get back to the airplanes.

As one aircraft crossed the landing threshold and the next was still five miles out, I put a Delta on the runway—or so I thought. "Delta Seven Nineteen, position and hold." Then, "Delta Seven Nineteen, cleared for takeoff." I *never* even noticed that Delta hadn't answered. I was in some kind of "cruise control" controller mode and obviously not paying attention to the read backs.

I next went into sheer panic and shouted throughout the Tower, "*Oh my God*, where did Delta go?" As I focused back on the ground radar, I couldn't see Delta on the runway. Had Delta already departed? By this time the supervisor, Bill Ewart, and half the Tower were breathing heavily down my neck, trying to help. I saw what appeared to be a target airborne about two miles to the southeast. Immediately, I inquired, "Delta, say your D-M-E." It was an unusual request on my part, because most controllers would have said, "Say position," but my assumption (ASS of yoU and ME) was that the aircraft was in the air.

DME is aviation language for "distance measuring equipment," which is a distance from a navigational aid at the airport. In other words, "Delta, how far are you from the airport?"

A confused Delta said, "Tower...err....ya...uh....Delta is one point five d-m-e." When I told Bill 1.5 DME, we both couldn't find anything resembling a Delta on the radar in any direction. The target that we had initially seen was simply a landmark etched into the radar screen. The reason we knew that was because it wasn't moving.

It was now back to panic mode, since if Delta wasn't airborne, maybe he was still on the ground in takeoff position, and worse yet about to be landed on by the next arrival. Without hesitation and any prompting from Bill, I sent the next arrival around, telling him "traffic on the runway." Quickly I begged Delta, *"Delta, say your DME, please!"*

An unusually quiet voice came back and without any sense of urgency, "Tower, still one point five DME." I was now totally in brain gridlock. When I looked back at Bill and told him Delta was still at 1.5, his eyes enlarged to twice their normal size. He was lost, too. Not knowing Delta's exact location, I couldn't take a chance with the next arrival, so I sent him around as well.

By this time I had the whole Tower standing around me, trying to figure out if maybe Delta was a flying saucer hovering 1.5 miles away from the airport. It was like an aviation three-ring circus—aircraft flying everywhere.

What about direction from the airport, someone said. Figuring I had the answer, I asked Delta his direction from the airport. Delta responded in a much louder voice, "Tower, we are one point five DME *west* of O'Hare."

I went back to the land of confusion. How could this be? That position report has Delta somewhere by the approach end of his departure runway.

Then a voice popped into my ear from a controller in the TRACON who had been listening as a monitor. "Calvin, ask him if he's in the run-up pad next to the runway." Without thinking, I just repeated the TRACON controller's instructions, and sure enough Delta responded with a resounding, *"Affirmative."* I quickly went back and cleared the next aircraft to land.

It turns out, the whole time, Delta was never anywhere near the runway, but in the holding pad right next to it. The first words Delta ever heard from the Tower were the questions about the DME. Delta never heard clearance for takeoff, and I never caught him *not* answering.

Needless to say, Bill relieved me and took me down-stairs for a "little discussion."

I had known Bill, nicknamed "ET" from his operator's initials, from the first day I came to O'Hare. He was always very sympathetic, kind, and tried often to be the voice of reason. He rarely elevated his voice when angry, but instead would shrug his shoulders in exasperation. For ET, it was better to quietly approach problems than make them worse with loud anger. When he worked with a certain area manager named "Captain Kangaroo," his nicknamed changed to "Dancing Bear," because all ET was allowed to do then was listen to the Area Manager try and run the Tower. Often ET would just stand around and flail his arms in disbelief, just like the dancing bear on the Captain Kangaroo show.

As we sat down in ET's office, the first thing he said was, "Calvin, I've known you for a long time and I think I can tell something is up. Are you OK?"

It was a valid question, but one I couldn't possibly an-swer in his lifetime. Or so I thought. "ET, I guess I just missed one," I jokingly replied.

ET just shook his head in the affirmative and then amusingly said, "You know, Calvin, are you sure you're not calling me at night, pretending you're the FBI?" ET totally left the Delta incident.

ET's reference was to suspicious phone calls he was get-ting at home from someone saying they were with the FBI. I think ET even alluded to the fact that it might have had some-thing to do with the Contras. I replied in the negative, because even though it might not have been beyond me to attempt such bad humor, I knew I was not responsible.

From that day on, anyone who was in Tower at the time of the "Delta DME" incident never forgot it. One of my fellow controllers, Bobbi Hoffman, even put the experience into a ballad, using the chorus of the song "Delta Dawn" by Helen Reddy. It went as follows:

"Delta Dawn, why's your transponder not on?
Could it be that you forgot to flip the switch
Or did I hear you say
"One point five D-M-E away"
I better send the guy two out around.
Delta, you dog, I can't see you in the fog
Recycle your transponder right away!
Or did I hear you say
"Not 'til the gear's all stowed away"
I think I'll send another guy around.
Delta Dog gone, go back to Atlanta where you belong -
Can't find you on the radar anywhere –
Or did I hear you say
"We're on the ground!" – NO WAY!
I better send another guy around.

I had it all coming to me. Bobbi, like everyone else in the Tower, had been the victim of many of my practical jokes. Her revenge was sweet but in good spirits. I even had to laugh.

My obsession with psychotherapy had become so great that I began to tune out everything around me. B.J. never did a lot of pontificating, but asked a lot of questions designed for me to understand what I was missing in my life. I was becoming less and less patient at work. I adopted an almost self-righteous attitude towards other controllers who I felt were being hard on everyone else, particularly the pilots.

One of those controllers was Kenny, the "Volcano Man." His nickname was indicative of the fact that pilots represented fuses on bombs while the controllers symbolized the fire that lit the fuse that blew up the volcano. He was intelligent, articulate, stubborn, and an excellent controller. He was one of the originals from 1984. I truly enjoyed being around Kenny. He was entertainment at its purest.

Without a headset on, Kenny was a good-humored, fun guy who enjoyed a good joke as long as it wasn't played on him. With a headset on, however, he would sometimes let his temper get the best of him. Anytime we saw Kenny's rage coming out, we knew we had to call in a specialist. A popular character amongst controllers was the use of the "phantom controller," who was designed to educate people who were in need of being taught one of life's many lessons. Once again, it was Marvin who showed Kenny the way.

One day, while Kenny was working outbound ground control, Marvin was working Ground Metering. Kenny was in a surly mood and proved it by screaming at a United in a very condescending manner, "Captain, I gave you the instructions *several* times—how many times you want them?"

Kenny's treatment of that pilot upset Marvin. Marvin decided to teach Kenny a lesson.

When an American called to taxi, Marvin replied, "American Four Twenty-one monitor ground on one-two-one point seven-five." The only problem was Marvin never really transmitted, but put the flight strip on Kenny's board without sending him to Kenny's frequency. In Kenny's mind, the aircraft was on his frequency, awaiting instructions because he had been told to monitor. With American, the only departure on Kenny's board came the "Volcano" taxi directions: "American Four Twenty-one, taxi to runway two-seven left via foxtrot and mike."

Meanwhile, as Kenny was talking to no one, Marvin said to the real American Four Twenty-one, "American Four

Twenty-one, taxi to runway two-seven left via bravo and delta." Given different instructions, American would be turning on bravo instead of the Kenny-assigned mike. Kenny watched intently, like a tiger waiting to pounce on its prey, as American moved out of his alley.

Then, as the American made the first wrong turn on bravo, the volcanic ash started to spew from Kenny's head, *"American Four Twenty-one, what are you doing? I told you to turn on mike, not bravo."*

Kenny had to think quickly now, because just ahead at the next intersection was a LOT flight approaching the same intersection as American. A traffic call was needed. Kenny calmly said, "American Four Twenty-one, give way to that LOT at the next intersection." Kenny's eyes were glazed on the American.

Meanwhile, at the same time Marvin was telling American to speed up to stay ahead of LOT. Even the inbound ground controller who was talking to LOT told the Polish airliner to "give way" to the American MD-80. It was all perfectly orchestrated by Marvin.

As American continued in front of LOT, the lava flow started to pour, *"American Four Twenty-one, I told you to give way to LOT—not cut him out! Geeeeeeez!"*

At this point, Kenny had the attention of everyone in the Tower. Most, of course, were laughing. Kenny wasn't transmitting to anything but air. Kenny continued, "American Four Twenty-one, I know you can hear me—make the next turn at mike five, please."

Marvin simultaneously, and very quietly so Kenny couldn't hear, transmitted, "American Four Twenty-one, don't turn at mike five but continue down delta. I'll have more for you."

As a horrified Kenny watched, American shot right past mike five. Even better was the fact that the Tower boom box was playing "Whipping Post" by the Allman Brothers. How appropriately came the words:

"Sometimes I feel...

Like I've been tied to the whipping post..."

Kenny was stuck on the post and didn't even know it.

Next was a full-blown, volcanic, almost nuclear explosion, *"American Four Twenty-one, American Four Twenty-one, I don't think it's possible for you to get anything right today! I know you can hear me. Just switch to the tower on one-two-zero-point seven-five. Any questions?"* Not getting an answer, Kenny just threw up his hands and slammed his strip board as hard as he could. Even though Marvin gave the American plane the correct Tower frequency for take off, other controllers couldn't resist a final parting shot.

The controller working frequency one-three-two point seven gingerly walked up to Kenny and asked, "Why is this American Four Twenty-one calling me?"

American, of course, never went to one-three-two point seven, but Kenny didn't know that, and sure enough, there was just a little lava left: *"These pilots are all idiots!"* And just one more time he drove his fist of anger back into the helpless strip board holder.

Many people pondered how Kenny's fury never translated into any health problems like a lot of other controllers. I simply thought Kenny was the best at sending anger out of his body and into the atmosphere.

Years later, when I revealed to Kenny the "lesson" Marvin had imparted, he erupted again, *"That was not funny."*

The irony of Kenny's outburst was that as soon as I mentioned the incident, another controller sitting nearby,

Johnny B., exploded in laughter. Johnny had remembered the whole thing as being hilarious. I just let other controllers decide what was funny, figuring they were the best judges.

Lighten up, Kenny—you're alive, living in America, and working at O'Hare.

Chapter 25

Bring in the Clowns

CONFLICT ALERT: *a function of air traffic control systems designed to alert controllers to existing or pending situations between tracked targets (known as IFR or VFR targets) or their own body that require his/her immediate attention/action.*

A s the millennium approached, I started to wonder if all the hype about the end of the world might be true. Well, at least in my universe it was. My wife and I were barely talking. As her issues became more centered on my behavior, I simply withdrew more and more, resorting to extra Vicodin. I was drinking so much that other controllers were *worried* about me. That was especially ironic. I was only an occasional drinker and not the type anyone would worry about.

When my wife and I separated near the end of 1999, I had lost all my bearings. I questioned the bigger questions in life. Where was I supposed to be heading? How could my wife and I work it out?

Every time the Tower radio played the song "Take the Long Way Home" by Supertramp, I would be reminded of my predicament. The lead singer, Roger Hodgson's, voice went straight into my soul:

"And when you're up on the stage,

it's so unbelievable, unforgettable,

how they adore you…

But then your wife seems to think you're losing your sanity,

oh, calamity, is there no way out?…

Does it feel that your life's become a catastrophe?

Oh, it has to be for you to grow, boy…

When you look through the years and see what you could have been, oh,

what you might have been, if you'd had more time…

So, when the day comes to settle down…

Who's to blame if you're not around?

You took the long way home…

You took the long way home…"

When my wife and I tried marriage therapy, it became a verbal wrestling match and, in just a few months, we stopped talking altogether. I had never felt comfortable confiding such extreme thoughts to my wife, much less in front of a marriage therapist. Admitting my weaknesses was not someplace I wanted to go. Without any close friends to confide in, B.J. became my only alternative. He knew I was drinking and taking prescription medications as fast as I could get them. He couldn't stop me, but only slow me down. He made me concentrate on my kids to avoid the obsessions with my own life. This worked fine for a short time, but then I'd have to deal with my marriage. I even fantasized about the days of Eden, when everything was so much easier and uncomplicated. With my marriage in shambles, I turned to a pilot for consolation.

For most of 1999, I had been trading quips on the radio with a Great Lakes Aviation pilot by the name of Katie. For many months, she was simply a soothing female voice on the frequency during a time of great pain. Katie's voice reminded me so much of Eden, I often imagined that this could be my childhood fantasy reincarnated. As bizarre as this might have sounded, my mind was capable of believing anything during this time in my life. We exchanged many cute and clever transmissions, until one day I decided to meet her down at a gate in the terminal for coffee. We had decided, on the ground frequency I was working, to meet at gate F-3, where her plane was parking. The meeting was convenient, since the Tower was located in the Terminal where F was located.

As I walked through security, I stopped at gate F2 and pondered the possibility of turning around. At least that way I would still have the fantasy without possibly losing it *again* and forever *again*.

When I first saw Katie, I couldn't believe my eyes. She was tall, cute, and had the most distinctive smile I had ever seen. Her short blond hair transported me back to the days of Eden. When I introduced myself, she smiled from ear to ear. All the anxiety I had been feeling for months disappeared.

Our mutual interests were virtually the same. She enjoyed sports, flying and, most of all, had a great sense of humor. I, of course, reveled in sports, observing flying, and laughing whenever I could.

For the next few months, we would meet at the terminal in between her flights. We literally spent hours on the phone, talking, never running out of things to say. While it seemed like the same communication I had as a kid with Eden, it still seemed too good be true.

B.J. never passed judgment on my actions, but he made me feel the consequences to a degree I had never felt in my life. Good times felt orgasmic, but bad times put me back in touch with alcohol and drugs. When I was with Katie I would forget all my problems—it was like being transported temporarily back to the innocence of childhood. Was Katie the answer to my problems, or simply a diversion I had created in my own mind?

The first half of 2000 was, without a doubt, the roughest year of my life. My two boys were becoming very sad and angry. Sad because of the separation, and angry because they couldn't understand what was wrong with Dad. In June of that same year, I decided to take my boys on a vacation to Zihuatanejo, Mexico, hoping to find an emotional escape, remove my kids' fears and possibly find an answer to that new fork in life's road.

The whole week in Mexico became the *biggest* departure from reality I had ever taken. As we arrived at the beautiful beachfront hotel, my two boys and I were whisked into one of the hotel restaurants for an "introduction" buffet. Before we could even sit down, one of the waiters, dressed in a *clown* outfit, brought over a bottle of tequila with three shot glasses. I was a little startled by this, since my boys were only seventeen and fourteen. Was there no drinking age limit in Mexico? Why were clowns serving drinks? At first I was apprehensive about even considering underage drinking, but then I had a novel thought.

Chances were that if my boys hadn't already tried some kind of liquor, it would only be a matter of time before they did. I didn't need someone's survey to tell me this. Just about everyone I knew had a story about his or her first drink of alcohol. Not one of those stories had the parents present on the day of initiation. I couldn't even remember one person saying they waited till age 21 to start drinking. So as the waiter placed the shot glasses in front of my two boys, both looked up at me with puppy dog eyes, as if to say "why not, Dad?" Well, if this *was* the first time they tried tequila, then what better time than with Dad? I felt, in a strange way, honored.

As the waiter poured the shots, I quickly reverted to my protective parental attitude: "Look, guys, I don't think this is a good idea."

Adam, my oldest, without hesitation gave me a macho reply, "C'mon, Dad, no big deal, this is nothing!"

Andy was a little less exuberant, but still confident. "Yeah, Dad, I want to try it."

Knowing Adam wasn't driving and Andy was always adventurous, I relented. As the waiter watched in amazement, all three of us did one of those on-your-mark, get-set, go routines. The tequila disappeared in 1.5 seconds.

I immediately knew I had made a big mistake. I didn't want my boys down the same road I was on. I was condoning underage drinking and I hated myself for it. A face of "bitter taste" disgust replaced the cockiness that had once been on Adam's face. Andy said he was ready to eat, but what he really meant was that he wasn't ready (now or ever) to have another shot. Adam, not ready to admit defeat, asked if we could do another. I told him he was a better man than I, but *no way* was that going to happen.

It was clear we needed food, so while Adam sat enjoying his "moral" victory, Andy and I hit the buffet table. It was a long 50-foot walk to the buffet. Andy was clearly teetering, and I knew my night ahead was not going to be without a headache. Adam, just to take the competition further, ate more food than Andy and I combined. With bloated bellies and slightly scrambled brains, we made it back to our room and straight onto our beds. More quality time with my boys.

As we dozed off, we were rudely awakened an hour later by a noise that sounded like someone had set off a foghorn in our bathroom. The noise was human and a cross between a loud scream and equally loud "Frankenstein" grunts. When the voice said, "My God," I recognized it as Adam. My guess was Adam must have had more than one when I wasn't looking. I felt horrible that I had caused Adam to endure this experience. I was the one who had allowed the first drink. He was learning from the additional drinks. It's every parent's nightmare.

The rest of the week, Adam got better while I, on the other hand, was getting worse. I was trying to get into the Guinness Book of Records for the most rum and tequila drinks in a one-week period. I had met another Chicago tourist named Gus. He spoke fluent Spanish and English, and was even more fluent in his drinking. The boys and I enjoyed Gus and his family immensely, laughing constantly. What I didn't realize, however, was that trying to keep up with the big, stocky, 300-pound Gus, drink for drink, day after day, was the biggest mistake I could make.

By the third day, Adam and I were so sunburned we resembled lobsters. Andy was always smarter and wore tee shirts most of time. By the fourth day, lying down at night and going to bed was a chore. On the fifth day, I was mixing a lethal cocktail of Tylenol P.M. and alcohol unknowingly. I needed relief from the painful sunburn to sleep. The active ingredient in P.M. is benadryl, which causes drowsiness and, eventually, a numbing siesta. What I failed to realize or pay attention to was the warning label on the Tylenol P.M.: "DO NOT MIX WITH ALCOHOL." I had probably seen that warning a million times on prescriptions and over-the-counter drugs and never given it a second thought. I wish I had.

On the last day of vacation, I couldn't walk ten feet without having the air sucked out of my lungs. A conflict alert went off in my head. My body was signaling me there was a problem. My boys sensed something wrong. My breathing became so labored I was just begging God to get me on the airplane back to Chicago. I knew something was wrong, but I didn't want to find out in Mexico. I had had enough "fun."

When I got off the airplane in Chicago, I felt relieved to be home and even rationalized that my shortness of breath would get better. I decided there was no need to see a doctor right away. The next day, I made it to work, but I could feel the shortness of breath was even more pronounced. As I got off the elevator to walk the one flight of stairs to the Tower, it all seemed impossible. By the time I made it to the top, I could barely breathe. After a few short minutes and finally catching my breath, I decided it was time to go to the hospital. Having several controllers, including the supervisor, Dave, staring at me in concerned shock, made that decision easier.

Dave didn't even say anything, except, in a very sympathetic tone, "See you later, buddy. I'll put you down for sick leave. Do you need any help?"

True to my stubbornness, I shook my head in the negative and sped for the hospital. Heading straight to the emergency room, I kept telling myself everything would be OK. When the nurse in the ER asked me what was wrong, I gave a casual, "I think I'm a little short of breath." Not sensing any urgency, the nurse put me into a cubicle and said to wait for the doctor. I can't believe I didn't tell her how I really felt—like dying.

After an hour of waiting, the ER doctor gave me a thorough examination, requested some blood tests and an EKG as a "precaution." He appeared not too worried about my condition, speculating maybe "asthma or allergy." As a technician finished the EKG and pulled the progress strip from the machine, a very concerned look flashed across his face. He ran over to the ER doctor who, with half the emergency room personnel, descended back into my cubicle.

"Mr. Richards, we need to get you upstairs as soon as possible!" exclaimed the now panicky doctor.

I was in shock. "What are you talking about?" I asked.

"Mr. Richards, your heart is in a very abnormal and life-threatening rhythm—we're taking you up to the ICU unit to stabilize you."

For the next few days, I was in the ICU. I didn't even tell people at work, except to say I would be off for a few days while the doctors tried to figure it out. I was being loaded up on blood thinners to prevent stroke and to dissolve a blood clot in my lung. The doctors' biggest fear was that my irregular heart rhythm would throw more clots. I couldn't even admit to myself *this* was serious enough for my friends and relatives to know about. I told my boys it was "no big deal." Again, I was too stupidly proud and afraid of showing a physical weakness that I had clearly brought upon myself.

On July 4th, I was deemed stable and transported to a regular room. Within a few months, I was cardioverted, a process where the heart is shocked back to its normal rhythm using those paddles so often seen in medical shows. As I found out later, the interaction of benadryl and alcohol is well documented in its deleterious outcomes.

I never looked at a Tylenol P.M. again. When I finally went back to work, I decided to stay positive and "bring in the clowns."

"Bringing in the clowns" was an expression to describe the idea that I would go back to concentrating more on just the positives and fun aspects in my life. At home, it was my kids and my new relationship with Katie. At work, it was working with one of my Tower "clown" friends, controller Jim Veronico.

Jimmy was funny, young, single, Italian, and *bald*. He was constantly mocked about his baldness and often referred to as "No-Hare Jim," which was a play on the word combinations "no hair" and "O'Hare." By the time I got back to work, I was ready to call in the "phantom clown." Sure enough, there was Marvin, ready to go. He loved the part of the clown.

Jim was training a transfer from Palwaukee, whom I'll call Paul, on inbound ground control. Very often, it was not possible to simulate all the possible training scenarios that a trainee might encounter. This was where Marvin came in. Marvin's plan was very simple. Would a trainee be able to have good enough vision to see all that was going on around the taxiways at O'Hare? To test the trainee's vision, Marvin picked up the portable radio (out of sight from Jim and Paul, of course) and tuned the transmitter to the inbound frequency.

Jim knew that something was up as he observed Marvin picking up the back-up radio. He had seen this many times before. Making eye contact with Marvin, Jim smiled and let out a slight chuckle. He could tell the education and entertainment were about to begin.

On the tower boom box, the group Pearl Jam was belting out the song "Even Flow":

"Even flow…

Thoughts arrive like butterflies…"

Inspired by Eddie Vedder, Marvin was about to grab the butterflies and perform his magic.

As Paul stared out the window looking over the airport, Marvin began transmitting, "Ground, this is American Seven Fifty-five, over."

A very cordial Paul responded, "Yes, American …uh… whatever your number, what can I do for you?"

Then Marvin: "Yes, Ground, this is American *Seven Fifty-five* on the bravo taxiway approaching taxiway foxtrot, and it looks like we have a *clown* standing out here off my right side."

Jim started to snicker. Paul paused in disbelief for a few seconds before replying, "American Seven Fifty-five, *understand* there's a *clown*… we'll get someone out there."

Before Marvin could speak again, Paul turned around and addressed Supervisor Tim across the Tower, "Timmy, call the City—there's a clown out by the foxtrot taxiway."

Initially, Tim didn't say a word, looked stunned, and then picked up the direct phone to the City. Finally understanding what had just been said, Tim put the phone back down and, to no one in particular, said, *"What?"*

After shaking his head in disbelief several times, Timmy asked aloud, "Understand you want me to call the City and tell them *what?*"

Without an answer, all Tim could do was wait. Things were happening too quickly.

Paul was looking intently at foxtrot, so whether he saw the clown or not was debatable, but Marvin had to make sure. "Ground, American Seven Fifty-five, oh my God, the clown just gave us the finger, he flipped us off!"

Instead of answering the pilot, Paul shot back to the supervisor, "*Tim*, the clown just flipped off that American pilot!"

Again Tim reached for the phone, but became confused when he looked over by foxtrot, and not only did he not see a clown, but there was no American jet there either.

Marvin came back, "Ground, did you copy, that is one crazy clown... hold on... I think he's up to something else..."

Paul was now curious, but what *he* was looking at, I had no clue. In an inquiring, serious voice, Paul replied, "American, what's the clown doing now?"

Marvin was ready to educate some more, since now he was in the air traffic "zone." "Ground, I think the clown is making something... Oh my God... Balloon animals! Ground, it looks like the clown is making balloon animals!"

At this point, I noticed Jim lying on the ground, holding his stomach. Jim's face was so red from holding in his laughter I thought he was going to self-implode. The clown was simply too much for Jim.

Somewhere in Paul's mind, the clown was out there, because he turned to Tim and explained, "Tim, it looks like the clown is making balloon animals—what do we do?"

Tim's confusion now turned to quiet, extreme laughter as he spotted Marvin off to the side, holding the hand-held radio and winking. Tim knew he was now part of something special.

Marvin now had had enough and decided to put an end to the clown, since he also couldn't stop laughing. Most of the eight controllers in the Tower were speechless from their own giggles. Tim also knew the lesson had reached its conclusion and signaled Marvin with a single index finger across the throat—end it, please.

Marvin went back for the last time, *"Uh,* Ground, American Seven Fifty-five, looks like we made a big mistake... That was simply a picture of a clown, not real... Sorry about that."

With a confused response, sensing he might have been duped, Paul replied, "OK, American, thanks for the info."

When Paul looked back at an overly smiling Tim, he sheepishly let out to the whole Tower, *"Oh,* nice one, guys."

Marvin had struck again. The clown had imparted another important lesson about O'Hare. For just a few minutes, the controllers' stress level was taken down a few notches. As the publication *Readers Digest* said, "Laughter *is* the best medicine." But had Marvin gone too far? Things were starting to get a little extreme. I heard a rumor later that the clown really did exist. Someone said they heard he went up to Oshkosh, Wisconsin. I decided to check it out. Maybe the answers to all my questions were with that clown.

Chapter 26

Oshkosh B'Gosh!

ACROBATIC FLIGHT: *Maneuvers intentionally performed by an aircraft involving an abrupt change in attitude, an abnormal attitude, or an abnormal variation in speed. The "best" are at Oshkosh.*

At the beginning of 2001, I was reminded of the movie *2001, A Space Odyssey*. I could remember watching that movie and thinking, "Wow, what a great place to be to get away from it all." I was yearning for some kind of break, or maybe even new challenges. The pace at O'Hare was becoming routine, though still fun. The daily grind at the big "O" was always special, but often I dreamed of a place that could take O'Hare and bring it to the next level. Could there be a place in the world that was actually *busier* than O'Hare?

How about a place where the rules were so bent that you could land airplanes on the runway three at a time? I'm not talking about formation flights, but rather one airplane right behind the other. A few times I tried that at Palwaukee. At O'Hare, though, the rules were simple: the first aircraft to land *had* to be clear of the runway before the second could land. Could there be a place where those rules could be changed? In January of 2001, another controller, Mike Blais, told me about such a place. He had been there the two previous years. He said, "Oshkosh, Wisconsin."

Initially, I thought Mike was just kidding around. Maybe he needed a new pair of jeans, you know, the "Oshkosh" blue jeans. After all, besides being a controller, Mike had a side job as a professional comedian. He always told grandiose and funny stories in his signature deep voice. Every time he got on position in the Tower, all the pilots knew his voice. It was always a laugh riot when visiting pilots came up into the Tower. Many of them would relate some experience they had with a controller and inevitably, in trying to explain the controller's identity, they would do an impression of Mike's deep voice.

Controllers in the Tower spent time imitating his voice, it was so distinctive. His exploits in the Tower were legendary. Like many of the O'Hare controllers, Mike loved to live on the edge, even outside the Tower.

In March 2003, a group of us, including Mike and the Mugavero brothers, Jim and John, went skiing in Breckenridge, Colorado. One day, during one of the worst blizzards in the history of the resort and Colorado, all four of us stood at the top of the mountain. We were debating what would be the safest and best path down the mountain. There were two choices.

One was the blue path or "run," which was for the intermediate skier and the *only* choice for Jim, John, and me. The other choice was the black path, known as the "black diamond." The black diamond was for the most advanced skier. It was about a 70° angle going down with the visibility at about *ten* feet from the approaching blizzard. I don't know anyone who would have tried this "dark" run. Mike, however, was the exception.

He looked at us and mockingly asked, "What's wrong with you guys? You afraid of this little black?"

John quickly shot back, "Mike, you're out of your mind!"

Mike, always challenging people, replied, "You guys are a bunch of pussies."

I couldn't believe it. Mike was questioning our manhood by using the "P" word. It was more than Jim could take. He calmly, mockingly replied, "OK, wise ass, you go down the black and us pussies will meet you where the two runs meet." Mike was called out. His "controller" ego couldn't turn back now. With the snow falling harder and visibility even more reduced, I knew Mike was in for an interesting ride. I don't think he would have had it any other way. This was who Mike was, proud and insane.

As Jim, John, and myself made it to the part of the hill where the blue met the black, we could see no sign of Mike. We pondered. Since we had taken so long to get to this point, could Mike have continued past our meeting area? We could barely see but a few feet in front of us. As we wondered out loud about Mike, we saw something cascading down the hill. It was a single ski casually moving past us by virtue of gravity —Mike's ski. Then a single pole skipped past us down the mountain—Mike's pole. Then a large, groaning man sliding down on his back—Mike.

At first, we were all concerned that Mike maybe had broken a bone or two. As John leaned over Mike, he asked the obvious, "Mike, are you OK, man?"

Mike was speechless, and for probably the first time as long as I had known him. After a few more minutes of moaning, Mike finally spoke, "I would have made it had it not been for a rock I got caught on and…"

"But are you OK, Mike?" John interrupted.

Mike shot back, "Of course!"

With Mike still on his back and no broken bones, John went in for the kill: "Well, Mike, who is the pussy now?"

To add insult to skiing injury, Mike decided that he was going to leave our vacation a day early since the blizzard was expected to be even worse the next day. As we waved goodbye to Mike, heading down highway 70 to Denver in the airport van, we started to think that maybe we should have left as well. If we got snowed in, there was no telling how long we might be stranded in the mountains.

As it turns out, as Mike's van was driving to Denver, the state troopers were closing the road behind him. By the time he got to the Denver airport, it was also closed—*for two more days*. Mike spent two nights and three days on the floor in the terminal of the Denver airport. The blizzard was that bad.

Back at Breckenridge, the Mugavero brothers and I went skiing. It was the best two days of skiing we had ever experienced. I never let Mike live that down. He hasn't used the "P" word since. Mike, however, had made me aware of a place as challenging as the Rocky Mountains. *Oshkosh.*

So what was Oshkosh, Wisconsin? Each year the EAA (Experimental Aircraft Association) puts on the biggest air show in the entire world, at Wittman Regional Airport in Oshkosh. Pilots from all over the earth come to this event. It's the largest single gathering of airplanes and flying machines you'll ever see. In the air show's one-week run, almost 10,000 airplanes will fly in, camp, and eventually fly out. The number of aircraft displayed to the public alone is around two and a half thousand.

Dick Knapinski, spokesman for the EAA, once said, *"If it has flown, is flying, or will fly, it comes to Oshkosh."* Every type, size, and mode of flying apparatus meets at Oshkosh. A lot of the spectators are pilots who fly in to camp for the entire week. Their numbers are right around 5000. When a visitor comes to Oshkosh airport during the beginning of the week for the first time, it's hard not to notice anything but rows of small airplanes lined up as far as the eye can see. Many of the parked planes have tents pitched right next to, or even over the airplane wings. You can save the cost of a hotel by doing this. And good luck trying to find a hotel room—most of the hotels are booked a year in advance. Not counting the "pilot campers," the daily average attendance at the air show is around 100,000. Oshkosh is, without question, the ultimate aeronautical "orgy".

Years before Mike told me about Oshkosh, one of my old O'Hare supervisors, Dennis Cunningham, always talked about how controlling airplanes at Oshkosh was the most fun he had ever had, next to outbound ground control at O'Hare. When I heard that, I really thought he was smoking something I needed. With Mike, Dennis, and Oshkosh in my brain, I put in an application to be a "rookie" controller at the world's other busiest Tower. When I was selected, I felt like I had been invited to an All-Star game for air traffic controllers. I would eventually get selected four more times before my retirement, and each time the experience was phenomenal.

It wasn't just a multitude of pilots descending into Oshkosh, it was also the nearly 70 controllers from all over the Midwest, from as far west as the Dakotas to as far east as Ohio. With three other controllers, I was placed on a crew composed of a supervisor, veteran, and limited. The veteran usually had two or more years of experience, while the limited had only one. I, of course, was the rookie. On day one of Oshkosh, in a classroom at the EAA museum, I was about to learn about a place that was crazier than O'Hare.

My new supervisor was John Moore from Minneapolis Tower. John was to be my mentor and supervise the other two crewmembers. The first time I met John, he barely uttered a word. One of the other controllers introduced me to John by saying, "Uh, John, this is Calvin, and he's from the 'big' house." John simply uttered "hello," and then walked out of the classroom. He had other things to do. I'm sure John wasn't too intimidated. He already had many years under his belt at Oshkosh, and had actually worked at the airport itself for many years before ending up in Minneapolis.

The class concentrated on all the new procedures controllers would learn for the week. At one point, the President of the EAA, Tom Poberezny, came in to give us a little speech on what Oshkosh was all about. Tom could hardly contain his own excitement. He spoke about the many thousands of pilots and spectators who would be present over the week. How it was up to us to show the world what air traffic controllers were all about. By the time he was done talking, I felt like I had drifted back to my college days and it was half time in the big game. *I couldn't wait to start the second half. Go team!*

They even gave me a uniform. It was a pink neon shirt and not the kind of thing I would wear around normally. The flaming color however was not without purpose. Apparently, it was the only color that pilots could see clearly from the cockpit. At times controllers were working next to the runways departing aircraft via small portable radios. The pink neon shirts were in effect saying, "Here I am, please don't run me over".

Walking around the air show in the pink shirts, controllers stood out in the crowds like an airplane landing light at night. It allowed easy invitations from pilots and the public in general to talk about air traffic and helping ourselves to some fine home cooked meals at the many "airplane campsites." There might have even been beer and other beverages at these areas but I honestly couldn't remember (till the next day).

It was time to go see my supervisor.

The next time I met up with John, it was much later in the day, at the controller "brat" party that took place after the first day's training session. While I had been in class, he was already working in the Tower, bringing in herds of airplanes. As I approached John, I could tell he was hammered out of his mind. I couldn't help but notice his incredible likeness to Davy Jones of The Monkees.

Feeling like I was at O'Hare, I had to give the guy a nickname: "Hey, Davy Jones, how are you doing?"

John again just stared and calmly asked, "What the *hell* are you talking about?"

I kept the charade going. "Hey, man, aren't you one of the Monkees?"

John put a finger to his head as if in disbelief. *"Oh, you're Calvin…* we're gonna have some fun in a few days. See you there in the Tower." A meandering John turned around and off he went, talking to the trees in the forest and occasionally even a few human beings.

After seeing John, I *couldn't* wait to see what was going on in that Oshkosh Tower.

My first day in Oshkosh Tower was unbelievable. When I first got to the top of the stairs, I noticed a group of four controllers working as one. In the group of four, one controller was the supervisor, who was plugged in next to the controller, doing the talking. The other two controllers were observers with binoculars, who looked out the windows for incoming airplanes. It was all quite simple. There were no departures. They would be controlled at the runway by another group of controllers. The Tower handled all the arrivals.

The two observers would tell the talking controller what to say to the pilots. The talker would simply parrot all that he/she was told. As the talker became more observant, he/she could then add in his or her own initiated transmissions, without the help of the observers. As the talker got better at spotting and keeping track of the airplanes, the observers would simply tell the talker where the airplanes were located in the sky.

Like outbound ground control at O'Hare, the pilots would do little or no talking. If a controller wanted verification from a pilot, he would simply tell the airplane to "rock his wings." For example, a controller might say, "Blue Cessna Skyhawk just north of the airport, rock your wings." Without answering on the radio, the Cessna would simply rock its wings up and down. This was how the Tower verified where each airplane was located.

As more airplanes came inbound, the pace would pick up. "Red Cessna turning final clear to land, blue Cherokee turn your base, yellow Mooney follow the blue Cherokee, Twin Cessna just north of the field, follow the Mooney ahead of you…" The stream of airplanes was endless, as were the instructions. It was even faster than the pace at O'Hare.

When I first started, I was the talker, and John was advising me on what to do and say. I had airplanes extended from the runway out to three miles. In that small amount of airspace, there were at least ten to 15 airplanes I was trying to get on the ground. On the runway were three dots, each about ten feet in diameter and at least 1500 feet apart. The first dot, at the beginning of the runway, was a fluorescent orange. It was an easy target for any pilot to see. Proceeding up the runway from the orange dot was a green dot, followed by a white one.

It took a few minutes, but I could feel a rhythm coming. "Red Cessna land on the white dot, red R-V land on the green dot, Bonanza on short final put in on the orange dot, and *everyone*, immediate right turns in the grass, *oh*, and welcome to Oshkosh and have a wonderful day." At O'Hare at times I was frowned upon for saying "have a wonderful day" while I was buried in large numbers of airplanes, but at Oshkosh it was actually encouraged. Because the whole "Oshkosh fly-in portion" of the event was about the small-plane pilot, many controllers felt it was important to put the pilots at ease.

I couldn't believe what I had just done. I was landing *three* aircraft at the same time on the same runway. Even controllers at O'Hare would have been scared by that move.

Once the aircraft had landed and turned off into the grass, the EAA Flagmen would take over. Dressed in bright orange crossing-guard outfits, these men and woman did the work of an inbound ground controller by pointing aircraft which way to proceed towards their respective parking areas. It was like watching parking attendants park cars at a rock concert. It was the most organized and largest line of parked airplanes I had ever seen.

As more airplanes filled the sky, I could tell I was starting to get a little behind. At times John would start talking, if he thought something needed to be said. Otherwise, all he had to do was look at me with that stare and I knew it was time to talk again. My two observers were Mike Dreger from Chicago-Midway and Wayne Roberson from Detroit. It was their job to sort out the "beehive" of airplanes approaching the airport.

Mike and Wayne had been to Oshkosh in past years and were always encouraging the whole time I was talking. This was teamwork at its best. I felt a part of something special.

After about twenty minutes of talking, I became so obsessed and excited I wasn't even hearing John give me instructions. John tried to get my attention: "Calvin, Calvin, *Calvin*!... You're doing fine, man, just relax."

I had that O'Hare "wound up" feeling surging through my body. At O'Hare it would have taken 300 airplanes and a few hours to feel it—at Oshkosh, a mere twenty minutes.

I was likening my new Tower experience to being in love with a woman. In my head and with "Davy Jones" standing next to me, all I could think about was the song "I'm a Believer" by the Monkees. The Monkees were equating love with Oshkosh when they were crooning,

Then I saw her face...

Not a trace of doubt in my mind...

Oshkosh made me a believer, and if it had been up to me, I would have made it last forever.

For some unknown reason, I even ripped my pants right down my rear end. Across the Tower, another controller, Jerry Kidd from Pontiac, Michigan, exclaimed, "Looks like the O'Hare guy is doing it half-ass." I couldn't have been having more fun.

During the 2002 air show, I was asked to do an interview with the *Wall Street Journal* about my experience at Oshkosh. I could hardly contain myself. I started out by reaching back into my musical background and labeled Oshkosh the "Woodstock of Aviation." To me, seeing all the happy people running around, watching the "airplane acts," was akin to being at a big outdoor rock concert. One of the main differences between Woodstock and Oshkosh was the organization.

Woodstock had a horrible problem with sanitation issues. At Oshkosh, there were over *1100* port-o-potties. They had learned from Woodstock.

At Woodstock, it was rock stars on stage. At Oshkosh, it was "rock star" pilots in the air. Walking through the fields of airplanes on my break, I could hear Crosby, Stills, Nash, and Young echoing Oshkosh in the song "Woodstock":

"By the time we got to Woodstock...

We were half a million strong...

And everywhere was a song and celebration...

And I dreamed I saw the bombers riding shotgun in the sky...

And they were turning into butterflies above our nation..."

As for "working" at Oshkosh, I simply said, "This [Oshkosh] has all the mayhem of O'Hare, only more. Landing three planes on a runway at the same time—you live to do stuff like that." Many of my peers thought I was crazy—so what else was new?

Every year at Oshkosh was a chance to meet and work with new controllers. Many of the temporary controllers at Oshkosh had backgrounds either as pilots or working in small towers that almost exclusively handled small airplanes. Identifying airplanes by types and company names for these controllers was a breeze. For myself, I was always learning airplane types. From my Palwaukee and Fullerton backgrounds, I knew the basic small airplanes such as Cessnas (the high-wings), Pipers (the low-wings), and Mooneys (the funny reverse tail). Having worked at O'Hare, I could tell every large commercial jet, including sub-models, such as the Boeing 737-200 versus the Boeing 737-800. The problem was that 95% of the airplanes at Oshkosh were not the ones that flew into O'Hare.

A few years later at Oshkosh, I was on a crew with Brad Hiatt from Fort Wayne, Indiana. Brad was a small airplane "genius." Not only did he know every make and model of small airplane, but he could also identify and name the "homebuilt" aircraft, since he himself built them. When I was the talker, Brad made my job incredibly fun and easy, since I rarely stumbled on the type of aircraft. He knew them all.

In fact, one time he got a little indignant when I mockingly questioned his ability to recognize aircraft. As I was looking through binoculars, I observed an airplane that I had never seen at Oshkosh. It was *so* unusual that I handed the binoculars to Brad and jokingly said, "Take a look at this one, Brad, there's *no* way you can know what that is!"

Brad simply took a quick peek and calmly stated, "Hyperbipe."

His answer even stunned the supervisor, Lynn McCarthy from Milwaukee. Lynn asked, "Are you sure, Brad?" None of us had ever even heard of a "Hyperbipe," unless it had something to do with the mouth. Still doubting Brad and thinking he had made it up, I asked the pilot directly, "Small red biplane airplane flying directly overhead, *say* your type." The answer was one word: "Hyperbipe."

My competitive nature would not allow me to let Brad off the hook. The next day in the Tower, while Brad was talking, I observed a very rarely seen airplane at Oshkosh. It was an ATA (American Trans Air) Boeing 737, and it was the "800" model. At the time, it was fairly new and had probably never been seen at Brad's home base in Fort Wayne. I, on the other hand, had seen enough of the airplane at O'Hare to know its identity.

As the Boeing airplane approached closer, I asked Brad, "Hey, Brad, what is that big jet three miles out?"

"Well, that's a Boeing 737, of course, Calvin," Brad proudly replied.

I had set him up, and then I pounced. "But Brad, what model Boeing 737 is it?"

Brad was now squirming. For the *first* time since we started working together, he was feeling uncertainty. After a dramatic ten-second pause, Brad fumbled around, "Calvin, that's a ... Uh... Boeing 737...500 series?"

I had him. I screamed, "*Wrong, Brad*, that's the 800 series, not 500, *what are you thinking?*"

The Tower immediately broke out into laughter, and for just one second, I had brought a puzzled look to Brad's face.

One of the constants amongst the Oshkosh controllers was the teamwork. It reminded me of O'Hare in the 1980s and the 1990s. I believe when people come together to work large numbers of airplanes, it is like an army waging war. If you don't control the airplanes, then they almost certainly will control you. Just like O'Hare in its heyday, Oshkosh controllers had a daily tradition of celebrating their amazing feats from the day's activities in their favorite watering hole.

At Oshkosh it was the Hojo's (Howard Johnson) bar. What became clear after a few years in Oshkosh was the oft-held theory that the amount of drinking a controller partakes in is proportional to the complexity and volume of traffic he/she controls. Controllers at Oshkosh made the controllers at O'Hare look like teetotalers. There simply was no comparison. The amount of traffic in one week at O'Hare was no match for the same at Oshkosh.

It was the combination of excitement and accomplishment that made just about every one of the 70 controllers at Oshkosh celebrate. Just when I thought I had eased up on drinking, Oshkosh would bring me back to overdosing on alcohol. Thank God all I had to do was *walk* back to my hotel room for just one week.

As years went by, other controllers at O'Hare would make the trip up to Oshkosh. One veteran and eventual Oshkosh supervisor was Jay Moffat. Jay had not only mastered Oshkosh but was very unselfish in teaching myself and others what he had learned. In a fitting tribute, he was voted "Controller of the Year" in 2006. It was a very prestigious award, given the fact it was voted on by the other 70 controllers and staff. Besides receiving a nice trophy, Jay would be invited to the other EAA air show, called Sun 'N' Fun, in Lakeland, Florida, as a guest and working controller. Jay had made O'Hare proud. It was time to go and watch the real airplane acts.

When I wasn't working airplanes, I would hang around and watch the air show. Every day, from around eleven in the morning till six at night, something was always going on. Some spectators simply enjoyed watching controllers landing the airplanes three at a time when the show wasn't in full swing. During the main air show, between two and six daily, came all the main acts. Each flying act by itself would have been a main attraction at any other air show, but at Oshkosh it was like a "cavalcade of the stars:" the most famous acrobatic pilots in the world, including Sean Tucker, in his biplane "the Oracle;" Patty Wagstaff, probably the best female acrobatic pilot in aviation; and my favorite stunt pilot, Jimmy Franklin.

Jimmy flew the most unusual and exciting act I had ever seen. His group was called the "X-Men" and their show was titled the "Masters of Disaster." Jimmy flew a "Waco" biplane that he had outfitted with a jet engine. One second he would be doing acrobatic maneuvers as a biplane, then all of a sudden he'd turn on that jet engine and really take off. It was a bizarre scene to see a plane alternating between prop and jet power. With his jet engine, Jimmy was performing stunts no one had ever seen, much less attempted.

To spice up matters, Jimmy would race an actual semi truck known as "Shock Wave." The semi on the runway was outfitted with two jet engines behind the top of the cab. This "jet truck" would position itself at the beginning of the runway, waiting to begin the show. As the "race" got started, the semi would show its power by revving up its two jet engines. Smoke and fire would shoot out from the truck like a fire-breathing dragon. By this time, the crowd was worked up into a frenzy, while kids hung on to their parents for their lives. It was like a NASCAR event of the future.

The drama became more pronounced when the public address system suddenly starting playing incredibly shrill emergency sirens, like the ones heard in a war raid. The race would start when Jimmy was about a half-mile behind the semi. That was when their start would be "equal," and Jimmy was over the runway.

As the Waco approached the rear of the semi, all hell broke loose. The semi's two engines shot out a fireball about 30 feet long. At the same time, Jimmy engaged the jet engine. The race was close, but I couldn't tell who won. I was too busy watching actual parachutes shoot out from the semi to slow its arrival at the end of the runway. The semi had all the characteristics of a jet fighter landing on an aircraft carrier. There was smoke everywhere and people cheering like someone had just hit a game-winning home run. I knew I was watching greatness.

My friend Duke and his family came up to Oshkosh one year to stay for the day. They had never seen an "Oshkosh" in their lives. After seeing Jimmy, they stayed an extra *three* days just so they could see his act repeated. To this day, they've never stopped talking about it. Sadly though, Jimmy died on July 10th, 2005, while performing in the Saskatchewan Centennial Air Show. Oshkosh and the world had lost a great pilot and friend. Nobody said flying was without risks.

As much fun as Oshkosh was, there was always an underlying fear that anything could go wrong at any time. A breathtaking 10,000 flights were screaming into Wittman Airport during the course of one week. Many of the pilots were simply flying as a hobby and not very experienced. It was only a matter of time before an incident occurred. Incidents *every year* at Oshkosh included crashes, spinouts, fires, injuries, and even deaths.

It was a given that sooner or later, a small airplane might miss a landing and become disabled near or on the runway. If this happened, it was everyone's job to determine if the aircraft was clear of the runway and the pilot was OK. During this process, the runway would be closed and potential landing aircraft would have to circle. Not a good thing with so many airplanes still in the air.

At a normal airport, the runway might stay closed for a long time so there could be an investigation and special equipment could be brought in to remove the aircraft from the runway. Not at Oshkosh. *As soon as* the pilot was verified to be without serious injury, the EAA would have special equipment standing by to remove a disabled airplane in seconds. If it was determined everything else was OK, then immediately the landings would commence.

The EAA ground crews were like some futurist "Mad Max." Mishaps at the runways were always cleared in record time. People on the ground watching aircraft landing rarely noticed incidents occurring, since the EAA would often have it all cleaned up in minutes. Knowing that herds of pilots were depending on them, the EAA had perfected their techniques from years of experience.

If the incidents at the runway were too serious, then the normal FAA protocol would take effect. Anytime the accident was serious, there would be no choice but to keep the runway closed. It was during this time that controllers were asked to work harder than ever.

I can recall one time when an RV aircraft flipped over on runway two-seven and the pilot was seriously injured. Immediately, the EAA closed the runway, but now there were at least ten to 15 aircraft that were headed to two-seven and had to divert to another runway. At the time I was working runway 18 right. Parallel to 18 right was runway 18 left. The plan was to give me the diverted planes. I decided to take them to 18 left while still landing my current traffic at 18 right. The plan was a disaster.

As all the airplanes were setting up to land from the north, all we could see in the Tower was a *mass* (or, in Oshkosh air traffic terms, "gaggle") of airplanes, probably at least 20 across the sky from west to east, *all* turning south into both 18s.

There was no way to sort that many airplanes out individually, so I thought of an old Palwaukee move I had seen performed by another controller. I made a blanket broadcast to everyone, "All the low wing aircraft head for runway one-eight-left and all the high wing aircraft head for runway one-eight-right."

As we looked out the window, it was like a puzzle putting itself together. All the low-wing Pipers and Bonanzas were lining up for the left, while the high-wing Cessnas were lining up for the right. Now the aircraft could be addressed more accurately as they got closer to the runway. Oshkosh was special that way, since it often required creative answers to the impossible questions it created. I was certain we had all lucked out. The pilots had performed like a finely tuned orchestra section.

After a week of Oshkosh, I was so tired and exhausted I was looking forward to going back to Chicago to see if I had anything left to give. It was time to go back and find out if there was any reality left in my life. I was satisfied, however, in knowing that I had accidentally visited one of those places we should all go before we die.

Chapter 27

The Delays and 9/11

EXPECT DEPARTURE CLEARANCE TIME (EDCT):
The runway release time assigned to an aircraft in a traffic management program and shown on the flight progress strip as an EDCT.

It seemed that as my body was breaking down, so was the air traffic system. Everyone around me in the Tower was complaining about the seemingly endless delays caused by the new "Traffic Management Units" (TMU) created by the FAA. Controllers acting as traffic management coordinators were imposing more restrictions on flights than at any time in the past. As the system was slowing down heading into 9/11, it was crawling *post* 9/11.

The day 9/11 is, of course, one everyone will remember, but at O'Hare it made everything we do seem insignificant. Technology not withstanding, it was the Tower boom box that informed O'Hare controllers about a "plane that had crashed into the World Trade Center." As soon as we heard that, one of the TMU controllers went downstairs and brought up a small portable black and white television from the Tower break room. As we worked airplanes in at a feverish rate, we would all occasionally glance back at the small black and white TV, starving for information.

When the second plane hit, management feared that maybe the Tower was next. While a few volunteers stayed in the Tower, myself and the rest of the controllers were told to grab the portable radios and get out of the Tower. The plan was for us to be transported on a City flatbed truck to a point in the middle of the airport, away from the Tower but near the runways. The controllers heading outside were the back-ups in case the Tower was to be *totally* evacuated. Thankfully we didn't have to implement the back-up plan.

Even so, confusion was everywhere. As we left the Tower entrance, located in terminal two, scurrying passengers were telling us that planes were being used in attacks everywhere. We all started to believe that maybe some other country was undertaking a sneak attack.

Controllers at O'Hare and across the country were presented with a scenario that had no real precedent. I don't know *any* person who could have pondered this horror as a reality. Prior to 9/11, hijackings were treated as "actions in progress." The first priority might have been to wait out the hijacker and hope the outcome would have a peaceful resolution. I dare say now if you were on an airplane and someone rushed the cockpit, you can be sure the rest of the passengers would take every measure to subdue the perpetrator. Many would not even think about risking their own lives. Some experts believe that the attacker has a better than 50-50 chance of losing his/her life.

In that one day, the "innocence" of the Tower and hustle and bustle that was Chicago O'Hare all but disappeared.

Controllers across the country had landed just about every airborne flight inside an hour.

The next few days, the airport was a ghost town as all flights were grounded, with the exception of military fighter jets patrolling major cities and airports. On 9/12, we spent the day shift watching two jet fighters circling over O'Hare for hours. On our ASD (Airport Situation Display, which shows all the airplanes in the air across the country), we could see nothing but military airplanes traversing the country, except for one. It was call sign "97 Illinois." It was the plane that normally transported the Governor of Illinois, George Ryan. The twin turbo-prop plane was observed by many in the Tower about halfway from Springfield, Illinois, to its destination of Boseman, Montana. This indeed was a very strange sight, since the FAA Command Center in Virginia wasn't allowing anything but military aircraft in the air. Even politicians in Washington, D.C., including congressmen and senators, were told to find other means of transportation to get home.

I never found out the exact story, but one TMU claimed the Governor was not canceling an "elk-hunting trip" he had planned. When I asked how he knew this, he said he had heard it from someone in the Command Center. I found this hard to believe, but never did I find someone to refute the story, either. I guess someone will have to ask George.

It was the most eerie feeling in the Tower not to hear the sounds of jet engines all around us. All this time we had taken the noise for granted. September 12th was a day that left people in the Tower sad, mad, and introspective. Many felt bad for the thousands of families who had lost loved ones. Many were angry at the terrorists and wanted revenge yesterday. Most others, though, just sat in the break room, pondering the future. Eventually, after the mourning period, life had to go on. It always does.

As flights began to recover, so did the delays. September 11th caused the whole system to become very tentative and cautious. Very often in the Tower, we could overhear the conversation between the TMUs and other facilities. At times the TMUs would become argumentative, always trying to get airplanes moving or lobbying to cut down the delay times.

I think, in a lot of ways, the shock of 9/11 at the Command Center took its toll on prioritizing maximum output at each airport. Within a few years, restrictions would become so numerous that controllers found their attention being taken away from separating airplanes out the window and instead directed to the restrictions written on each flight progress strip. The written restriction known as the "EDCT" (Expect Departure Clearance Time) was displayed as the time the aircraft could depart the airport. Controllers had a five-minute cushion after the time to get the aircraft airborne. If, for some reason, the controller missed the departure time, the TMU would have to re-coordinate a new time for departure. It can be very painful if you're the passenger in this situation. This happened more often than you might think, because by 2005, EDCTs were becoming commonplace to a multitude of destinations.

A typical group of airplanes waiting in line at the runway might have many different "EDCT" times to depart O'Hare. Like a puzzle, you had to determine which flights could depart and which had to wait. One flight might not be able to go to Newark until five minutes hence, while the aircraft right behind him, going to San Francisco, had been released two minutes ago. The problem is the first one can't go nor can the second because he's stuck behind the first. Controllers would be pulling their hair out trying to maneuver the aircraft near the entrance to the runway just to get *one* aircraft airborne.

This new traffic "management" system became such a distraction for controllers that often they would start making such stupid mistakes as forgetting if someone was cleared for takeoff while trying to figure out what to do with the next several airplanes. In 2006, a position was created just to put the new TMU puzzle together. A new controller, called a "local assist," was brought in to stand next to the controller clearing airplanes for takeoff. His/her job was to attempt to put the airplanes in some kind of logical order at the runway. That way the controller departing the airplanes could concentrate more on his *primary* job—*rolling airplanes*. This is where O'Hare is, at present day. Controllers are continuously trying to adapt to FAA "EDiCTS."

We have become so bureaucratic that restrictions are the norm, when years ago they only existed when the weather went bad. The government needs to find better ways to regulate the flow of aircraft across the country. Over-regulation is not the answer. At the very least, it is fast becoming unsafe. Tower controllers, burdened with so many extra tasks, will eventually miss something. They already have. In March, 2006, at O'Hare, a controller cleared two aircraft for takeoff at the same time on intersecting runways. One was a Lufthansa jet and the other an United regional jet. Both aircraft just missed where the two runways intersected.

One can only wonder when real corrective action will be taken. Chances are it will be when the NTSB is brought in to investigate another accident. It's a shame that blood is often the determining factor for change.

The O'Hare TMUs have gotten smarter, though, and begun to question the people at the top. One of the TMUs,

Dwight "the Genius" Kuzanek, from the class of 1991, had no problems questioning restrictions put on O'Hare departures. Having spent over ten years as a controller, he understood the frustration of delays at O'Hare. When delays to other airports started to get a little excessive, Dwight would grill the Command Center and other TMUs into exasperation in getting releases. I'd thrive in the Tower on challenging Dwight when I felt airplanes were sitting far too long. I'd say, "*Hey, Jackass,*" jackass being a term of endearment in the Tower, "when are we going to get some of these guys outta here?"

Dwight would view my words as a personal challenge and, amazingly, when he put his mind to it, he could do just about anything. He was one of my favorite "jackasses."

One day, the delays were so bad to the New York airports that some planes were sitting on the ground for up to four hours. One of the TMUs was fairly new and, in fact, had only been an O'Hare controller for a few years. His name was Brian Cugno. He was young, intelligent, and full of enthusiasm, but we needed to put a little meanness in him so he would speak up on behalf of the flights that were sitting and waiting far too long.

I pointed out to Brian some Newark flights that had been sitting at the airport for over two hours under the excuse of "volume." As I started to taxi out another Newark just leaving the gate, I mockingly handed the flight progress strip to Brian and said, "And how many hours is this guy going to sit on the ground?"

Brian took the strip and walked away without a word.

Again I grilled Brian, "C'mon, man, how long are you going to make these passengers suffer?"

A condescending Brian finally answered, "Are you asking me or telling me?"

At that point, hearing the Tower radio echoing "Aeroplane" by the Red Hot Chili Peppers could not have been more appropriate. The radio was sending a message through the Peppers:

"I like pleasure spiked with pain...
Music is my AEROPLANE..."

Brian became unglued. His anger was obvious. He threw the strip at me and, as I put my hand up to block it, I ended up knocking over my strip board, which was keeping track of around 15 airplanes I was taxiing to the runway. Now I had to reorganize all my airplanes, but before I did that, I had a better idea. I grabbed Brian's clipboard with all his "paper" restrictions, opened up the clip, and let all the papers fall everywhere. I then pulled his coordination phone out of the jack and threw it on the floor. Everyone laughed and then Brian understood.

My years of frustration were only starting to become his. Brian was still a young O'Hare controller, but would now quickly learn in a day what had taken many controllers' years. As time went by, Brian became more compassionate about delays when dealing with other facilities. He had learned to question incompetence when it reared its ugly head. Oh, and by the way, before Brian picked up his papers, he made a call to the Command Center, and within a few minutes, the flights to Newark were airborne. A new "punk kid" was born. The future for John/Jane Q. Public has hope.

Sensing the new "kids" of O'Hare were going to try and help put the system back together, I decided it was time to coast into retirement.

Chapter 28

Reasons For Waiting

CLEARED TO LAND: *ATC authorization for an aircraft to land. It is predicated on known traffic, known physical airport conditions, and the ability to touch down to a new "starting point."*

As my life with Katie was getting started, I became officially divorced in March of 2001. Even though I knew it was inevitable, I still couldn't help feel that sense of failure I had often despised. Too often, I would think about the uncertainty of my relationships with people and then plunge into depression all over again.

Because of her job as an airline pilot, Katie spent a lot of time traveling across the country. At times, to be together, I would either travel along with her or have lunch at the airport. It wasn't a normal relationship. Months later, when Katie was promoted to work at a major airline, the short flights in and out of O'Hare were replaced by long trips and layovers. When she was gone, I would spend far too much time sitting at home, brooding about my loneliness. As it became harder to sleep, I would revert to drug therapy. It's amazing that we can sometimes rationalize that having a prescription for a drug means there's no way we can abuse it. Vicodin was always there for me.

When I went to see B.J., he insisted I had to work out my personal conflicts. If I was going to keep on believing I couldn't trust in anyone, then I would almost certainly be doomed. Something would have to give. In time, because of my growing isolation, my depression would deepen. B.J. knew I was taking the easy way out by using Vicodin and alcohol. I was constantly aware that the only person who could change me was myself. Easier said than done.

My anxiety level at work was on the rise. My patience started to wear thin. One time, I even had a flashback to a long-ago childhood experience. During a day shift, one of the supervisors, Clifford "Scott" Mulbarger, took note of my performance on ground control. He came up behind me to point out an inbound United jet trying to get in his alley to park at a gate. The jet, instead of turning into the alley, stopped on the taxiway, a cardinal sin at O'Hare. Any aircraft moving on the same taxiway behind the United would be delayed in getting to their gate.

At the time, I was busy talking to other aircraft on the other side of the terminal where conflicts needed to be resolved ASAP. Without my timely traffic calls, there could be a problem. The lone United jet wasn't delaying anyone, since there wasn't anyone behind him.

Without this complete picture, Scott exclaimed, "Calvin, get that United moving!"

I ignored him. There were more important things I needed to be saying.

Scott persisted, *"Calvin, move that United now!"*

All of a sudden, *I* became the "volcano man."

At the top of my voice. I yelled, *"Hey, asshole, is my wiffle ball on your lawn?"*

Scott looked at me with the most startled and confused look you could imagine and said, "What *are* you talking about...wiffle ball...on my lawn?"

For just a few seconds, I had equated Scott with my old next-door neighbors, the Vashinkos. I was pointing out the insignificance of Scott's demands.

Later, when I got off position, I explained to Scott what I had said. He simply laughed and understood. From then on, whenever Scott saw me working ground and saw potential for problems, he would cleverly say, "Hey, Calvin, I'm seeing a wiffle ball on my lawn, take care of it please!" Even supervisors can learn.

I was letting my personal relationships enter the work environment. Anytime I was frustrated in my relationship with Katie, my patience at work became minimal. I was never sure where my relationship with Katie was headed.

What bothered me about Katie was her unexplained need to keep my existence from her mom and family. It was as if I was her "little secret." Everyone in *my* family knew who Katie was. I simply believed if you *truly* loved someone, then you wouldn't care what anyone else thought or said. We had lived together for over two years, and yet I had never met her family.

At one point, her mom in Minneapolis insisted on visiting her at our place in Illinois. After Katie reluctantly gave in, she asked me if I would leave the house for the day with my son, because she still didn't want her mom to know about me. I was dumbfounded. After a short argument, I just gave in. To add insult to injury, while her mother was visiting, Katie removed any pictures having to do with us. Apparently, she wanted to convince her mother she lived alone.

As different holidays passed, such as Christmas, Easter, and Thanksgiving, I kept waiting for Katie to say, "Well, it looks like we're going up to my family's house and you can come with." When the time passed without any invitation, we would get into *another* argument. Katie's answer to the question was always, "Well, my mother might not understand." At one point she argued that her mother wouldn't understand our 14-year age difference. I could only throw up my hands.

Things started to really unravel on our vacation to Punta Cana in June of 2002. While we had planned to spend a week in the Caribbean with my two boys, Katie had expressed a desire to leave halfway through the vacation to attend a "basketball camp" for officials. While I expressed some resistance to her leaving during the middle of our vacation, I wanted *her* to decide what was most important. Which would she choose? She chose the camp, and ended up leaving three days into our trip. I was angry, but at the same time, I knew I couldn't force the issue. If her priority was not to stay the whole trip, then I wasn't going to force it. She had often said she was in love with me, but her actions said something different. As Katie left Punta Cana in the middle of our vacation, I decided to change my whole attitude.

With only a few days left of vacation, I decided I was going to have a great time with my boys and not worry about where my life was headed with Katie. On June 28, 2002, I strolled over to the large, outdoor "in the round" hotel bar of the Fiesta Americana. The bar was so enormous it could easily handle around 50 people. Even with that capacity, I noticed only one open seat. As I sat down and ordered a Piña Colada, all I could hear was the sound of foreign languages. Most of the patrons were from South and Central America. Spanish was everywhere. Next to me was a lady with long, blond hair, with her back to me. Maybe she spoke English, I thought.

When I tapped her on the back, she jumped slightly, as if I had scared her. When she turned around, I didn't know what to say. She was exquisite. I was so happily surprised that I said the first thing that came into my mind. "Hi, how old are you?"

I had no clue what I had just said, but the lady smiled and, in her polite New England accent, calmly said, "Wow, that's a great pick-up line."

Her name was Kim. Feeling a little embarrassed, I couldn't help but notice her sweet smile and pleasant demeanor. From that moment on, it was as if Kim and I were the only people in Punta Cana. There might have been 50 or 60 people around us, but I wasn't aware of any of them. All I could see was Kim.

It wasn't anything like Eden. In fact, it was so much more powerful. My life stopped being so hurried. Working at the Tower often made it hard for me to slow down the pace of my body when I came home. Sitting and talking to Kim made time stand still. I wasn't worried about what was coming next. I was wonderfully stuck in the moment of her presence. It was all I needed.

The best part of all, though, was the fact that I didn't feel the need to drink to enjoy my "chat" with Kim. I was stone-cold sober, and for once was enjoying it. It took me 20 minutes before I started on my Piña Colada. It was a drink I wanted to celebrate with her. I suggested we take a walk on the nearby beach. It was the perfect night. Stars everywhere, warm ocean breeze, waves rolling lazily, no place to go. I was overwhelmed by a feeling that told me I was involved in something very special. I had a revelation. It was now time to put the past behind me. Kim was *all* that mattered.

When I turned to kiss her on the beach, I could tell it was special. We stretched out on a beach chair for a few hours, talking about our hopes and dreams. We had so much in common that I felt as if I had known her for years. It was the most peaceful conversation I ever had with another human being. I felt it was on the spiritual level that Kim and I connected. For a half hour, we didn't talk, but just looked into each other's eyes. It was a time I had only previously dreamed about, full of joy and happiness. Our eyes spoke the words we had both desired to hear our whole lives.

Later that night, we went to retrieve our kids at the local disco. By coincidence, my boys had run into Kim's daughter. They were also enjoying their time together. Every one of our teenage kids had been drinking—what a surprise. The examples we sow can become the habits our kids reap. I knew I had to stop my own drinking before I could expect the same of anyone else.

After leaving Punta Cana, Kim and I would e-mail each other and talk on the phone endlessly. Meanwhile, Katie and I were already quickly growing apart. Before I even met Kim, my relationship with Katie had been deteriorating fast. Months after 9/11, Katie was laid off from her dream job as an airline pilot. Her world was falling apart faster than mine.

In August of 2002, when Katie went on her yearly vacation with her mom, I figured I would be a ghost in her family forever. Enough was enough. I decided then to meet Kim in Maine. I was also writing feverishly at the time, since I had no other way to express myself.

When Katie found out about my trip to Maine, we broke up for good. It appeared that in the GPS of life, I was being sent on an alternate route.

As a parting shot, and after our two-and-a-half-year relationship, Katie said, "It's all just a shame, since I was going to take you up to Minneapolis to meet my family for Thanksgiving." Of course you were.

There was no doubt where I was headed next—Massachusetts. Kim and I started dating long distance, and every trip became more interesting than the next. I never wanted to leave when I was at her house. Saying goodbye till the next time was getting harder and harder, because it reminded me of the time I had said goodbye for the last time to someone when I was in high school. I vowed history was not going to repeat itself.

I knew I had to be patient. In time, Kim and I would talk about her moving to Chicago. We adopted the song "Reasons for Waiting" by Jethro Tull, which described how lovers waited patiently, dreaming about the day they would be together forever. It would constantly play in my mind:

"What a sight for my eyes to see you in sleep
Could it stop the sunrise hearing you weep...
You're not seen, you're not heard
But I stand by my word...
Came a thousand miles just to catch you while you're
smiling."

I must have played it hundreds of times for comfort.

Kim was getting me to open up to her. For the first time in my life, I was able to tell another human being how I felt, good and bad. I had one battle left to fight. I knew I had to free myself from the drugs and alcohol that would come in and out of my life like a bad cold. Freedom from Vicodin and alcohol meant freedom to live life to its fullest and with Kim. I was always afraid of telling Kim about my weaknesses, fearing she would be put off or even disappointed. Nothing could have been farther from the truth.

When I finally found enough courage to explain my fears to Kim about my abuse of Vicodin, she gave me hope. She said she understood and would support me in any way I needed. That was all I needed to hear. I cried tears of joy over the phone. Kim had saved me. I now had the courage to take the next step. The next time I went to see B.J., I brought in two large vials of Vicodin. B.J. immediately understood its meaning. As he dumped the contents in the trash can, he turned to me and said, "Are you sure this is what you want?"

I simply nodded my head in the affirmative.

B.J. next smiled for a second, but then became very serious. "We have one more thing we need to do, and do you know what that is?"

I could feel myself starting to break down in tears—I knew it was coming, and when it did, I still wasn't prepared. All of a sudden, B.J. stood up and pleaded, *"Bob, you have to stop holding in all the years of frustration in your life and your job. Enough already, are you ready to give it up?"*

He had hit the target. I had *never* cried harder in my life. Years of stress, loneliness, frustration, lies, and uncontrollable emotions disappeared.

Anytime I felt myself wanting to lapse into old habits, I would think about Kim, my boys, family and friends. Many had stayed loyal throughout my ordeals over the years, even when they couldn't understand them. Kim was my salvation.

In August 2005, doctors were advising me to have an operation that would hopefully, once and for all, fix my abnormal heart rhythm. With Kim at my side, I knew I would never be alone. Initially, the procedure, called "pulmonary vein isolation," was a success, but then came the complication that changed my life and brought me back to the "starting point." What is that, you ask? The starting point represents that second chance I was given to start my life over with a new outlook and attitude. Hope you can *still* understand.

I can never say enough for all the kids, both my own and Kim's. Kim and I were both divorced, but were very lucky to have children who, at times, were wise beyond their years. The kids' support carried Kim and me through some very hard times. My own sons, Adam and Andy, were always there when I needed them. Kim's sons, Ben, Greg, and Andrew, made my life fun and interesting. Even Kim's daughters-in-law, Lis and Kim, always had kind words to say at the right moments. Kim's daughter, Julia, "the Princess," became the daughter I had only dreamed about.

On November 26th, 2005, Kim and I, with *all* the kids, went back to Punta Cana and got married. Having the kids together at one time was more than special. It was the start of a new life. We had *all* come back to the new starting point.

In 2006, the O'Hare Tower and TRACON combined to commit 28 operational errors. This was the most errors in the history of aviation at O'Hare. It was a sign of the current trend which also includes greater delays with future ramifications for passengers everywhere. Air Traffic Control is at the crossroads as is the rest of commercial aviation. It's now up to the class of 2007 to step up again.

On February 2nd, 2007, Groundhog Day, and after 25 years of government service, I didn't see my shadow, so I retired. Peace had finally come.

Chapter 29

How We Treat Each Other

NEGATIVE CONTACT: *Used by pilots to inform ATC that previously issued traffic is not in sight. It may be followed by the pilot's request for the controller to provide assistance in avoiding the traffic. Any positive contact is, of course, appreciated.*

Hopefully we are all enjoying our trip through life. Our journey has taken us many places. The things that make our life meaningful revolve around the people in our lives. If we live by the golden rule, then surely the trip will not encounter as much turbulence then if we lived by some other set of nondescript rules. Our roles in the workplace should follow in that same manner.

The relationship between the FAA and its employees is symptomatic of what is happening in every other facet of society across the earth. It's the way we *treat each other*.

For years, the controllers at O'Hare and facilities all across the country have made the air traffic system safe and a model for the world. Even when they are stretched to the limit and their morale is low, controllers still find ways to overcome. They are proud, mischievous, and passionate about helping people, particularly the flying public. Kiss one the next time you see one in the airport; that's "positive reinforcement."

Since the FAA adopted its new "negative reinforcement" policy, job satisfaction among controllers is currently at an all-time low. How does that translate for the flying public, or even the controllers themselves? I think anyone can figure that out based on how we *treat each other.*

My solution for the FAA and the world is simple. Learn from Michael Hurley. Mike taught many controllers how to treat each other. Mike was a man I met about 20 years ago while walking through the terminal on my break. He was stricken with cerebral palsy and barely able to walk. He walked with a pronounced limp and often found it hard to get from place to place. He had the use of only one of his arms, while the other was often stiff and unmanageable. I saw him walking through the terminal one day with his hand-held VHF radio. I was struck by the fact he was holding it only about an inch from his ear. He was listening to transmissions from the Tower and seemed totally fixated on every word that was being said.

When I walked up to him and asked him how it was going, he immediately showed me a great big smile, answering, "I'm listening to the air traffic controllers. I like to listen to them." When I inquired further about his interest, he proudly proclaimed, "I come to the airport every week. I really enjoy listening to the controllers because they're always having lots of fun and I like to watch the airplanes."

His enthusiasm was contagious, and when I told him I was a controller, his mouth opened up as if in total awe and surprise. "How would you like to come up to the Tower and watch?" I asked. To Mike this must have been like a kid winning a trip to Disneyland.

By the time we got up into the Tower, Mike could hardly contain himself. As soon as he got his first look out the windows, all he could do was say, "*Wow!*" When I introduced him to some of the controllers, the smiles got bigger and bigger. Not just on Mike, but everyone who shook his hand. All the controllers were fascinated by his good nature. He even remembered everyone's name after only the first introduction. Mike was *never* angry or upset about anything. People in the Tower envied his positive outlook. Many wondered how someone with so much to overcome could *never* have a complaining moment.

We would help Mike up into one of the controller high chairs and give him a headset to listen. He had in effect become our "best friend." To the controllers at O'Hare, Mike was one of them.

People loved Mike because he gave back one simple quality—*hope*. The hope he gave to all controllers was one of happiness and joy. He gave *all* people he met the hope that anything was possible. Very often people in the Tower would feel the need to whine about something. As soon as they saw Mike in the Tower, they thought again and instead smiled. This is how Mike *treated us* and what he gave to all those around him.

At one point, when airport security was at level whatever-color-is-bad, Mike was told by TSA (Transportation Security Administration) personnel he could not bring his radio into the airport. No longer could Mike come to the airport and have fun listening. The scanner was somehow thought to be an "instrument of terrorism." This was Mike being treated in the worst way.

Mike was so intimidated by his experience that he rarely came back to O'Hare, except to attend Catholic Mass at the Airport Chapel. In spite of the way he was treated, he did not complain and *still* kept smiling. When the controllers brought Mike back to the Tower in 2006 last year for his 50th birthday, he was the same Mike. *Every one* of us has a Mike *inside* us.

One day during my last year at O'Hare, while I was walking in the terminal on my break, *Mike's spirit came out of me*. I happened upon an old man lying on the ground by the US Air ticket counter. He must have just collapsed, since there were only two TSA people standing over him, not sure what to do.

With the old man lying on his back, I bent over to see what I could do. As I held his wrist to check his pulse, I inquired, "Hello, sir, how are you feeling?"

The man answered, "I feel a little dizzy."

I announced, "Your pulse is a little fast. How's your breathing?"

"My breathing is good," he explained.

I was starting to wonder if maybe he was a diabetic. "Sir, did you eat today?"

"No, not really," he anxiously retorted.

I had one more question, "Sir, are you a diabetic?"

The man now seemed amazed, "*Yes*, I am, how did you know..."

Just at that moment, the sound of the paramedics' ambulance was right outside the terminal door. While I was still crouched over the man, he started to regain his energy. One of the TSA guys, upon seeing this, said to me, "Are you a doctor?"

Then it hit me. I smiled immediately. My answer was right out of a television ad: "No, but I stayed in a Holiday Inn Express once."

The man on the ground laughed so hard he started to get up. As paramedics made it to the scene, it must have been quite puzzling for them to see their patient and the TSA people laughing. But laugh they did and, as the man was rolled out of the terminal, he smiled, waved, and winked back at me. I finally understood how to treat a stranger.

The world is a good place. We all need to believe in it.
Treat each other well.

Appendix 1

The Last Flight Home

RESUME OWN NAVIGATION: *used by ATC to advise a pilot to resume his/her own navigational responsibility. It is issued after completion of a radar vector or when radar contact is lost while the aircraft is being radar vectored.*

For all the years I have been on this wonderful thing we call "Earth," it has been with a constant source of amazement for all the people who come and go in all of our lives. Many people we meet have all in some way helped us acquire knowledge, learn new things, and entertained us, sometimes without us even knowing it. From time to time, whether in a dream or a simple state of reflection, it is possible to bring back to life all those who have passed on. Many have left this life after having spent many wonderful years, while others have left much too early. The most constant and saddest fact throughout my years at O'Hare was that watching young controllers die was the norm and not the exception.

All the people I speak of in this chapter are my co-workers, who were not only inspirations to me but to all those around them, and probably never even aware of it. Very few people I have met ever take the time to sit back, look into themselves and see how special they really are. Too often we are all consumed by everyday life and its responsibilities, schedules, appointments, computers, cell phones, cable television, etc. All these very mundane activities only vaguely seem to inspire our *inner* spirits.

In the movie *Parenthood*, the wise great-grandmother states that when she was a child, everyone she knew rode on the merry-go-round, while she preferred the roller coaster. This, of course, is the idea that if you search out life to its fullest, chances are your experience will be more full and more complete than anyone could imagine. I was totally taken aback by this analogy, because upon hearing it for the first time, I realized that not only was I on the roller coaster, but all the people I've known were on it as well. They are all people I wish everyone could have known, because they would all still be riding the coasters had the "Big Man" in the sky not booked their last flight home. I salute these people and give you just a small slice of their lives, just to show how simple, personal experiences are sometimes the most powerful.

Stephen (Steve) Perkins was born February 10th, 1959. He was a south side Chicago guy who had a real zest for life, and someone who never seemed to have enough friends. Steve started his air traffic career as an ATA (Air Traffic Assistant) in the TRACON in 1985. ATA was a starting point for someone considering entering the air traffic field. They assisted the regular controllers by doing such simple tasks as disseminating weather, distributing flight plans from the printer, and issuing flight plans to pilots over the phone or on a frequency. Many ATAs would become full-fledged controllers, while others might be furloughed pilots waiting to be called back by their employers, the airlines.

Steve's gregarious nature made him very popular with the people in the TRACON. Anytime we talked, he always had a good joke ready to go. One of the best jokes he played on me was after work in May of 1988, just a day before my birthday. Steve lived down the road from me, so occasionally after work we would head out for some "post-game" cocktails. One day, Steve suggested we go to "church." It was 9:00 p.m. and we were just getting off work. When I asked him what the hell he was talking about, he said, "Never mind, you drive and I'll show you where to go. Trust me, it's almost your birthday."

A half hour later, we pulled up in front of "St. James Place" on the south side. It was the name of the local watering hole in Steve's neighborhood, and where many of Steve's friends "prayed." As we pulled up to the front of the bar, ten of Steve's "Irish" friends I never met were buying me drinks and wishing me a happy birthday. I felt like I was the King of Ireland. This was how Steve treated people, with kindness and compassion. He loved to see people having a great time. I learned a lot from Steve.

Steve died in August of 1988 of heart failure at the ripe age of 29 years old, only months before his 30th birthday. When his sister went to awaken him for work one morning, Steve was already gone. He had died in his sleep.

One of Steve's best friends and south side carpooler, TRACON controller Mike (Doc) Egan, would like all to know that Steve "was a great man who showed me the way." When he first told me the idea of going to "church," I was a bit skeptical. I sure was glad that he insisted. There weren't many days we missed the daily service on our way home from the TRACON. When Steve passed away, I spent the majority of my time at "church," trying to ease the pain of my lost friend. His wit, sense of humor, compassion and his way with words remain with me today. I take great comfort knowing he will be a part of Chicago O'Hare Air Traffic Control forever, because anytime the radar system is down for maintenance or a failure, there is a large piece of airspace Northwest of Chicago that has been named the "Perkins airspace"."

Dan Eagan was born on March 17th, 1958. He came to O'Hare from Chicago Midway Airport in 1986. Dan was a mountain of a man. At over six feet tall and nearly 250 pounds, Dan towered over just about everyone in the Tower. Dan was a very kind man who had one of those laughs that was contagious. If you heard Dan laughing on the other side of the Tower, chances were other people throughout the Tower would be snickering, just listening to Dan's cackling.

Most of all, Dan was the *hardest*-working controller I had ever seen in the Tower. When working ground, he would literally sweat buckets of water. If I'd had a towel to wipe Dan down, it would probably have yielded a gallon of water each day I worked with him. The most fun I had with Dan, though, was when he was training someone. Even if he were training and not talking, he would sweat profusely. Some trainees had that effect on Dan. He was a tough but caring trainer, and would often allow me to help him in creative ways to get points across to his trainees.

One of Dan's favorite trainees was a controller by the name of Dave Swanson. Nicknamed "Bullethead" for his pointed head, Dave was a "rocket full of energy" and at times more than anyone could handle. Dave mixed with Dan most of the time was like oil and water. Anytime Dan sensed Dave was about to make a mistake while training on ground, his lips would curl up, waiting to pounce. Once, while Dan was training Dave on outbound ground, I handed over a strip for Dave to taxi. The strip was on Japan Air Flight #10, a Boeing 747 non-stop to Narita, Japan. It would be Dave's job to assign a runway. Now Dave had been training for months and every day when this flight came out, it always had the same runway request, runway 14 right or 32 left, the longest and *only* runway this overly weighted, 13-hour flight could handle.

To see if Dave was paying attention, I wrote on the strip that Japan Air #10 was requesting runway 22 left, a blatant impossibility for this flight at any time because of its short length.

As Dave started to mouth the words, "Japan Air Ten Heavy taxi to runway two-two-left...." Dan's head turned completely red with anger. *"Dave, what the fuck are you thinking?"* Dan shouted. As Dave tried to reply, Dan interrupted with, "C'mon, Dave, what part of your head is stuck in your ass?"

Then Dan just laughed hysterically. It had all been an act, albeit a very convincing one.

Dave had learned a valuable lesson and, even though he was sent back to his previous airport, Dupage Airport, for some more seasoning, he came back a few years later, breezed through the training, and has been a mainstay at the Tower to the present day. In my last few years at O'Hare, I worked on the same crew as Dave. I could tell Dave had benefited from Dan, because when it was time for Dave to be a trainer, it was like watching a mirror image of Dan. Dan's training lived on through Dave—a fitting tribute.

Dan died the night of September 7th, 1988, of a sudden and massive heart attack while babysitting his infant son, John. He was *only* 30 years old. I had just walked out of work, laughing with him, the day before he died. It just didn't make any sense. I remember the supervisor in the Tower, Bill Ewart, making the announcement of his death just after I had plugged in local control to start the morning shift the following day. I couldn't talk to one pilot, I was in such a state of confusion. I was promptly relieved, as were many others. We would never hear Dan's laugh again.

Dan's wife, Marge, would like all to know what a special person her husband was. Marge said, "What can I say about Daniel Mark Eagan? He was the kindest, most loving gentleman. His laughter would light up a room and I am blessed to say he was my best friend, my husband and the father of our son, John Robert. Dan would always try to find the humor in the situation. We shared an apartment on Archer Ave, not far from Midway (Airport). One evening we came home to an unwelcome visitor, a mouse. Dan was called to rescue us from the creature. Knowing the seriousness of a mouse in our apartment, he left Midway Tower, drove to Oak Lawn and returned to the apartment on Archer equipped with his Mickey Mouse ears, a huge smile and mouse traps. Dan also loved trivia. I was always glad he was my partner, playing the then-popular Trivial Pursuit. He would remember interesting facts, such as one evening we met some friends for dinner, a discussion came up about shoestring potatoes. Dan informed us that all you need to make shoestring potatoes was a straight straw and a raw potato. Yes, you can make shoe string potatoes using a straight straw and a raw potato."

"Dan also loved to find bargains. He loved to travel, so finding a bargain involving travel was his forte. Some new airline was flying to Minnesota from Midway. Dan decided we should see the MN zoo in November. We had a great time. We left Chicago at 7:00 a.m., arrived in MN, and went to the zoo. We also went shopping and were back in Chicago by 9:00 p.m. that same night, ready to go to work the next day. Another time, Dan found a great airfare to Nashville—road trip. Dan booked airline tickets, made hotel reservations and rented cars for about 20 friends. We saw the Grand Ole Opry, Jack Daniels Brewery, and some nightclubs. Since Dan did such a good job on the Nashville trip, he was given control over the 'turning 30' outing in 1988. He decided California and Vegas in February would be appropriate. It was the last big trip he planned, but one none of us will forget. Our son was seven months old at the time, Dan's motto was 'have son, will travel,' so we packed up and had an incredible ten-day trip."

"Dan enjoyed life. His life was short, but his memory will live forever with his friends and through his son. John is his own person, but so many of Dan's qualities shine through him. His father would be very proud of the person he has become."

Chester (Andy) Anderson was born on September 23, 1931. He was a controller at O'Hare in both the Tower and TRACON throughout his almost 40-year career. As the chief of O'Hare Tower and TRACON, Andy was primarily known for his fierce loyalty to the controllers he served. Andy sought solutions to problems, usually in very constructive and creative ways. I can vouch for that firsthand. Controllers to Andy were all "good people," just like Father Flanagan said at Boys' Town. Andy saw the good in everyone and was often patient with the "bad" boys and girls of O'Hare.

Andy died November 9th, 1997, of heart failure at the age of 66. There wasn't one controller who wasn't directly or indirectly influenced by Andy's gentle nature. Andy's ability to use positive reinforcement over negative reinforcement is what made him successful in the upward movement of the airline industry and air traffic control from the 1970s through the 1990s. Andy was one of the few in management who created the pride that all controllers, both past and present, feel to this day.

Andy's wife, Anne, would like all to know that "Andy was a very private person. He was not one to brag or gloat on his achievements. So much so that when he went to Washington, D.C., to receive the Secretary's Award in September 1983, I knew nothing of this until he returned. In his briefcase there was a small, velvet-covered box, and I inquired about the contents. He explained that it was a medal that was presented to him by Elizabeth Dole, Secretary of Transportation at the time. The inscription read 'For outstanding management of the nation's busiest terminal air traffic control facility under extremely critical circumstances.' When I told him I would have loved to be there for the presentation, his remark was, 'why, that's what they pay me for,' in his usual calm manner. I'm sure his thoughts were 'why all the fuss?'"

The rest of the Anderson Family would like all to know that "the Great Lakes Region personnel signed a petition in 1998 to have a local aeronautical aid on runway 14 right renamed 'CHSTR' in his honor. The petition was sent to Washington, D.C., and approved. This non-directional beacon was officially renamed on April 23, 1998. It is a fitting tribute to his legacy and dedication to O'Hare and one that we are extremely proud of. He will now always be a part of the facility he loved so dearly. So next time you are flying into O'Hare, grab the headphones, tune into Channel Nine (or whatever channel lets you listen to the air traffic controllers) and hopefully 'CHSTR' will guide you in to his beloved O'Hare!"

Bill (Woody) Norwood, Jr., was born on December 16, 1960. Woody was one of only three African-American controllers in the Towers after 1985. He was always very personable in the Tower and had a way of being amusingly politically incorrect with everyone, including himself. He broke the barrier of race relationships in the Tower by simply being open and comedic. He was extremely proud of his father, who was the first black captain at United Air Lines, and his young family, which he adored.

Woody died on September 13th, 2003, at the age of 42 after a 14-month bout with liver and pancreatic cancer. It was hard to conceive of a man built so strong and athletic succumbing to such a debilitating cancer. We all thought Woody could beat cancer, just like he beat everyone on the softball field. Those controllers who spent time with Woody in his final days cried unashamedly. They understood the paradox.

Woody's wife, Cindy, would like all to know "what a phenomenal father he was. He could never get enough time with his girls (Emma and Rianna). Emma and Woody were inseparable. Woody also took a major interest in his two step-children (Tiffany and Reed), caring for them and loving them like they were his own. He was 'Dad' to them both. His parenting skills always amazed me (I guess we can thank his father for that). Friends would ask if they could send their young children to Camp Woody to learn respect and manners, since he did such a wonderful job with Emma. He was the best!

Woody was also one of the biggest family men I ever knew. He would call his relatives on a weekly basis to check in. He talked to his parents almost daily. If someone was ill, he was there cooking a meal, visiting at the hospital, taking them to doctor's appointments... whatever they needed, he was offering to help. His heart was as big as the world, and we miss him terribly."

Woody's parents and brother would like all to know that "Bill, Jr. was a loving son who was very family-oriented. He would often sacrifice his last dime to give it to a friend. He was confident in his abilities and very competitive. He was once described as 'being cocky,' to which he replied it was confidence. This belief in himself and hard work allowed him to be successful in a variety of fields. He was also a leader, and this trait was exhibited as early as his elementary and high school years."

"During his final months and during many chemotherapy sessions, he was continually encouraging others in similar situations. He had strong will power to accomplish difficult things. An example was when he was diagnosed with liver and pancreatic cancer; he said more than once that he would never give up or give in to the dreadful disease. As a result, instead of the predicted four to six months after diagnosis, he lived 14 months. He was courageous and brave until his last day. He was realistic about his illness and, at the time, remained hopeful. He often told us that we should not look back—only to look forward and to take care of Cindy and the girls. Bill, Jr. will be missed by all who knew him for his outgoing and cheerful attitude."

Mike Gschwendtner was born on March 7th, 1964. He came to O'Hare from San Francisco in 1995 and made an immediate impression on everyone in the Tower, with his big farm boy attitude and innocent smile, which was always a disguise for some kind of mischievous act about to take place. Case in point: very often Mike and I would come back early from our breaks so that we could get what we considered the "fun" positions in the Tower. Both our favorites in the Tower were the outbound ground position, because at certain times during our shifts, we could potentially work as many as 100 departures in an hour. This is what we lived for at O'Hare—the challenge and fun of it.

Like kids in a frenzy playing their video games, Mike and I competed to see who could plug in his jack first to work one of the hourly outbound extravaganzas of airplanes. Very often we would hit the door to the Tower at the same time, wrestle each other, heading over to the ground position while grabbing our headsets, and then, with remarkable timing, both put our headset jacks in at the same time. Now it was a game of chicken to see who would flinch first. As we both gasped for air from our friendly wrestling match, Mike would say, "Hey, I got here first," and then I quickly replied, "No way, man, I'm first!"

After a few more exchanges about who got where first came the stare down. For thirty seconds, we simply looked into each other's eyes, trying not to laugh, while we pondered another resolution to our dilemma. Mike, in his classic style, ended it all with a loud, muffled noise coming from the back of his pants. I wasn't sure at first what the noise was, but within five seconds I could smell it.

Mike was the only human being on this earth I knew that could pass his own gas on cue. I unplugged my jack and ran for cover, as did everyone else within ten feet of Mike.

Instead of being upset at Mike, everyone instead cursed me, saying, "Way to go, Calvin, you just had to get him going!" They were, of course, absolutely correct, and I never challenged Mike again. With that big farm boy smile on his face, Mike said to no one in particular, "It's a beautiful day in paradise." Hope to see you there someday, Mike.

Mike died on November 25th, 2003, of a sudden heart attack at the age of 39, just before midnight and two days before Thanksgiving, while playing hockey at a local ice rink. He had no previous symptoms, and as far as anyone knew, he was strong as an ox his whole life. He left behind a young wife, three small kids, and a lot of friends. The day shift on the morning of November 26th could not have been quieter.

Mike's family, including his wife, Anita, and sons, Kerry and Tracey, would like all to know that "Mike's number one priority was his family. He always put us before anything else. His kids were the most important thing to him and he was dedicated to all of their activities. He would be on the ice four times a week, helping out with hockey classes, and he also helped coach a soccer team. He had a passion for snowmobiling and the kids enjoyed that passion with him and, whenever we had a chance, we would all head up north to ride. In his spare time he loved to help his dad with the family farm, and in July and August, he would head down south to the farm and pick fresh, sweet corn and bring it to everyone up in the tower. Mike was one of the easiest guys to get along with, was never without a smile, and everyone loved him. He would do absolutely anything to help out a friend. At work, he loved to play practical jokes on some of his fellow workers. One time, he and his friend, Todd, moved all the furniture around in one of the offices."

Mike's now 12-year-old daughter, Ellie, would like all to know that "one of the funniest things about my dad was that one day he was fixing the upstairs bedroom floor, when all of a sudden he fell through the floor into the kitchen. What was left was this gigantic hole."

Ellie continued further, saying, "the best thing about my dad was that he could carry all three of us (my two brothers and me) on his back. Another funny thing was that when it was bedtime, my father would climb up the stairs while speaking loud enough for us to hear, "Fe Fi Foe Fum! I smell three little kids!" It would always be fun, trying to race into bed so he wouldn't discover that we weren't sleeping. Finally, he would sit on a couch and watch a wood-working channel, and learn everything about it by sitting there. As a result, we have beautiful hand-crafted shelves full of books and all of our games. He also built a set of bunk beds and a two-level fort in the backyard (which he couldn't get done soon enough for us). Every day, we wait for him to come home, thinking that he's still with us, and in the end he is, in spirit."

Terry Arneson was born on January 30th, 1955. He was one of the supervisors in the Tower and an original from the class of 1984. Terry liked to invoke his Navy background with such colorful phrases as, "Hey, Calvin, if you have a better idea, then let them pay you to steer this battleship!" In the years I worked with Terry, I never heard him utter a four-letter expletive bomb. With all the bombs flying in the Tower, this was an amazing act of self-discipline in itself.

Terry died of pancreatic cancer on January 18th, 2005, just days shy of his 50th birthday. His bout with cancer never stopped him from making the over one-hour commute from Rockford while still fighting for his life. He loved being an air traffic controller. He never said "why me?" His faith in God sustained him throughout.

Terry's wife, Jo Ann, would like all to know that her "husband was God's greatest gift." Terry was a "gentle, soft-spoken man who loved the Lord and reflected Him so beautifully. He was always there to encourage, comfort and to reach out to help whenever help was needed. I feel blessed that we had 27 years together. His love will sustain me until the Lord calls me home."

Terry's 19-year-old daughter, Ashleigh, stated, "the proudest moments in my life are when people ask me about my father. He was brave, kind and passionate about Jesus Christ. My father always challenged me to remember why I was 'a daughter of the King.' Every day I wait in anticipation for the moment when Jesus and my dad together welcome me home."

Even the TRACON wasn't spared unfortunate, heartbreaking stories. TRACON controllers Mike Fanucce, Charlie Bunting, and Roger Graybeal took the "last flight home." Roger's death was especially tragic. He collapsed and died of a heart attack while playing in a softball game in the summer of 2004. He was the coach of the TRACON softball team and only 38 years old. He had no history of heart trouble. It was an experience many of the TRACON players never forgot.

Like many of the Tower controllers, all the TRACON deaths were people still very young and in the prime of their lives. There must be a plan in all these tragedies. Could it be that God needs a Tower and TRACON in heaven, so he recruited the best? Maybe they'll get to ride the coaster one more time.

Ian Anderson of Jethro Tull wrote a beautiful song about life and its brevity, entitled "Life's a Long Song." It is a song that is always close to us all.

When you're falling awake and you take stock of the new day,

And you hear your voice croak as you choke on what you need to say,

Well, don't you fret, don't you fear,
I will give you good cheer.
Life's a long song...
Life's a long song...
Life's a long song...
If you wait then your plate I will fill
As the verses unfold and your soul suffers the long day,
And the twelve o'clock gloom spins the room,

You struggle on your way...

Well, don't you sigh, don't you cry,

Lick the dust from your eye.

Life's a long song...

Life's a long song...

Life's a long song...

But the tune ends too soon for us all.

Appendix 2

"Save the Airlines" Top Ten List

EXPECT FURTHER CLEARANCE: *the time a pilot can expect to receive clearance beyond a clearance limit, or the time an airline can expect to receive a clearance beyond government bureaucracy.*

Anytime a controller retires from his job, it is usually a time for great celebration. The job satisfaction of knowing you did the best you could to get the flying public from place to place is a noble undertaking. The part I can't get out of my mind is that I know *more* can be done. As often as the FAA and the airlines meet to discuss issues, it has always been clear to me that someone is withholding information. It is not a conscious conspiracy, but rather one borne out of ignorance, apathy, and plain laziness. The FAA and the government are very passive when it comes to helping the airlines save the bottom line. Uncle Sam will answer questions when posed by the airlines, but rarely is he proactive when initiating creative plans of his own.

Often, the attitude between corporate America and the government is an attitude of "you mind your store and I'll mind my own." The FAA upper management bureaucracy is so bogged down by the day-to-day running of the "store" that to find ways to improve the airlines is often cost prohibitive. I've *never* seen one, just one, FAA manager say, "What is it that we could do to help the airlines make money?" It saddens me because we in the government are excellent at helping people in foreign countries in their times of need, but when it comes to our own people, we're asleep at the wheel. If you want to understand this last point, all you have to do is to sit down and talk with any airline employee.

The morale of most airline employees is as low as it has ever been. In my last year at O'Hare, I had the opportunity to teach a runway safety class to most of the mechanics at both United and American Airlines. Most of the mechanics took great pride in what they had accomplished and were extremely receptive to all the information I was feeding them. They are the lifelines of the airlines.

The experience level of the majority of mechanics averages over 20 years. In better fiscal times, many of the mechanics I met would have been retired. Unfortunately, most mechanics hinged their retirements on the company stock options. When United and American Airlines were selling at $70 to $80 per share, the outlook for retirement looked great, but as times declined and 9/11 reared its ugly head, the bottom fell out. Bankruptcy spelled the end of most retirements.

Many of the airline employees are only working for the health benefits. Many others are simply too old to find a new career. At the time most of the airline employees were hired, loyalty was everything. One might argue that most airline employees should have had a back-up plan for retirement.

That's a great argument when you have money to burn, but what if you're just getting by? When times were good, no one could have predicted the collapse of the airlines, with the exception of the CEOs, who always had their "financial buyout parachutes" available. They never worried and always felt they had nothing to lose.

So it is time to submit, to *all the airlines, my top ten list* on how the Federal Aviation Administration (FAA) can personally save the airlines not only from further bankruptcies but a brighter future in the area of $$$$$ and ☺ ☺ ☺.

Everyone pay attention. The information I am presenting is simply what "the Towers" across the country can do. I won't speak for the TRACONS and the Centers, but the right people in those areas could easily do the same. My examples will use O'Hare Tower as the starting point. To quote an old aviation maxim, "as O'Hare goes, so does the rest of the country." *In the last few years,* the common working men and women at the airlines have been exploited by the FAA *so badly* they haven't even noticed the cattle prod extended from their back orifices. It's time to *take it out!* Starting with

#10 – FAA STAFFING AT TOWERS

Very often, the government sets limits on how many Tower personnel are required or needed for each shift. At O'Hare, for instance, the day shift requirement is 15, while the night shift is 17. Those are great numbers if you're just getting by and the weather is perfect. I believe the controllers could work the same two shifts at eight and ten if they had to. They are that flexible. But give me an extra four to five controllers per shift and watch what happens.

I would split up the workloads more, thereby moving airplanes faster and more efficiently. At O'Hare and other large airports, *because of the staffing,* we are stuck to the idea that one person works one outbound ground and one person works one inbound ground.

The sad part of watching these operations is most often I see *one* ground controller working ten to 30 planes. We *do* it, of course, because that's our job, and most pilots love to marvel at us. We've become used to working large amounts of airplanes. But could we move those same airplanes faster if *two* people were working 30 planes instead of *one*? And what happens when the weather goes south and the workloads automatically double and triple? Could more people help? Often, if we are overstaffed on a shift and we are overwhelmed by airplanes, we *will* open up another ground, but at this time, this is a luxury, not the norm. If it sounds simple, that's because it is. The problem is the FAA reluctance to spend your tax dollars.

The FAA is not in business to make money for the airlines, but they should not be satisfied with a minimum effort of service to the public, either. The FAA will tell you of the endless studies they use to get their staffing numbers. Most of these studies are done by bean counters who have no understanding of the daily nuts-and-bolts operation at the Tower or the dynamics that determine how quickly airplanes move in and out of an airport. Guess what happens when you decide to save money on staffing?

The answer is Lexington, Kentucky, on August 27th, 2006. That was the day a Comair jet crashed and killed 49 people. Why was only one controller working the midnight shift and performing the tasks of several controllers, when two were required, according to the FAA's own memos? You're not going to find anyone in the FAA to answer that question—they'll be too busy in court. The FAA spends a lot of money in court time because of its shortsightedness and *thriftiness*.

Airlines have always felt uncomfortable about questioning the FAA on how they distribute their employees, but *they shouldn't. Please, speak up or continue to lose money and lives.*

#9 – MORE TMUs (TRAFFIC MANAGEMENT UNIT) PER SHIFT

Traffic Management Controllers are a recent addition to the towers in the last ten years. They oversee the traffic flow of airplanes across the United States by coordinating with other air traffic facilities, as well as the FAA Command Center. If there are delays at other airports, it is the TMU that updates the length of those delays and distributes that information to controllers throughout the Tower. On most shifts at O'Hare, there are one and sometimes two TMU controllers. If the weather is pristine *across the whole country*, then it's possible to get by a whole shift with one TMU. (Pristine accounts for a total of around ten days a year.)

The major problem involves what happens locally at the airport when bad weather approaches. If, for example, a thunderstorm to the west stops the departures that are routed westbound, it is usually up to the TMU to reroute *each* individual aircraft around the bad weather. If a group of ten to 30 aircraft are affected, then the workload becomes unbearable for just one TMU to handle. Time after time I'd watch *one* TMU make incredibly valiant efforts to keep up with the new routes. The volume simply was more than any *one* human being could handle. It would become a time of anger and frustration for most TMUs. Two TMUs might be able to keep up, but having a third would certainly almost guarantee all flights would have their new routes faster than they could get to the departure runway.

Each flight has to be given a new route obtained and approved by the TMU. This process per aircraft may only take a few minutes, but multiply it times 20 or more flights, and you end up with a lot of airplanes sitting on the tarmac, burning fuel, waiting for a new route. Having *three* TMUs per shift guarantees smooth transitions when the really bad weather hits.

I know my fellow controllers will ask what happens when the weather is good and the TMU's workload is at a minimum? Do we need three then? Maybe not, but then an extra TMU is also an extra controller who can work airplanes. What better way to get the hours needed to stay proficient as an air traffic controller and help out with #10 on the list? Having three TMUs per shift allows flexibility to be a TMU and also work airplanes to maintain Tower currency. It creates even better teamwork.

So, to the airlines: call your local FAA and get more TMU staffing in the tower. Speak up or continue to lose money when bad weather hits.

#8 - SAVING FUEL ON THE GROUND

This is an aspect of air traffic control that is a product of years of experience on outbound ground control. Too often, whether the issue is volume of aircraft or bad weather, the lines at the departure runways can easily exceed 20 airplanes. Very often, we as controllers can save the airlines fuel by simply asking them to shut down their engines when and where it is convenient to do so.

For example, when a controller is given a restriction, such as 20 miles between westbound departures, chances are the number ten in line and beyond won't be leaving for some time. Why have their engines running when they could shut down for 15 or even 20 minutes, and save the fuel? In the controllers' defense, it becomes very hard to do this when another 20 aircraft are waiting to taxi. It is a technique, however, that can be more quickly learned if #10 was implemented. Every ground controller would then *have* the time to set up engine start and stop times.

Hey, Mr. Airline, gas is very expensive these days. Speak up or continue to lose money.

#7 – EDUCATION AND INFORMAL COMMUNICATION BETWEEN CONTROLLERS AND FLIGHT CREWS

This area of the aviation industry is often overlooked because it is hard to quantify it in actual dollar terms. Prior to 9/11, controllers were allowed "familiarization" privileges. Riding in the cockpit jump seat up to eight times a year, controllers could learn what goes on in the flight deck during landing and takeoff. I became a much better controller by knowing, for example, what questions to ask a pilot when bad weather was in the area, or what the capabilities were of a particular aircraft.

Conversely, pilots could ask questions about how the Tower works. For example, many pilots received valuable tips on how to file flight plans when weather was bad. By learning the air traffic system, a lot of pilots found ways to avoid big flight delays and make their day-to-day jobs easier. I doubt the "FAM" program for controllers will ever return in the short term because of the current security cockpit issues, but maybe it will be possible to bring it back in a safer future. As far as I can remember, though, of the millions of FAM rides taken by controllers, not one was hijacked.

Overall education for Tower controllers could be better improved with more staffing in the Tower administration. At O'Hare, the training department has always been stretched out. The only *two* training specialists presently in the department too often would be used to cover staffing shortages in the Tower. Of the two specialists, one is dedicated entirely to running the new "Tower Simulator."

The other specialist oversees the training and records for up to 60 controllers. Often, he might have little time to prepare classes for new hires and no time to create new and advanced training for people already in the Tower. He was doing the work of many specialists, but still kept up and did a phenomenal job. Having spent most of his career at O'Hare, he always had the O'Hare "can do" attitude.

Opposite the training department is the quality assurance. Here, there is only one specialist to handle all the day-to-day issues, including investigations, reports, and studies that could be done to improve the Tower environment. One manager is in charge of *both* the training and quality assurance departments. She is often tasked with having to do all the jobs of the specialists, simply because there is no one else who can help. Most of the training staff gave up complaining years ago, having reached deaf ears on numerous occasions, with the same answers each time: we don't have the money.

In the 1980s and even the 1990s, it was common practice to allow flight crews visits to the Tower. Normally, a staff person in the administrative area would conduct such tours. Many airline employees, including pilots and mechanics, who visited the Tower, came away with a *much* better understanding of their own jobs. Today, there are barely enough staff people to support the controllers, so allowing visitors to the Tower has become non-existent. It would be a novel idea to pay someone, whether a retired FAA controller or simply any-one, to give tours to educate airline employees. Again it's not something you can quantify in terms of dollars, but the expe-rience to all is **priceless.**

#6 – BETTER SEPARATION STANDARDS

The FAA and the airlines *together* need to take a bet-ter look at the standards of separation currently in use today. There are many LAHSO issues still to be resolved. I believe there has to be some consistency in the way we enforce cer-tain standards. For example, if the separation is three miles and the aircraft separation goes down to 2.9 miles, is it an error or is there some flexibility or accepted degree of error in the system that measures these distances? The *safety* factor of 2.9 versus three should not be an issue, since it is only barely measurable.

The problem has become that the FAA has decided to rigidly enforce outdated rules, thereby creating paranoia among controllers. Controllers who used to work around the three miles now start out at four, five, and even six miles to get the same result. No one wants to be right at three miles and take the risk of being tagged with an operational error. Remember, three strikes and you could be out. This new atti-tude of the millennium has caused a domino effect, described earlier in this book. It is one of the main reasons for delays when weather is not a factor. They are simply called "volume" or "air traffic" delays. Unfortunately, they have become *routine* in the last few years.

So, to the airlines: tell the FAA to be clear about this issue. Speak up or continue to be delayed and lose money.

#5 – BUILD MORE RUNWAYS

To the National Air Traffic Controllers Association (NATCA) and to the Mayor of Chicago, congratulations on making *most* people understand this issue. A few years ago, John (Bulldog) Carr, then president of NATCA; Ray Gibbons, head of the TRACON NATCA; and Craig Burzych of the Tower NATCA put this issue center stage. Mayor Richard Daley never backed down. Controllers at O'Hare, such as Bill Spence and Kevin Markwell, are currently working on the procedures for the new runways and taxiways. O'Hare will be ready for the future. Each year, the amount of flights at O'Hare and most airports will continue to increase. We all need to stop making this issue brain surgery. The more runways you have, the more aircraft can land and take off. End of story.

So, to the airlines: I hope you can find ways to make this happen. I know the FAA was asking you for donations.

#4 – REPAIR THE FAA MANAGEMENT TRAIN WRECK

This issue is something that, unfortunately, is part of a bigger problem. Over the past few years, labor, particularly in the airline industry, has taken a beating. Employers have made it as simple as either "take a pay cut" or "lose your jobs." At O'Hare, if you talk to any United or American employee, they'll tell you they have little or no say in their contracts. It became no different for air traffic controllers.

The FAA, led by administrator Marion Blakey, had been unable to hammer out an agreement with controllers since George Bush took control in 2001. According to the law regarding FAA workforce negotiations, if the negotiations reached an impasse, then the FAA could send its "last and best offer" to Congress. In 2006, that was exactly what happened.

When the Congress didn't act to force the FAA back to the bargaining table, controllers lost all say in their job conditions. The FAA was given carte blanche and allowed to implement its own rules and, in effect, force it down the throats of air traffic controllers. All the benefits the controllers had worked for were now at the discretion of the FAA. On September 3, 2006, the new FAA rules went into effect.

Marion had preached for years that controllers were overpaid and, as she put it, "more than compensated for." She immediately instituted a B pay scale, thereby scaling down new controller salaries for years to come. New hires wasted no time in letting their feelings be known. One new controller in Memphis left to start a new mowing business because it provided a higher salary. Two Department of Defense controllers turned down job offers at Louisville, Kentucky Tower because it would have been a $20,000 cut in pay.

The cycle is eerily similar to what happened to O'Hare in the early 1990s. Controllers left O'Hare when they realized the pay at some of the neighboring airports was only a few thousand dollars less. Why work your ass off when you could take it easy somewhere else, for almost the same amount of money? It became hard to get people to come to O'Hare, until the government instituted a ten percent bonus system. A few years later, the bonus was rolled into a new pay band. Finally, O'Hare was being fairly compensated for the number of airplanes worked.

The next election, in 2008, will probably have a lot to say about the future of aviation. If we continue on the present road, we will certainly become more divisive. When Bill Clinton was President, the relationship between controllers and the government was as good as any of the years previous.

I suppose it's possible that a Clinton will be President again, in the form of Presidential candidate Hillary.

My personal knowledge of Hillary was always fleeting. I spent a few brief episodes with her and the Secret Service in 1994. One was at a speech she made on healthcare at the Berwyn-Cicero Council on Aging in my hometown. In that little episode, I was exchanging a few quips about life and marriage with another Secret Service agent. Hillary was standing a few feet away, waiting to be introduced to a small group. When I made a remark about how hard marriage could be, the agent laughed. Then, all of sudden, with a broad smile on her face, Hillary interjected, "Isn't that the truth?"

I thought it was nice that as a politician, she could let her guard down and be open and frank emotionally, if only for a few seconds. We *all* need to have that sense of humor and be able to laugh at ourselves. That was the only time I saw Hillary not "official." At least I know she has it in her.

I believe Hillary's success, or lack thereof, will come down to that simple quality of being "genuine." Watching Marion Blakey, on the other hand, *always* made me uncomfortable. The last time I saw her, on a visit to the O'Hare Tower, she was totally political, smile and all. She never took the time to sit down with *any* of the "working stiffs" in the Tower, known as the controllers. It was always show your face and out the door, like some bad movie star on the red carpet. How could you possibly learn about the people under you if you never *talk* to them?

It always amazed me that Marion, or anyone in FAA's upper management, for that matter, knew what was fair compensation for any air traffic controller, much less those at the busiest airports in the world. The health issues at O'Hare were and are still staggering. Many have died. Many more have had heart problems, numerous cancers, blood pressure issues, and a host of other ailments. Most of these controllers are only in their 30s and 40s. How do you put a price on that?

I wish *uninformed* Marion would do something to address these issues. In an April 10th, 2007 letter to Marion from the National Transportation Safety Board (NTSB), Board members criticized the FAA for "*ignoring* the Board's previous findings that air traffic controller fatigue is a problem." There's the understatement of the millennium. *Most* ironic of all, though: prior to being the FAA Administrator, Marion was the "NTSB *Chairman.*" Apparently, she forgot where she came from.

So, to the airlines: good luck finding someone with a heart at the FAA. Most I know don't have one. They do, however, smile a lot and give good speeches.

#3 – TOWER SIMULATOR

This is an item that has the potential to save the airlines millions of dollars, not just at O'Hare, but also at every airport across the country. The summer of 2006 ushered in a new method of training at O'Hare. Trainees would now spend time learning the O'Hare Airport in its new "state of the art" simulator. This simulator is such a realistic representation of the actual O'Hare Tower that it might be possible to have a trainee spend most of his/her training in it before ever heading up into the real Tower environment. This was an idea that was long overdue.

Two O'Hare controllers, Jonathan (Johnny B) Bremseth and Dave Jennings, were given the task of making it work at O'Hare. Dave was a retired O'Hare controller who knew the airport in and out and went to work for the simulator contractor. Johnny B, currently on staff at O'Hare, was used because of his computer savvy and O'Hare controller experience from the class of 1983. Both have transformed the simulator into "another O'Hare airport." When I first worked in the simulator as a "practice" trainee, I could hardly tell the difference between the simulator and the real Tower.

Before the simulator, trainees would go directly up into the Tower and work airplanes. Initially, training was very tentative, taking months for trainees to get up to the same speed as a journeyman. Since trainees tend to be less efficient and make mistakes, a lot of learning was done at the airlines' expense. Slower taxi rates induced by trainees translated into higher fuel bills. Accidentally sending an aircraft to the wrong runway could cause a longer taxi, as well as a delay, also translating into higher energy expenses. The longer you can keep a trainee in the simulator, the more money you save the airlines.

So, to the airlines: support your local Tower simulator and demand trainees stay in the simulator as long as possible until they become proficient enough to work in the Tower.

#2 – TOWER-TRACON BREAKUPS

One of the primary reasons for the decline at O'Hare in the new millennium was the separation of the TRACON from the Tower. *Nothing* was done to remedy the problems caused years after the split. Controllers at each facility continue to question the other's competence and abilities. On a weekly basis, investigations are occurring to see if "*they* had another one" (operational error). A few years ago, the FAA tried to put out a catchy slogan to inspire teamwork. It was called "ONE FAA." Like a lot of FAA "catch" words, it never got off the ground. Simply saying it and putting out little buttons ☹ isn't going to make it happen.

One-day field trips between the facilities are not the solution. Without the teamwork that existed when both facilities were collocated, delays have become the norm and not the exception. With controllers at the Tower and the TRACON not wanting to risk their jobs, they have instead built in such large cushions of *extra* separation that the airspace for airplanes across the United States has shrunk measurably. This is not a safety issue. There is simply *too* much distance between airplanes, caused by paranoia. Fear is the main thing guiding controllers, and no one is doing anything about it.

In 2007, I talked to Kevin Winn, a controller I started out with in 1985 at O'Hare, who is now at Boston Tower. When we compared notes, it became crystal clear that the same low morale at O'Hare had already invaded the east coast. Kevin put it simply: "It just isn't fun anymore." This was coming from a guy who was "high" on air traffic control his whole life.

Matt Dunne, a TRACON controller, once said, "I love the work but I hate the job." Matt knew, like a lot of other controllers, that any time politics got involved in the facilities, controlling airplanes soon became a "job."

So, to the airlines: get your local FAA to stop its infighting. Speak up or find ways to deal with more angry and delayed passengers.

AND THE #1 MEASURE TO HELP THE AIRLINES:

#1 – PUT THE RADIO BACK IN THE TOWER, BRUCE!

On September 3rd, 2006, when the FAA new rules went into effect, the aviation industry hit a new low. The first thing the Great Lakes Regional Office did was impose its own set of rules on the controllers at O'Hare Tower. It was FAA National Vice-President of Terminal Operations Bruce Johnson who, in a moment of brilliant thought, decided one of the first things that needed to be done was to "get the radio out of the Tower." Bruce was in charge of *all* Towers across the country.

You might have thought one of the first things he could have done would be to create an environment of reconciliation. How about working towards healing the wounds caused by bad contract negotiations? Or maybe even use this time to get the flying public back on track and out of delays? But *no*. His move reminded me of when Captain Kangaroo desecrated government pens so they wouldn't be stolen. At first, many didn't understand why the radio was so important to Bruce.

From a practical standpoint, the radio, over the years, was nothing more than a resource for information and entertainment. It was from the radio we received most of our information right after the planes hit the World Trade Center. The radio had more information at the time than we were receiving from our own Command Center.

On severe weather days, the radio was used to hear up-to-the-minute weather warnings in the local area. At O'Hare it was incumbent on the supervisors and TMUs to use "every resource and aid" that could provide information to the controllers. The radio was just one of those tools. I couldn't recall one example in 25 years of working airplanes where the radio caused an operational error. Its ability to pump out music created a very harmonious atmosphere in the Tower. Personally, its rock and roll value always had me working at peak performance, even when I felt a little down. It was *more* of a distraction when it was removed from the tower.

So what did the radio represent? As more edicts came down the pipe to O'Hare, it was clear what the radio was all about in Bruce's world. It was the opportunity to show the "punk kids" at O'Hare and the country who was the "new

Boss." It was testosterone out of control. As the rock group The Who once said, *"Meet the new boss, same as the old boss."* Bruce even imposed a "lockdown" at O'Hare Tower and all the Towers across the country.

Controllers at O'Hare, who often on their breaks took strolls into the adjacent terminal to get some relief from the pressures of the job, were told, *"no more."* You couldn't even walk out the door to get a cup of coffee. His reasoning was never clear, but for three decades previous, controllers had enjoyed the option of spending their breaks by stepping out of the facility, sometimes just to get some fresh air or a meal. Controllers were now to be treated as prisoners in the Tower "compound."

Joseph M. Bellino, the Tower NATCA President and a controller for nearly 30 years at both the Tower and the TRACON, could not recall a time, short of the air traffic controllers' strike, when working conditions were worse.

To make matters worse, O'Hare installed a new Chief, Bill Mumper, to help implement the new rules. All Bill could do was apologize and say how sorry he was that these tactics were being used. He even said he would fight to have some of the "privileges" restored. Bill wasn't even a home-grown O'Hare controller, and yet he understood the significance of the region's actions.

What the region viewed as "privileges," we as controllers viewed as "survival." I'm certain Bruce purposely avoided installing a new chief with O'Hare experience. Most of the previous O'Hare pipeline chiefs, including Chester (Andy) Anderson, and Pete Salmon, would have quit before accepting such ridiculous conditions.

Bill just shrugged his shoulders and, last I heard, used a lot of his vacation so as not to deal with any of it. He was caught between the proverbial Bruce "rock" and the O'Hare "hard place." Only time will tell if Bill and the O'Hare controllers can withstand Hurricane Bruce. It would appear that this is an "MTV" world and Bruce is simply AM Radio. In the end, the biggest losers will be the airlines and the passengers who fly them.

God help us all. And to the airlines: one last request. Get a petition started to get the radio back in the tower. Speak up so you, the flying public, and the controllers, will be happy again.

Appendix 3

Chicago-O'Hare Airport Runway and Taxiway Map

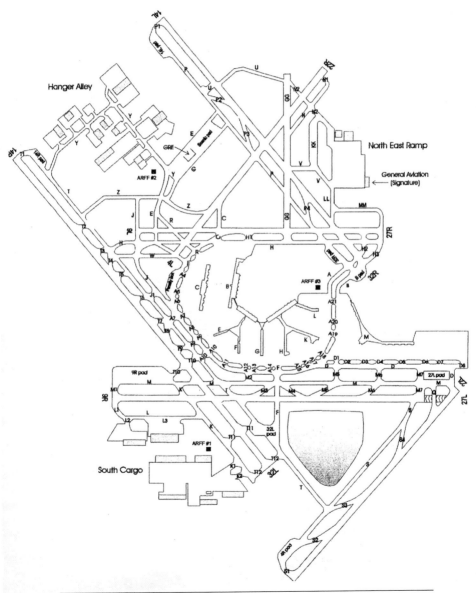

About the Author

Bob Richards is a former air traffic controller who recently retired in February, 2007, after spending the last 22 years, in the tower at one of the world's busiest airports, Chicago-O'Hare International Airport. *Secrets from the Tower* shows his dedication and passion about keeping the aviation industry safe, profitable, and sensitive to the health and well-being of its employees. Bob currently resides with his wife, Kim, and family in the Chicago area.